VERBES IRRÉGULIERS

W0321176

ISBN 2.85232.245.5

1 - THE WORK ETHIC AND ITS EVOLUTION

TRADITIONAL CONCEPTIONS

Profane

It is summed up in a statement of Richard Nixon's : " The work ethic holds that labor is good in itself ; that a man or woman at work only makes a contribution to his fellow man but becomes a better person by virtue of the act of working. " In other words, the work ethic is a desire to do the best work possible, irrespective of pay or any other reward than the satisfaction of doing a fine piece of work and being useful to the community.

There are of course other motivations than working only for work's sake.

-Ambition sways a good many people :

-Immigrants from poorer countries want to " make it " in America or other industrialized nations in order that they and their families may climb up the social ladder.

-Happiness in a consumer society is proportional to purchasing power and some people are apt to become workaholics to increase their earnings.

-Japan is famous for its dedicated labour force : workers will toil to make their companies thrive, making do without holidays and sacrificing family life.

-Philosophers emphasize the dignity that a job confers on man. Thomas Carlyle, for instance, holds that " all work is noble ; work is alone noble ". Workers can judge how apposite that view is when they are made redundant and feel humiliated to have to depend on welfare.

Religious

- According to the Bible, work is a punishment imposed by God on man for his disobedience : " You shall earn your daily bread by the sweat of your brow ! "
- Quotations from holy men :

  -St Paul : " If anyone will not work, let him not eat "

  -St Benedict : " Laborare is orare " = " To work is to pray "
- According to Luther and Calvin, workers are God's collaborators in the work of the universe.
- Popular sayings of Christian inspiration :

  " The devil finds work for idle hands "

  " Idleness is the root of all evils "

  " Idleness breeds vice "

  " God helps those who help themselves "

Patriotic

The motherland needs the work of her citizens to achieve victory over the enemy in war-time. Work is also essential in peace-time to enhance the prestige of the nation.

Fatalistic

However reluctant you may be, you must work to earn a living ! No matter how unrewarding, work is inevitable !

THE CHALLENGE

Leisure is gradually losing its sinful nature. Our society has a marked leaning towards hedonism : we were not born for a life of toil ; we are eager to derive from life as much enjoyment as possible. " Carpe diem " is modern man's motto. The uncertainty of the future : the economic crisis, the energy shortage, the different wars being waged in the world, the threat of nuclear warfare undoubtedly account for that tendency : what has tomorrow in store for us ?

Some younger people lay stress on the spiritual side of life and condemn the pursuit of wordly ambitions and success through hard work. They claim that their elders are on the wrong track when they hold that happiness varies in direct ratio to the acquisition of riches. Happiness does not go hand in hand with wealth and status or, as the popular saying goes : " money cannot buy happiness "

In all fields, machinery, robots, computers are eating away at jobs. Ousted workers fall back on the jobs which are still available, but which do not necessarily correspond with their skills or tastes. Hence a feeling of frustration. They have to put up with the irksome task of earning their daily bread, fulfilling themselves only in creative pastimes : hence a longing for more leisure !

Longer periods of leisure are indispensable, so that people in industrialized countries may keep their balance. Without rest and relaxation, they would not keep up the hectic tempo of life, or bear the relentless and humdrum recurrence of nights curtailed by their having to commute to the daily " grind ".

The enjoyment of rest and relaxation is made possible by the development of social services within the framework of the Welfare State. Unfortunately some people who are not hampered by scruples are apt to value leisure so much that they yield to the temptation of taking undue advantage of sick leave and pay.

The Welfare State makes it also possible for some people to be fastidious about the employment they are offered. They can afford to remain idle, refusing work that they consider menial, unskilled, irksome or dirty, as they are granted unemployment benefits until they find a job that they regard as suitable.

Mass media, collective entertainments, the numerous amenities that are to be found in towns, make it very pleasant to idle one's time away, and entice one into asking for more leisure.

(to be continued)

TEST YOUR KNOWLEDGE

1 - WHAT MAKES PEOPLE WORK ?
- AMBITIOUS PEOPLE ?
- CONSUMERS ?
- FATALISTS ?

2 - OUR SOCIETY IS HEDONISTIC. WHAT DOES IT MEAN ?

3 - WHY DO SOME YOUNG PEOPLE THINK THAT THEIR ELDERS ARE ON THE WRONG TRACK AS REGARDS HAPPINESS ?

4 - WHY ARE A NUMBER OF PEOPLE LONGING FOR MORE LEISURE ?
- BECAUSE OF THE NATURE OR THEIR WORK ?
- BECAUSE OF THE NATURE OF EVERYDAY LIFE ?
- ANOTHER REASON ?

5 - HOW CAN UNSCRUPULOUS PEOPLE ENJOY MORE LEISURE ?

6 - WHY CAN SOME UNEMPLOYED PEOPLE PROVE FASTIDIOUS WHEN THEY ARE OFFERED A JOB ?

7 - WHAT IS **YOUR OWN** MOTIVATION ?

1 - TO ABIDE - ABODE - ABODE

R : peut aussi être régulier.
+ by : to respect, to be faithful to
- A law-abiding citizen : *un citoyen respectueux des lois*
- To abide by a promise, a decision : *tenir une promesse*
- To abide by the therms of a contract : *s'en tenir aux termes d'un contrat*

2 - TO ARISE - AROSE - ARISEN

s'élever, surgir, résulter
- Unexpected difficulties arose in the negotiations.

Synonyme : to spring up - sprang - sprung ; to crop up ; to turn up
- Social unrest may arise from that package of measures.
Il se peut que de ce train (cette série) de mesures résultent des troubles sociaux.

Synonyme : to result from

3 - TO AWAKE - AWOKE - AWOKE (awaked)

se réveiller, s'éveiller

4 - TO BE - I WAS - BEEN

mais I was bor**n** : je suis né

5 - TO BEAR - BORE - BORNE

porter, supporter (figuré)

Synonyme : to endure, to put up with, to tolerate, to stand - stood - stood
- To bear injustice, sexual or racial discrimination, a bad treatment, etc.

Expressions : You should allways bear in mind that self-management cannot work miracles.
Vous devriez toujours vous rappeler que l'autogestion ne peut pas faire de miracles.
- If I don't raise her salary, she will bear a grudge against me (she will bear me a grudge).
- It is born**e** out by statistics : it is confirmed...
- Migrant workers will bear the brunt of the shake out.
Les travailleurs immigrés feront les frais des compressions de personnel.

6 - TO BEAT - BEAT - BEATEN

battre (propre et figuré)

Composés : An upbeat assessment (downbeat) of the economic situation : *une évaluation optimiste (pessimiste) de la situation économique.*

7 - TO BECOME - BECAME - BECOME

devenir + of : *advenir*
- What will become of the staff if you wind up the business ?
Qu'adviendra-t-il du personnel si vous liquidez l'affaire ?
(to wind - wound - wound)

8 - TO BEGIN - BEGAN - BEGUN

commencer
cf. *se mettre à* : to set about + gérondif

Substantif : The beginning (the end). Aussi : the onset of a crisis, of shortages, of winter.

9 - TO BEND - BENT - BENT

(se) plier, courber
cf. to be bent on ; set upon ; determined on + gérondif :
tenir absolument à ce que, vouloir absolument que

10 - TO BESET - BESET - BESET

assaillir (figuré)

Synonyme : to assail
- All industrialized countries are beset with economic difficulties.
" Assaillir " au sens propre : to attack, to assault

11 - TO BET - BET - BET

parier

Synonyme : to wager
- To lay (laid - laid) a bet, a wager : *faire un pari*
- To bet on horses : *jouer aux courses*
- The odds are that... *Il y a gros à parier que...*

12 - TO BIND - BOUND - BOUND

1) *Lier, attacher*

Synonymes : to tie, to fasten (≠ to unbind, untie, unfasten)

- Not only did the strikers confine the boss in the boiler room, but they bound his wrists with a piece of wire.
Non seulement les grévistes ont-ils séquestré le patron dans la chaufferie mais ils lui ont attaché les poignets avec un morceau de fil électrique.

2) *Obliger, forcer*

Synonymes : to oblige, to compel
- A civil servant binds himself by contract to work for the State for 10 years when he/she passes that competitive examination.
Un fonctionnaire s'engage par contrat à travailler 10 ans pour l'Etat quand il réussit ce concours.
- You are not bound (compelled) to work overtime.
Vous n'êtes pas tenu de faire des heures supplémentaires.

Expression : The firm **is bound to** make a profit this year. The firm **cannot fail to** make - **cannot but** make a profit...
La firme ne peut que faire des bénéfices cette année, ne peut manquer de faire...
Cf. a bond : *un lien,* mais aussi *un bon, un titre.*
Treasury bonds : *bons du trésor.*

Composés : The harbour is ice bound : *...paralysé par la glace.*
The docks are strike bound : *...paralysés par la grève.*

13 - TO BITE - BIT - BITTEN

mordre (propre et figuré)
- My secretary never files her nails : she bites them !
Ma secrétaire ne se lime pas les ongles : elle les ronge !
- Spray some insecticide around not to be bitten by mosquitoes !

14 - TO BLEED - BLED - BLED

saigner. Cf. blood : *le sang*
Attention à la prononciation de blood et flood : *l'inondation*
[blʌd] [flʌd]

15 - TO BLEND - BLENT - BLENT

R : *mélanger, mêler*
A blend : *un mélange (café, thé, tabac, spiritueux, etc.)*

16 - TO BLOW - BLEW - BLOWN

souffler
mais aussi : The tornado has blown a great many roofs away.
La tornade a emporté nombre de toits.
- They blew up all the bridges to hinder the enemy's progress or retreat !
Ils ont fait sauter tous les ponts pour gêner la progression ou la retraite de l'ennemi.
- Here's a tissue : blow your nose !
Voici un mouchoir en papier : mouche-toi !

Attention ! a blow : *un coup*
to deal (dealt - dealt) someone a blow :
asséner un coup à quelqu'un

1 - STRUCTURES VARIABLES

Comparatifs

1 - ÉGALITÉ

a) Affirmatif : He is **as** lazy **as** his brother.
b) Négatif : He is **not so** lazy **as** his brother.
He is **not as** lazy **as** his brother.

Traduction de : **autant (de)**

■ Singulier
- You spend **as much** electricity **as** we do.
- You do **not** spend **so much** electricity **as** we do.
- You do **not** spend **as much** electricity **as** we do.

■ Pluriel
- He smokes **as** many cigarettes **as** I do.
- He does **not** smoke **so many** cigarettes **as** I do.
- He does **not** smoke **as many** cigarettes **as** I do.

Attention à la place de l'article après " as " (cf. " so " et " too ").
- He is not **as** intelligent **a** boy as his brother.
Ce n'est pas un garçon aussi intelligent que son frère.
- He is **so** intelligent **a** boy that everybody admires him.
- He is **too** intelligent **a** boy to believe those lies *(ces mensonges).*

2 - INFÉRIORITÉ

Couramment : A bus is **not so** fast **as** a car.
Adjectifs longs : A bus is **less** comfortable **than** a car.
Traduction de : **" moins (de) "**

■ Quantités mesurables
- The mine yields **less** coal **than** it used to.
La mine produit moins de charbon qu'auparavant.

■ Éléments comptables
- There are **fewer** trees around here **than** over there.
Il y a moins d'arbres ici que là-bas.

3 - SUPÉRIORITÉ

■ Adjectifs longs
- This scheme is **more** attractive **than** I thought.
Ce projet est plus séduisant que je ne le pensais.

■ Adjectifs courts
- A car is fast**er** **than** a bus.

N.B. : BIEN + COMPARATIF = MUCH ou FAR : It is far more attractive, much less expensive.

Assimilés aux adjectifs courts :
- Adj. de 2 syllabes en
  - -y : lazy, pretty, crazy
  - -er : clever
  - -ow : narrow, shallow (peu profond)
  - -le : noble, gentle

Exemples :

- He is **cleverer** but **lazier** than I.
- The Strait of Gribaltar is narrower than the Strait of Dover,
  Le Détroit de Gibraltar est plus étroit que le Pas-de-Calais.

Traduction de : **" plus (de) ":**

Singulier et pluriel : more

- He earns **more** money **than** I do.
- They have got **more** friends **than** we have.

Remarques

a) Traduction de : **" tant de "**

■ Singulier : - He has drunk **so much** wine **that** he is drunk.

■ Pluriel : - I have read the book **so many times that** I know it by heart.

b) Traduction de : **" si peu de "**

■ Singulier

- They earn **so little** money **that** they cannot make ends meet.
  Ils gagnent si peu d'argent qu'ils n'arrivent pas à joindre les deux bouts.

■ Pluriel

- They have got **so few** tools **that** they could not repair the engine.
  Ils ont si peu d'outils qu'ils ne pourraient pas réparer le moteur.

THEME D'APPLICATION NUMERO 1

1 - *Tant de difficultés imprévues peuvent surgir au cours des négociations !*

2 - *Cette firme a supporté si peu de difficultés économiques* qu'elle ne peut manquer *(3 traductions) de faire des bénéfices cette année.*

3 - *Des troubles sociaux vont résulter d'un train de mesures aussi impopulaire (2 constructions ; unpopular).*

4 - *Vous devriez toujours vous rappeler* (locution) *que les femmes aujourd'hui subissent moins de discrimination que leurs mères.*

5 - *Moins de jeunes gens passent ce concours maintenant : ils ne veulent pas s'engager par contrat à travailler 10 ans pour l'État !*

6 - *Il a si peu de conscience professionnelle (conscientiousness) qu'il ne s'en tiendra pas aux termes du contrat.*

7 - *C'est un travail (a task) trop pénible (arduous) vous n'êtes pas tenu de faire des heures supplémentaires !*

8 - *C'est une jeune fille aussi rancunière (spiteful) que sa sœur ; elle m'en voudra si je n'augmente pas son salaire !*

9 - *Il n'aurait pas perdu tant de sang si vous ne lui aviez pas asséné un coup aussi violent (2 constructions).*

10 - *La tornade a emporté moins de toits que nous (ne) le pensions.*

11 - *Les travailleurs immigrés sont moins (2 constructions) chanceux (fortunate) que leurs camarades de travail (a workmate) européens : ils feront les frais des compressions de personnel.*

12 - *La grève des dockers sera plus longue que prévu (expected) : tous les ports sont paralysés !*

13 - *Les troubles sociaux qui résultent de ce train de mesures seront bien plus graves (serious) qu'en 1970.*

14 - *Il y a gros à parier qu'il aurait été bien moins décidé à liquider l'affaire si le personnel ne l'avait pas séquestré dans la chaufferie !*

15 - *La firme a fait si peu de bénéfices (singulier) cette année que cela gênera son expansion.*

2 - THE WORK ETHIC AND ITS EVOLUTION

(Deuxième partie)

THE NEW ETHIC : SPECIAL EMPHASIS IS LAID ON THE "QUALITY OF LIFE"

BETTER HUMAN RELATIONSHIPS

- Labour relations are improved. Conflicts between Management and Labour are slowly evolving from protest movements based on strikes, wildcat strikes, massive walkouts, working-to-rule, demonstrations..., towards collective bargaining, labour contract policies...
- Worker participation (co-determination, co-management). Workers' delegates are members of the Board and take part in the management of the firm : they are involved in the running of the firm and no longer excluded from decision-making.
- Social advancement. Employees are granted every opportunity of getting promotion through further education and training (sandwich courses, work-study programmes). In accordance with redeployment programmes, retraining enables them to find another job more easily in this or that branch of industry or commerce.
- Importance of each worker in the manufacturing process : by taking workers round the different workshops after they are engaged, by showing them the end product of their work, they no longer feel as if they were useless cogs in the machinery.

HUMANIZATION OF WORKING CONDITIONS

- Improved environment. Workshops become larger ; they are heated or cooled more efficiently ; they are well-lit, less noisy and grimy.
- Increased safety.

  1 - New equipment is installed, more inspectors make sure that safety regulations are respected. Rates of production are less frantic : workers may pause and have refreshments, especially those with mind-numbing or nerve-racking work.

  2 - Dirty, irksome, hazardous tasks are performed by robots.
- Improved social services. To attend more efficiently to industrial accidents, medical services and equipment are brought up-to-date. Creches are created on behalf of working mothers. Canteens provide attractive and

NEW METHODS OF WORK

They restore man's dignity. He is no longer reduced to the level of the automaton, of the robot. He can use his powers of reflection, of imagination and his sense of beauty

- Gradual replacement of repetitive work on the production line by team work, pioneered by Volvo and Saab in Sweden.
- Individual workers are trusted with a totality of tasks ; the latter are no longer divided up among several workers. Each one is thus aware of creating something from start to finish.
- Quality circles.

  The 8 to 12 volunteer workers and foremen who make up these circles share the responsibility for the quality of the products that they manufacture : they feel involved in the manufacturing process.
- Matching people and jobs.

  Workers are entrusted with the jobs for which they have a liking or a gift, and encouraged to acquire or improve the skills that they require.
- Telecommuting. It is the modern version of cottage industry. The employee works at home as he/she is linked to the company by telecommunications, most often by a computer terminal.

DURATION OF WORK

- The workweek (U.S. ; G.B. : the working week) is progressively being reduced to 35 working hours (U.S. : work hours).
- Workers are little by little granted longer paid holidays.
- They are entitled to retire at 55 or 60.
- Employees are allowed to set their own work schedules (U.S. : flextime ; G.B. : flexitime).
- Working part-time enables mothers to lead a professional life, bring up their children as well, or devote themselves to other activities.
- Three shift schedules are being gradually done away with.

Financial incentives

- PRP : Profit-related pay. The workers are paid a basic wage plus a share of profit. Studies confirm that such a scheme improves industrial relations, boosts productivity as the prospect of a fatter take-home pay (disposable income) spurs a worker on to work harder.
- Profit sharing schemes. Companies earmark part of the profits for trusts which deal out shares to employees. Employees become shareholders, attend the meetings of the Board, and have a say in the management of the firm, in decision-making, in short-term and long-term policy-making.
- Share option schemes (U.S. : stock options schemes). Employees are granted options to buy shares at a preferential price.
- ESOP (U.S.) : Employee Stock Ownership Plans. Under such plans, employees become "employee-owners" since they have got a stake in the company (U.S. : corporation) according to salary and seniority.
- Incentive payment schemes (bonus schemes) to encourage workers to work harder or better by granting bonuses linked to performance.
- Fringe benefits (perquisites, perks). They do not concern only top-management. There is a wide range of "perks" : a company-car, free housing or very cheap rents, free uniforms, free or very cheap meals, sports facilities, loans at low interest rates, free transport, goods at a discount, etc.
- "Well pay" (U.S.) : employees are given extra pay for their punctuality or their regular attendance at work.

Mavericks

"Yuppies" — young upwardly mobile professionals — in the United States, and their European counterparts "Yaps" — young aspirant professionals — in Great Britain ; "Les Naps" — Neuilly-Auteuil-Passy — in France ; the "3 S" generation — soldi, successo e sport — in Italy ; "Die Aufsteiger" — in Germany ; "Los jóvenes lobos" — the young wolves — in Spain… So many names for one category of young people who swim decidedly against the tide, who do not share the generous ideal which gave rise to the Welfare State.

They pretend not to work hard, but they are actual workaholics who seek *power* and *money* in such sectors as business, banking, the import-export trade, or high-profit ventures, for they are not averse to risk, provided it pays ! Shamelessly *self-centred* and *materialistic*, they enjoy "the good life" : powerful cars, fashionable clothes, dining out, holidays abroad, etc.

When they happen to get married, they form "Dinks" — double-income, no kids couples — who pursue the same ideal…

TEST YOUR KNOWLEDGE

1 - What is labour unrest being gradually replaced by ?

2 - What is worker participation ?

3 - What are quality circles ?

4 - What makes it easier for mothers today to lead a professional life ? (two reasons)

5 - Why does profit-related pay improve industrial relations ?

6 - What are fringe benefits ?

7 - Why is "well pay" a paradox ?

17 - **TO BREAK-BROKE-BROKEN**

casser, briser, rompre (propre et figuré).
- To break even : *ne faire ni pertes ni profits, rentrer dans ses frais.*
+ down : the duplicator is out of order : it broke down yesterday.
La machine à ronéotyper est en panne : elle est tombée en panne hier.
+ into : we have broken into the American market : *nous avons fait une percée sur...*
+ out : a flu (influenza) epidemic has broken out in the department : *une épidémie de grippe s'est déclarée dans le service.*
+ up : a compromise in order to break up the deadlock in the pay negociations : *...pour sortir de l'impasse dans les négociations salariales.*

Substantifs :
- A nervous breakdown = collapse : *une dépression nerveuse.*
- The breakdown was not serious, the machine is now in working order : *en état de marche.*
- A breakdown of expenses : *un décompte des dépenses.*
- A secretary's job is more pleasant now thanks to the breakthroughs achieved in electronics : *le travail d'une secrétaire est plus agréable maintenant grâce aux découvertes réalisées en électronique.*
- We have reached breakeven point : *nous avons atteint le seuil de rentabilité.*
- A further outbreak (bout - upsurge) of inflation : *une nouvelle poussée de, une recrudescence...*
- An outbreak of labour unrest (labour turmoil) : *une vague d'agitation sociale.*
- A breach of contract : *une rupture de contrat.*

18 - **TO BREED-BRED-BRED**

élever (des animaux), se reproduire ; engendrer (figuré)
- Lots of people used to breed hens and rabbits during the war owing to the scarcity of eggs and meat.
- Idleness breeds vice : *l'oisiveté engendre le vice.*
mais : *élever des enfants :* to bring up (brought - brought)
A thoroughbred : *un pur sang.*
A breed of cattle : *une race de bovins.*

19 - **TO BRING-BROUGHT-BROUGHT**

apporter, amener
- Should you not comply with this deadline, we would bring an action against you : *au cas où vous ne respecteriez pas ce délai (cette date limite), nous vous intenterions un procès.*
- I can't bring myself to allocate the entire sum to the purchase of machinery : *je ne puis me résoudre à consacrer la somme entière à l'achat de machines.*

Expression :
- Our Governments will bring pressure to bear on the Japanese authorities for car exports to Europe to be reduced by half : *Nos gouvernements feront pression sur les autorités japonaises pour que les exportations de voitures vers l'Europe soient réduites de moitié* (will put - apply - exert pressure on the Japanese).

Synonymes :
+ about : to lead (led-led) up to, to cause, to give rise to : *mener à, donner naissance à, causer.*
- This policy has brought about (has led up to) the imbalance between the volume of our imports and that of our exports : *cette politique a entraîné le déséquilibre entre le volume de nos importations et celui de nos exportations.*
+ down : to lower. Banks have brought down their lending rates : *les banques ont baissé leur taux d'escompte.*
+ in : to yield, to earn interest : *rapporter.*
- No investment brings in (yields) 20 % a year - earns 20 % interest a year.
+ up : *élever des enfants* (to breed-bred-bred : *élever des animaux*).
Ne pas confondre : a good upbringing : *une bonne éducation.*
a good education : *une bonne instruction.*

Inflation has been brought under control : *...a été maîtrisée...*

To curb, to bridle, to rein in ; to stem, to check, to stamp out.

20 - **TO BROADCAST-BROADCAST-BROADCAST**

diffuser, émettre
- The BBC - The British Broadcasting Corporation.

- A recorded broadcast : *une émission en différé* ≠ live : *en direct.* To record : *enregistrer.*
mais : the Government have issued a package of measures : *...a émis une série (un train) de mesures.*

21 - TO BUILD-BUILT-BUILT

bâtir, construire
The building trade (building industry) was thriving (flourishing) in the 50s : *l'industrie du bâtiment (le bâtiment) a été prospère au cours de années 50.*
- High-rise buildings, (mot proche : skyscrapers : *gratte-ciel*) mar the beauty of (disfigure) cities like Paris, London, etc. *Des « tours » enlaidissent (déparent) des villes comme Paris, Londres, etc.*
+up : *constituer, amasser, s'accumuler*
- A few building constractors built up a fortune after the war.
- To build up reserves, a stock of st.
- Evidence continues to build up : *les preuves continuent à s'accumuler.*

participe passé : Built-in : *incorporé*
- A tape recorder with a built-in loudspeaker : *un magnétophone avec haut-parleur incorporé.*
- A flat with built-in cupboards : *...placards encastrés.*

22 - TO BURN-BURNT-BURNT

brûler
- To burn to ashes : *réduire en cendres.*
- A burn : *une brûlure.*

23 - TO BURST-BURST-BURST

(faire) éclater, exploser
sens figuré : industrialized countries are bursting with food *(regorgent de nourriture)* whereas the Third World's populations are starving.
+ into : the secretary burst into sobs when she saw the pile of letters she had to type : *...éclata en sanglots...*
+ out : to burst out laughing : *éclater de rire.*

substantif : The boss is notorious for his outbursts of anger : *le patron est (tristement) célèbre pour ses accès de colère.*

24 - TO BUY-BOUGHT-BOUGHT

acheter
She can't afford to buy a fur-coat : it's beyond her means (≠ it's within her means). *Elle ne peut se permettre d'acheter un manteau de fourrure : elle n'en a pas les moyens (≠ elle en a...)*

Attention ! He has bought his wife a car - He has bought a car *for* his wife.
I bought that typewriter second-hand *from* a colleague of mine : *...à une de mes collègues (elle me l'a vendue).*
to make purchases : *faire des achats, des emplettes.*

Substantif : Cf. purchasing power : *le pouvoir d'achat.*

25 - TO CAST-CAST-CAST

jeter, lancer (propre et figuré) ; couler (métal)
- It's no use casting your line into the water if you have forgotten the bait ! *(l'appât)*
- A huge tanker has cast anchor off the island (≠ to heave anchor).
Un énorme pétrolier a jeté l'ancre au large de l'île (≠ lever l'ancre).
- The boss cast a glance at the letter : " It's badly set out ! "
Le patron jeta un coup d'œil sur la lettre : " Elle est mal présentée ! "
- The chairman has a casting vote : ... *a une voix prépondérante.*
- To cast molten metal into a mould : *couler du métal en fusion dans un moule.*
- Cast-iron : *la fonte*
+ about for (around for) - try to find : They are casting about for funds : *ils recherchent des capitaux.*

Substantif : a live broadcast : *une émission en direct*
the weather forecast : *les prévisions météorologiques*
- Migrant workers are sometimes treated as outcasts.
On traite parfois les travailleurs immigrés comme des parias.
- When the weather is overcast, I feel downcast !
Quand le temps est couvert, je me sens déprimé (depressed).

Superlatifs

1 - ABSOLU

Traduction de très, fort, bien, des plus.

a) Adjectifs ou participes présents
- It was a **very** good match.
- It is a **very** interesting film.

b) Participes passés
- He was **very much** embarrassed.
- It is a **much** coveted jewel *(très convoité).*

Sauf les participes passés courants : I am very tired, pleased, etc.

c) Dans tous les cas
- He was **most** astonished when they told him : *il fut des plus étonnés...*
- I find it **most** revolting : *je trouve cela des plus révoltants.*
- He is a **most** intelligent dog : *c'est un chien des plus intelligents.*

2 - RELATIF

a) Supériorité

■ Adjectifs longs
- He is **the most** formidable character that I have ever met.

C'est le personnage le plus impressionnant que j'aie jamais rencontré.

■ Adjectifs courts
- Mount Everest is **the** high**est** mountain in the world.
- He is the laziest member of the family.

b) Infériorité : l'éviter, surtout avec les **adjectifs courts**
- She is certainly **the least** attractive girl of all.

Elle est certainement la moins séduisante de toutes. Mais : " the smallest " remplacera " the least big ", etc.

Remarque : Le complément du superlatif : " in " + nom de lieu
" of " dans les autres cas
- The church is the highest building **in** the village.
- She is the prettiest girl of the class.

Comparatifs et superlatifs irréguliers

■ Good, well : better, the best
- His English is better than yours.
- He speaks English better than you do.

■ Bad : worse, the worst
- The economic situation is worse than it is generally believed to be.

La situation économique est pire qu'on ne le croit généralement.

■ Far : farther, the farthest : idée de distance
further, the furthest : sens figuré
- Walk **far**ther back.

Reculez davantage.
- Give me **fur**ther information.

Donnez-moi des renseignements complémentaires.

- Old, older, the eldest : employés comme épithètes pour les membres d'une même famille.
  - She is their eldest child.
    Elle est leur aînée, l'aînée de leurs enfants.

Mais : My sister is **older** than I (attribut).
  - He is my oldest friend (il appartient à une autre famille).

Emplois divers

1 - COMPARAISON ENTRE DEUX ÉLÉMENTS : COMPARATIF EN ANGLAIS

- Paint the upper part in red, the lower part in blue
  Peins la partie la plus haute en rouge, la plus basse en bleu.
- The **weaker** prisoners would be killed ; the **stronger** ones would work in the mine.
  Les prisonniers les plus faibles étaient tués ; les plus forts travaillaient à la mine.
- Pupils in the upper forms (≠ the lower forms).
  Les élèves des grandes classes (≠ des petites classes).
- The weak**er** sex : *le sexe faible.*

2 - TRADUCTION DE : " DE PLUS EN PLUS "

Accroissement progressif
- The story is getting **more and more** exciting.
- If you use that soap, your complexion *(votre teint)* will become prettier and prettier.
- That pig is getting fatter and fatter.

Attention ! En Anglais économique :
- Raw materials are **increasingly** expensive.
  Les matières premières sont de plus en plus chères.

- Gradually less + adjectif ou adverbe — *" De moins en moins ".*
- Fewer and fewer + nom pluriel - Fewer and fewer people go to the cinema : it is becoming gradually less popular.

3 - TRADUCTION DE : " PLUS... PLUS ", " MOINS... MOINS '

Accroissement parallèle
- The more, the merrier.
  Plus il y a de fous, plus on rit. (Textuellement : plus on est, plus on est joyeux).
- The angrier he is, the redder he becomes !
  Plus il est en colère, plus il rougit !
- The better he knows men, the better he loves animals.
- The faster you drive, the more dangerous you are.
- The less you will drink, the longer you will live.

THEME D'APPLICATION NUMERO 2

1 - Ce pays n'est pas très industrialisé, son Président doit se résoudre à consacrer des sommes importantes (= large) à l'achat de machines.
2 - L'industrie du bâtiment n'a pas été l'activité la moins prospère (2 traductions) cette année mais les " tours " enlaidissent maintenant les plus beaux quartiers (area) de nos villes.
3 - Il n'y a pas de pire investissement sur le marché car il rapporte moins de 2 % par an !
4 - Les pays riches (wealthy) regorgent de nourriture et les populations meurent de faim dans les pays pauvres !
5 - Le travail d'une secrétaire devient de plus en plus agréable grâce aux découvertes réalisées en électronique.
6 - Notre politique est de moins en moins rationnelle (rational) car elle entraîne le déséquilibre entre le volume de nos importations et celui de nos exportations.
7 - Plus le temps est couvert, plus elle se sent déprimée et comme les accès de colère du patron sont de plus en plus violents, une dépression nerveuse est inévitable.
8 - Moins elle a de lettres à taper, mieux elle les présente ! C'est une conséquence des plus logiques (logical) !
9 - Nous sommes très intéressés par (in) les nouveaux taux d'escompte : les banques les ont baissés.
10 - Les preuves s'accumulent ; les pires prédictions s'avèrent (to prove) justes, nous ne rentrerons pas dans nos frais cette année.
11 - Si nous ne sortons pas de l'impasse dans les négociations salariales, nous pouvons nous attendre à une vague d'agitation sociale des plus déplaisantes (unpleasant).
12 - Le plus petit lapin était très apprécié pendant la guerre à cause de la rareté de la viande.
13 - Nos gouvernements ne peuvent aller plus loin dans leurs interventions pour que les Japonais exportent de moins en moins de voitures vers l'Europe.
14 - (En ce moment) Ils recherchent des capitaux pour acheter des machines, mais il est de moins en moins certain qu'ils en trouveront !
15 - La pression que nous exerçons sur les salaires et sur les prix est de moins en moins efficace (effective) : nous ne pourrons pas juguler l'inflation !

3 - THE WELFARE STATE

DEFINITION

A country is said to be a Welfare State when it aims at ensuring the welfare (the well-being) of all its inhabitants by means of state-financed social services.

ORIGIN

It was born in Europe, especially in Scandinavia (Sweden, Norway, Denmark, Finland), the Benelux countries (Belgium, the Netherlands, Luxembourg), Great Britain, West Germany and France.
Rudimentary between the two World Wars, it was to develop rapidly after World War II, spurred by economic expansion. The rising welfare costs would then be covered by increasing tax revenues. Unfortunately there occurred a slowdown in economic expansion following upon the successive oil price shocks in the Seventies. Unemployment swelled, and inflation gnawed at consumers' purchasing power, which weakened production all the more. Paradoxically, governments had to face soaring welfare outlays at the very moment when their resources - in this case tax revenues - were shrinking.

Unlike the above-mentioned European countries, the United States are not a fully-fledged Welfare State yet. This is probably due to the fact that they are a nation of immigrants, tough people who are more accustomed to relying on themselves than on the community. The pioneers of old used to believe in the " American dream ", and it still obtains with immigrants today, though probably to a lesser extent.

The " American dream " is the assurance that America offers its citizens equality of opportunity : even if you start from scratch, you can be confident that you will " make it " by fending for yourself. That belief in the virtues of self-reliance can explain why the welfare system in the United States is still a patchwork of social programmes which is slowly evolving towards its European model.

By contrast, Old Europe, after all its trials and tribulations, wanted to create a more humane society by atoning for the injustice of fate ; it wanted the aged, the unemployed, the sick, the disabled, the widowed - in a word, the underprivileged - to have a share in the benefits of an affluent society that so far only the well-to-do could enjoy.

EVOLUTION

The lofty goal of the Welfare States' founders was that all citizens should be entitled to benefits " from the womb to the tomb " or " from the cradle to the grave " ; it was unfortunately to spell their undoing ! That egalitarian ideal was generous, but when the system was in its prime, it was over-ambitious and short-sighted. When - among other reasons - their economies ran out of steam, the Welfare States found themselves in a sorry plight. To meet their commitments they had to resort to domestic and foreign loans, thus running into debt.

Today the media expatiate on their woes, and wonder how they will extricate themselves from the morass !

CAUSES OF THE DECLINE

- *A drop in tax revenues.* Social programmes depend on taxes and the contributions paid by companies and the active population. In a slump, contributions will be less substantial, and the problem is compounded by the fact that a good many workers are made redundant : not only do they not pay their contributions any longer, but they qualify for unemployment benefits ! Moreover, ailing companies get support from the State !
- *The aging of populations.* In all industrialized countries, the birth rate is undergoing a sharp drop, and demographers denounce the " graying " of those countries, i. e., the aging of their populations. Thanks to better nutrition, progress in medicine, scientific breakthroughs which lead up to high-technology health care, the aged enjoy a longer life expectancy. They are unfortunately more susceptible to disease than the young, and as their number keeps rising, more and more geriatric hospitals and old people's homes are needed. Concurrently, the age of retirement has been lowered to sixty, or even earlier sometimes ; and more elderly people are now eligible for a pension, which puts an extra strain on the states' coffers at the very moment when the drop in the birth rate whittles away the active population !
- *Index-linked benefits.* In the heyday of Welfare States, welfare benefits used to be pegged to the Consumer Price Index. Cost-of-living adjustments would be

carried out regularly. Whenever inflation flared up, it would accordingly bloat the benefits. Unfortunately, contributions did not follow suit !

- *Black labour.* As unemployment is rife, a number of workers resort to black labour (moonlighting). As their earnings are illegal, neither employers nor employees need to pay any contributions.
- *Cheating.* Unscrupulous people take advantage of the system. Some of them will make false claims in order to receive higher or unwarranted benefits. Others, who are officially on the dole eke out the benefits by moonlighting.
- *The system's extravagance.* Part of the blame can be laid on the unstinted generosity of the Welfare State which at one time used to be profligate ; it would also lavish benefits on undeserving people without checking carefully whether they were rightfully entitled to them.
- *Paradoxical effects.* Worse still, social programmes are reproached for making people fall into either the unemployment or the poverty traps, for pushing up the rates of unemployment and inflation.

The unemployment trap concerns the unemployed people whose incomes, after adding up various benefits, are not far from being as substantial as the paypackets that they would bring home from the regular jobs that they are offered. So, why work ?

The poverty trap concerns the people who draw meagre wages and are consequently granted supplementary benefits. Their income may then reach a higher bracket, and the Inland Revenue claws back what welfare had granted.

The contributions that companies have to pay are certainly not likely to break the vicious circle, and even less if Governments try to raise them in order to meet their commitments. In one way or another, companies recoup them by raising the prices of their lines, or by refusing to raise salaries and wages, and they balk at hiring more workers.

(to be continued)

TEST YOUR KNOWLEDGE

1 - What is a " Welfare State " ?

2 - Which countries are to be found in Scandinavia ?

3 - Why did the oil-price shocks lead up to a slowdown in economic expansion ?

4 - What is " the American dream " ?

5 - What was " old Europe's " ideal ?

6 - How did the Welfare States meet their commitments at one time ?

7 - Why, in a recession, is the Welfare State in a vicious circle ?

8 - Why are industrialized countries " graying " ?

9 - What is the unemployment trap ?

10 - What is the poverty trap ?

26 - **TO CATCH-CAUGHT-CAUGHT**

attraper, prendre (propre et figuré)
- She was caught in the act : she was filing her nails instead of filing the invoices.
Elle a été prise sur le fait : elle se limait les ongles au lieu de classer les factures.
- Everybody catches cold owing to the oil shortage.
Tout le monde attrape le rhume à cause de la pénurie de pétrole.
To catch up with : *rattraper*
- Their development was already sluggish, but the oil-price shock has made them fall very far behind ; they will never catch up with our standard of living.
Leur développement était déjà très lent (a slug = une limace) *mais le choc pétrolier leur a fait prendre beaucoup de retard ; ils ne rattraperont jamais notre niveau de vie.*
Mais : I am behindhand in my work and I want to make up for lost time : *je suis en retard dans mon travail et je veux rattraper le temps perdu.*
- When the mechanic caught sight of the foreman...
Quand le mécanicien aperçut le contremaître...
- I just caught a glimpse of the shop-steward talking with the strike-picket.
Je n'ai fait qu'entrevoir le délégué syndical en train de discuter avec le piquet de grève.

Substantifs : Advertisers use catch-phrases such as " Drinka Pinta Milka Day " in their marketing campaigns (sales campaigns - sales drives).
Les annonceurs utilisent des slogans accrocheurs tels que... dans leurs campagnes commerciales.
Cf. an adman : *un publicitaire, un spécialiste de la publicité* (***mais :*** *un publiciste = un journaliste).*

27 - **TO CHIDE-CHID-CHIDDEN**

R - : *gronder*
to scold, to reprimand sont plus courants
Cf. to find fault with : *trouver à redire à* (≠ to praise - *louer, faire l'éloge de + for*)
- Although she is a dedicated (devoted) secretary, he is always finding fault with her work.
Cf. to reproach sb. **with** st., **for** doing st.
- They reproach the Minister for failing to redress the trade balance.
Ils reprochent au Ministre de ne pas arriver à redresser la balance commerciale.

28- **TO CHOOSE-CHOSE-CHOSEN**

choisir :

Synonyme : to pick out, to select (propre et figuré)
- **Which** package (d) tour are you going to choose for the Summer ?
Quel voyage organisé allez-vous choisir pour cet été ?
- As you choose - as you like - as you please - as you wish !
Comme vous voudrez !

Substantif : We have no choice (alternative) ! Refusing (turning down) the merger would be tantamount to committing suicide !
Nous n'avons pas le choix ! Refuser la fusion reviendrait à nous suicider !

Attention ! You **take** a choice but you **make** a decision

29 - **TO CLEAVE-CLEFT-CLEFT**

ou clove - cloven ou R :
fendre, diviser moins courant que to split - split - split

Substantif : The cleavage (split-division) between capital and labour (the employers and the workers, the management and the shopfloor, etc.).
Le clivage entre le capital et le travail (le patronat et les travailleurs, la direction et les ateliers, etc.)

30 - **TO CLING-CLUNG-CLUNG**

s'accrocher à (propre et figuré)
- A great many illegal migrant workers cling to the hope of being able to straighten out their position and get a residence and work permit.
Bon nombre de travailleurs étrangers clandestins s'accrochent à l'espoir de pouvoir régulariser leur situation et obtenir un permis de séjour et de travail.

31 - **TO COME-CAME-COME**

venir, arriver

Attention !

■ *Arriver* (*événement* = event) : to happen, to take place, to occur (prétérit occu**rr**ed)
■ Arriver à (*réussir à - parvenir à*) :
to manage to + infinitif
to succeed in + gérondif
Ne pas arriver à : to fail to + infinitif
I fail to understand why...

Passé récent :

venir de - to have just + participe passé
- We've won ! The Board have just earmarked 3m dollars for research and development.
Nous avons gagné ! Le Conseil (d'administration) vient d'affecter 3 millions de dollars à la recherche fondamentale et appliquée.

Expressions :

- The law will come into force as from March 1st : *entrera en vigueur.*
... All of a sudden, the oil rig (the drilling rig) came into sight.
Soudain, la plateforme pétrolière (la plateforme de forage) apparut.
- When you come of age, your parents will no longer be entitled to family allowances.
Quand vous atteindrez votre majorité, vos parents n'auront plus droit aux allocations familiales.
- Will the dream of " The United States of Europe " ever come true (ever be realized) ?
... se réalisera-t-il jamais ?
- The recession has come to an end : the economic recovery (the economic revival) is becoming more marked (more pronounced) day after day.
La récession est arrivée à son terme : la reprise économique s'accentue (devient plus sensible) jour après jour.
- These items come in different colours : *ces articles existent en différentes couleurs.*
+ to : to add up to, to amount to : *atteindre, se chiffrer à, se monter à, revenir à* (aussi : to total up to, to run up to)
- His earnings come to an astronomical sum : *ses gains atteignent...*
- Production has come to a standstill... : *s'est arrêtée, est paralysée.*

Substantifs composés :

- All increments in your salary must of course appear in your income tax return**s** ! They are not under-the-table perquisites !
Toutes vos augmentations de salaire doivent bien sûr figurer dans votre déclaration d'impôts sur le revenu ! Ce ne sont pas des " dessous de table " !
- A civil servant does not need a computer to reckon his yearly income !
Un fonctionnaire n'a pas besoin d'ordinateur pour calculer son revenu annuel !
- What was the outcome of the collective bargaining that took place in Paris last week ?
Quelle a été l'issue des négotiations pour une convention collective qui ont eu lieu à Paris la semaine dernière ?
- The forthcoming conference of the O.P.E.**C**. in Geneva heralds (foreshadows) a further increase in the price of crude (oil).
*La prochaine conférence de l'O.P.E.**P**.* à Genève présage une nouvelle augmentation du prix du (pétrole) brut.
- Obvious as the shortcomings (faults - defects - failings) of his policy are, he is convinced that it is able to stave off the collapse of our economy.
Quelque évidents que soient les défauts de sa politique, il est convaincu qu'elle peut éviter l'effondrement de notre économie . (to stave off-fend off-ward off : avert)

4 - TRADUCTION DE " D'AUTANT PLUS, D'AUTANT MOINS "

- A nuclear war is **the more** improbable **as** it would destroy the world.
- Their reaction is **the less** understandable **as** they had been warned (avertis).

Remarques : Se construisent comme des comparatifs :
- You have given me **the same** answer **as** all the others.
- Couldn't you have **other** friends **than** those long-haired rascals ? (ces vauriens à cheveux longs)
- He would **rather** die **than** betray his country (trahir son pays).
- **No sooner** had the pilots landed **than** they had to take off again.
A peine les pilotes eurent-ils atterri qu'ils durent redécoller.

Mais :
- He won't drink anything **else but** wine.
  Il ne veut rien boire d'autre que du vin.
- Their output (leur production) is superior (≠ inferior) **to** ours.

5 - TRADUCTION DE DEUX FOIS (ETC.) PLUS, MOINS

- Prices rise twice **as** fast **as** wages (≠ half as fast as wages).
  Les prix montent 2 fois plus vite que les salaires (≠ 2 fois moins vite).
- He earns three or four times **as much as** a manual worker.
  Il gagne trois ou quatre fois plus qu'un travailleur manuel.
- He eats half as much as his sister.
  Il mange deux fois moins que sa soeur.
- The human heart beats one tenth as fast as that insect's.
  Le coeur humain bat dix fois moins vite que celui de cet insecte.

THÈME D'APPLICATION NUMÉRO 3

1 - Les secrétaires courageuses (courageous) classent les factures, les paresseuses se liment les ongles !
2 - Leur développement est de plus en plus lent (pas " slow ") : ils ne rattraperont jamais notre niveau de vie qui s'élève de plus en plus (devient de plus en plus élevé).
3 - Plus une secrétaire est dévouée, plus il est désagréable (unpleasant) envers elle, trouvant toujours à redire à son travail !
4 - Le clivage entre le patronat et les ouvriers est d'autant moins important (considerable) de nos jours que ceux-ci obtiennent de meilleurs salaires.
5 - La conférence présage (2 traductions) une nouvelle augmentation du prix du brut : il sera un jour deux fois plus cher qu'il ne l'est aujourd'hui.
6 - Les sondages (public opinion polls) trouvent dix fois moins de défauts dans notre politique que dans la précédente (previous) : si c'est vrai, nous éviterons (4 traductions) l'effondrement de notre économie.
7 - Le Conseil est de moins en moins généreux (generous) ; il affecte de moins en moins de fonds (funds) à la recherche et cela revient à nous suicider !
8 - Quand nous serons majeurs, nos parents toucheront trois fois moins d'allocations qu'ils n'en touchent aujourd'hui.
9 - L'issue des négociations collectives est d'autant moins acceptable que les décisions n'entreront en vigueur que l'an prochain.
10 - Grâce aux nouvelles lois, il y a environ deux fois moins de travailleurs étrangers clandestins qu'il y a quatre ans.
11 - Nos deux sociétés ont accepté la fusion d'autant plus facilement que la reprise économique s'accentue.
12 - Les bénéfices ne peuvent qu'atteindre des sommes de plus en plus substantielles car nos articles seront cinq fois moins chers que ceux de nos concurrents !
13 - Nous arriverons à redresser la balance commerciale d'autant moins facilement que notre production est paralysée !
14 - Je crois que sa secrétaire lui était d'autant plus dévouée que chaque année elle obtenait de généreuses augmentations de salaire !
15 - A cause des chocs pétroliers ils achètent trois fois moins de pétrole qu'en 1969 mais ils s'accrochent à l'espoir de devenir producteurs grâce à leurs plateformes de forage en (dans la) Mer du Nord.

4 - THE WELFARE STATE

(Deuxième partie)

THE FUTURE

The rising generations take for granted the rights acquired by their elders, and there is no question of depriving them of benefits obtained after arduous negotiations - sometimes fierce tugs-of-war - between unions and management, and after countless parliamentary debates. All the more so as the work ethic is on the wane - at least in its traditional version - and people are no longer ashamed of being aided : they are even eager to obtain more !

Moreover, which politician would be courageous enough to canvass a so far coddled constituency with a political platform that undertakes to prune the welfare system ? It would result in political suicide to try and tamper with it !

REMEDIES

Governments are on the horns of a dilemma : they cannot jettison the Welfare State although the huge sums gobbled up by social services have not succeeded in wiping out inequalities. They cannot go on borrowing money and bequeath the debts to posterity. On the other hand, everyone acknowledges that social objectives - noble as they are - should not jeopardize the economy.

Since it is imperative that welfare programmes should be revamped, Governments must resign themselves to choosing from the following array the measures that they deem most appropriate, bearing in mind all the while that they must rein in soaring public expenditure without spurning the legitimate needs of the ill-fated.

- Increase contributions to shore up the system and bridge the gap between income and outflow. A most unwelcome measure !
- Retrench the expenditure by trimming benefits and pensions. For instance, retirement pensions could very well be made up of one third only from the state, one third from private schemes (occupational pension schemes) and one third from savings (deposits with Savings Banks, Building Societies, Unit Trusts (US : Mutual Funds) ; shares, debentures, etc.)

  Scaling down benefits and pensions would be tantamount to regressing to the original concept of welfare : a mere safety net devised to stave off utter poverty. It would raise a general outcry !
- Encourage people to retire later or discourage them from early retirement. But that is contingent upon people's positions : a successful engineer will undoubtedly be more inclined towards late retirement than a toiling manual worker.
- Incite and help families to keep their aged parents or relatives at home, and look after them instead of shrugging off that responsibility and passing it on to the state.
- Call upon voluntary helpers, private associations, charitable institutions, churches, etc., so as to ease the strain on public services. In short, call for a return to a self-help society !
- Appeal to citizens' sense of civic responsibility, and try to instil it into children at school as early as possible. Accustom people to coping with minor ailments.
- Institute a two-tier system. The state would meet only part of health expenses, and people would be induced to take out private insurance policies to make up the coverage.
- Check the validity of claim more carefully, track down abuses, hunt down the scroungers of all types who shamelessly will make it a habit of sponging upon society.
- Enhance the work ethic by suppressing the unemployment trap. Avoid by all means making of a number of poor wretches the permanent wards of society.
- Workfare. It is because they value the work ethic, and to prevent children from growing up with the feeling that they are dependent upon the state, that a good many American states have launched out into that new scheme. It concerns single women in good health with school-age children - a matter of four million mothers and their seven million children, or so - who are entirely supported by A.F.D.C. : Aid to Families with Dependent Children. After completing a period of training, they are helped to find a job. If they do not comply with the regulations, if they refuse the job, they are struck off the list of welfare recipients.

  Great Britain might adopt a form of workfare for its long-term unemployed ; recalcitrants might be denied benefits.
- Workfare is not running too smoothly in the United States because of a lack of day care centres for the children of working mothers. A large number of

" latchkey children " are left too much to themselves. That is why firms are invited to create their own centres, relieving the state of the outlay.

■ Governments should clamp down on illegal immigration since illegal migrant workers work on the side, and end up living at society's expense.

■ Since it is patently obvious that alcoholism, drug-addiction and chain-smoking put a great strain on the Health-Service resources, Governments ought to take all possible steps to do away with these scourges. " Prevention is better than cure ! "

■ Hopes. Governments are reduced to pinning their hopes on a renewed surge in birth rates - all the financial incentives that they have devised to trigger it have not

THE LIBERALITIES OF THE MODEL WELFARE STATE

GB : The National Health Service (NHS)
The Department of Health and Social Security
US : The Department of Health, Education and Welfare
Medicaid - programme providing medical aid for the poor.
Medicare - programme providing medical care for the aged.
Social Security - Social Insurance - National Insurance, etc.

HEALTH

■ - Free hospitals and maternity hospitals
- Free surgical, medical, dental and ophthalmic care
- Free remedies

■ Protection of public health :
- Control of infectious diseases (free screening for cancer, Aids, etc., free vaccination)
- Prevention and treatment of drug dependence (alcoholics and drug addicts)
- Adequate sanitation : sewers ; effective sewage disposal works ; refuse disposal ; burial grounds ; rodent disinfestation, etc.
- Supply of wholesome water
- Prevention of air, water, land pollution
- Purity and safety of food (Additives, preservatives, colourings, flavourings, etc.)

■ Medical research

FAMILY PROBLEMS

- Maternity benefits -Pre-and post-natal allowances
- Family allowances - Allowances for non-salaried mothers
- Allowances for widows and orphans
- Allowances for dependants
- Allowances for single mothers
- War pensions (disablement - widows and orphans)
- Death grants

HOUSING

- Subsidized housing (coucil houses or flats) - Housing benefits
- Cheap loans and mortgages : interest rate subsidies
- Rent allowances
- Slum and shanty town clearing campaigns ; rehousing
- Shelters and hostels (for the down-and-outs)

EDUCATION

- Subsidized or free creches and day-nurseries (US : day-care centers)
- Free education (scholarships, grants)
- Free school lunches
- Free or subsidized transport for school children

FOOD

- Subsidized staple commodities : bread, eggs, dairy produce and meat
- Food coupons (stamps) - " Meals-on-wheels " - Soup kitchens

TRANSPORT

- Subsidized public transport

WORK

- Industrial injury benefits
- Industrial disablement benefits
- Unemployment benefits : the dole
- Retirement pensions (old age pensions)
- Supplementary benefits for workers whose incomes are below a given level.
- etc.

TEST YOUR KNOWLEDGE

1 - Why would younger people object to the Welfare State being phased out ?

2 - Why are governments at a loss as regards the future of the Welfare State ?

3 - What could pensions be composed of in future ?

4 - What was the original concept of welfare ?

5 - As regards health what would the two-tier system consist in ?

6 - What is "workfare " in the United States ?

7 - What are "latchkey children " ?

8 - Why should governments crack down on illegal immigration ?

9 - Which three scourges in our societies ought to be eradicated ?

10 - How could a surge in birthrates contribute to solving the problem ?

32 - TO COST-COST-COST

coûter (propre et figuré)

Attention ! R dans le sens de : *chiffrer, établir le prix de revient de quelque chose.*

- There are so many variations in the price of copper ore that we have not costed our products once and for all !
Il y a tant de variations dans le prix du minerai de cuivre que nous n'avons pas chiffré le prix de nos produits une fois pour toutes.
- We have received the contractors' tenders ; the lowest bidder has **costed** the work at X dollards.
Nous avons reçu les soumissions des entrepreneurs ; le mieux disant a chiffré les travaux à X dollars.

Cf. an estimate - *un devis*

Mais : The alterations have **cost** us a fortune !
Les transformations nous ont coûté une fortune !

Substantif : The cost of living
The cost-of-living index
The cost price : *le prix de revient*
- Lots of supermarkets boast of selling a few items at cost price.
Des quantités de supermarchés se targuent de vendre quelques articles au prix coûtant.

Expressions : At all costs, at any cost : *coûte que coûte, à tous prix.*
At great cost ≠ at little cost.
A grands frais ≠ à peu de frais.

Adjectif : - He lavishes costly furs and jewels **on** her, but she does not deserve it !
Il lui prodigue des fourrures et des bijoux de grande valeur, mais elle ne le mérite pas !

Composé : - An investment must be cost-effective : *rentable (aussi : profitable)*

33 - TO CREEP-CREPT-CREPT

ramper, se glisser, s'insinuer
Cf. *ramper au sens propre* : to crawl (like snakes ; snails : *escargots*)
- The Sahara desert is creeping southward.
- Creeping inflation : *rampante.*

Mais : rampant inflation : *inflation galopante.*

34 - TO CROW-CREW-CROWED

(R) : *chanter (coq)*
- The cock left the poultry-yard *(basse-cour)*, climbed on to the dunghill (manure heap - *tas de fumier*) and crew (crowed) to reassure the hens and their chicks (*poussins*).
- It is no use crowing over your victory, we have not landed the contract yet !
Cela ne sert à rien de chanter victoire, nous n'avons pas encore décroché le contrat !

35 - TO CUT-CUT-CUT

couper (propre et figuré)
Souvent + down : *réduire, diminuer.*

Synonymes : to reduce, to lower, to curtail
- To cut (down) taxes, production, working hours, wages, expenses...

Substantif : a wage cut - a cut **in** wages
a tax cut - a cut **in** taxes :
une réduction de salaire, d'impôts.
- A merger entails staff cuts : *une fusion entraîne des compressions de personnel.*
- Trade unions demand (claim) a cut in working hours : *les syndicats revendiquent une réduction des heures de travail.*
- A power cut has disrupted the traffic : *une coupure d'électricité a perturbé la circulation.*

Substantifs composés : - Cut-price books : *des livres à prix réduit.*
- Cut-throat competition : *concurrence acharnée.*
- Cutbacks in spending (in expenditure) are needed to balance the budget : *des compressions budgétaires* (*aussi : budget restrictions*) *sont nécessaires pour équilibrer le budget.*

- To undercut : conventional shops cannot prevent hypermarkets from undercutting them ; ... *de vendre meilleur marché.*

36 - TO DARE

R - Prétérit parfois durst : *oser*
Comme to need, peut se conjuguer soit comme un verbe normal, soit comme un défectif.
- He dare not strike a bargain (he do**es** not dare **to** strike a bargain) with a company which is reputedly on the verge (brink) of bankruptcy !
Il n'ose pas conclure un marché avec une société qui, selon la rumeur publique, est au bord de la faillite !
(to strike a bargain - to clinch a deal)
- He need not worry (he do**es** not need **to** worry) about his bills : they are automatically deducted **from** his account : ... *prélevées sur son compte.*

Substantif et adjectif :

daring
- A daring company head : *un chef d'entreprise audacieux* (synonyme : bold).
- You'll need plenty of daring and drive to start a business right in the middle of the slump !
Il te faudra beaucoup d'audace et d'allant pour lancer une affaire en pleine crise économique (au beau milieu de la dépression) !

37 - TO DEAL-DEALT-DEALT

distribuer (souvent + out)
You deal out cards, money, gifts (*cadeaux*)

Mots proches :

répartir, partager : to share out something **among** (to distribute)
- The foreman shares out the tasks among the workers of his team.
Le contremaître répartit les tâches entre les ouvriers de son équipe.
- To deal somebody a blow : *asséner un coup à quelqu'un.*
- The slackening off of trade, soaring taxation and social security contributions have dealt scores of small and medium-sized concerns a death-blow !
Le ralentissement du commerce, la montée en flèche des impôts et des charges sociales ont asséné le coup de grâce à des dizaines de petites et moyennes entreprises.
+ in - to trade in : *faire le négoce de, être dans le commerce de.*
+ with : *traiter de :* What does the report deal with ?
s'occuper de, aborder

Synonymes :

to handle, to tackle ; to cope with, to grapple with
- The government has to deal with a difficult problem.

Substantifs :

- Business is looking up : we have just clinched a big deal with Saudi Arabia !
Les affaires reprennent : nous venons de conclure un gros marché avec l'Arabie Saoudite.
cf. to strike a bargain, struck - struck)
- It's a deal ! : *Marché conclu !*
Cf. the New Deal : Roosevelt's program of reforms (1933-1940) which favoured the United States economic recovery : ... *qui favorisa la reprise économique...* (US : program ; GB : programme)
A good (great) deal of : beaucoup + **singulier**
A good (great) many + **pluriel**
A dealer : *un négociant, un marchand* (a trader)
a horse dealer, a secondhand car dealer
- That Lebanese dealer trades **in** Indian fancy goods.
Ce marchand libanais fait commerce de bimbeloterie indienne. (that Lebanese trader deals **in**...)
- The end of the month is the absolute deadline ; if the goods have not been delivered by that date, we will not have any more dealings (business relations) with them.
La fin du mois est le dernier délai... nous cesserons toutes relations commerciales avec eux.
- Deal furniture is all the rage these days !
Le mobilier en bois blanc fait fureur en ce moment !

4 - STRUCTURES

PRETERIT ET PRESENT PERFECT

TOUTE ACTION SE DÉROULE AU COURS D'UNE ÉPOQUE.

1 - L'époque au cours de laquelle l'événement s'est produit est terminée au moment où l'on parle : un adverbe, une date ou simplement le contexte l'indiquent : **preterit**.
- I saw your mother last week.
- Napoleon died in 1821.

2 - Même si l'action s'est déroulée pendant longtemps, on emploie le prétérit simple si l'époque est révolue :
- The First World War lasted 4 years, from 1914 to 1918.
- My brother learnt English from 1945 to 1952 (for seven years).

3 - L'époque au cours de laquelle l'action s'est déroulée n'est pas terminée au moment où l'on parle : **present perfect.**
- I have seen your mother this week.
- Grandfather has died this year.

NB. Si l'action s'est déroulée jusqu'au moment où l'on parle, on emploie la forme progressive :
- I've been working hard this morning.

" I have worked hard this morning " implique que pendant un certain laps de temps j'ai travaillé dur ce matin.

4 - On s'intéresse seulement au résultat présent de l'action passée même si l'action s'est déroulée au cours d'une époque révolue au moment où l'on parle : **present perfect.**

Comparer :
- " Have you learnt your lesson ? " " Yes, Dad, I learnt it yesterday ".
- " Has he written to the boss ? " " Yes, he did it last week ".

THÈME D'APPLICATION NUMÉRO 4

1 - Nous avons chiffré le prix de nos produits une fois pour toutes, à savoir X dollars la (une) tonne.

2 - L'année dernière, le ralentissement du commerce et la montée en flèche des impôts et des charges sociales ont asséné le coup de grâce à notre entreprise.

3 - Leurs marchandises ont été livrées la semaine dernière, donc avant le dernier délai, et pourtant nous avons cessé toutes relations commerciales avec eux !

4 - De 1981 à 1982 leur société a été au bord de la faillite, c'est pourquoi (that is why) il n'ose pas (2 constructions) conclure un marché avec eux.

5 - " Avez-vous conclu un gros marché (traduction différente de Phrase 4) avec l'Arabie Saoudite ? " - " Oui, en Janvier, ils nous ont acheté X tonnes de minerai de cuivre ! "

6 - Il a si peu d'audace et d'allant qu'il ne pourra pas lancer une affaire au beau milieu de la dépression !

7 - Cette année, il y a eu moins de variations dans le prix des minerais ; vous n'avez pas besoin (2 constructions) de vous faire de souci pour l'avenir (the future).

8 - Les transformations nous ont coûté une somme si importante (2 constructions) que des compressions budgétaires sont nécessaires pour équilibrer le budget !

9 - Les investissements que nous avons effectués (to effect) ce mois-ci seront-ils rentables ?

10 - Tout au long de (throughout) l'année, nous avons réduit les dépenses, baissé les salaires, diminué les heures de travail, mais en vain (in vain) : une fusion entraîne des compressions de personnel.

11 - Bien sûr les syndicats revendiquent une réduction des heures de travail mais c'est impossible : ces derniers mois nous avons souffert (to suffer from) d'une concurrence acharnée !

12 - " Le contremaître a-t-il réparti les tâches ? " - " Il l'a fait à 8 heures "

13 - Il fait commerce de mobilier en bois blanc ; ce type de mobilier a fait fureur ces deux dernières années.

14 - De 1980 à 1984, à cause du ralentissement du commerce et de la montée en flèche de impôts et des charges sociales, beaucoup de petites et moyennes entreprises ont fait faillite (to go bankrupt).

15 - " Pourquoi ont-ils chanté victoire toute la journée (la journée entière) ? " - " Ils ont enfin décroché le contrat ! "

5 - TRADE-UNIONS : EVOLUTION

It is a fact that in all Western industrialized countries trade unions have been undergoing a decline in membership these last years, and that today they wield a weakening clout at the negotiation table.

CAUSES OF THE DECLINE

COMMON TO ALL COUNTRIES

■ A decline in smokestack industries (cars, steel, rubber, mining), and others : textiles, ship-building, etc, which used to be the stronghold of unions. Union rolls keep dwindling because a large number of unionized workers have been gradually laid off, and the trend is going on, on account of automation, computerization, competition from abroad (cars, steel), bankruptcies, shutdowns, etc.

■ A shift towards service industries. White-and pink-collar workers are not so interested in joining a union as blue-collar ones ; moreover in the so-called tertiary sector, there is quite a number of part-time and temporary workers. Full-time workers are wary of compromising their " career " by taking part in union activities ; they are not so responsive to ideology and rather impervious to solidarity.

■ Governments' austerity programmes. In a recession, Governments are not prone to comply with the demands of trade unions, strapped as they are for money, and compelled to run their budgets on a shoe string, hence a freeze on salaries and wages. The working of welfare states have ground to a halt, existing social benefits are ebbing, and there is no question of meeting unions' claims for additional ones !

■ Fading public support. If we are to believe public opinion polls, people are not hostile to unions ; they acknowledge that unions have been, and still are, though to a lesser degree, protecting workers' rights. But they are becoming weary of their principal means of action -strikes- which disrupt their lives by preventing them from commuting to their work, from getting mail, medical care or foodstuffs, etc., in exchange for meagre results.

■ The shift from large to smaller concerns. Unions find it more difficult to establish themselves in them as their employees tend to obtain more easily from management what they reasonably wish for.

■ Subcontracting, and the use of temporary workers. The latter seldom belong to a union, and no law prevents industrialists from farming out work to subsidiaries or subcontractors whose workforce is not unionized.

■ Management by-pass unions. To stave off the unionization of their employees, management take the initiative and deal directly with their workforce : they offer work conditions, such as flextime, continuity of employment, etc., hence employees' reaction : " why belong to a union when we are being well done by ! "

■ Dissension.

1. among unions. Consensus is sometimes difficult to reach regarding for instance the tactics to be adopted in order to bring pressure to bear on governments or employers. This can often be ascribed to the political leaning peculiar to each union. Although they perfectly know how apposite the proverbs are - " united we stand, divided we fall ", or " strength through unity " - they cannot agree on a joint platform and they pull in different or sometimes opposite directions !
2. within unions. Squabbling among union members leads up to the rank-and-file's defying the leaders, scorning their orders and acting on their own. Their possible success does not help matters, and sullies all the more the union's public image !

■ The scourge of unemployment. When so many workers are laid off, those who are lucky enough to have had a job for some time, or who have just found a suitable one, want to hold on to it and keep a low profile to that end ! After all, a bird in the hand is worth two in the bush !

■ New forms of work.

1. Temporary, part-time, seasonal work. Job-seekers, especially the long-term ones whose unemployment benefits have petered out, school-leavers, with or without qualifications, who are denied a steady job on account of their lack of experience, are only too glad to be offered employment for short periods. The increasing number of working mothers who divide their time between their families and their workplace, the people who are engaged for a season in the hotel - and catering trade, in camping sites, in amusement parks (theme parks), in agriculture at harvest time, etc., elude as a general rule the approaches and the hold of unions.

2. Telecommuting. Communication technology makes it possible for employees to stay at home and perform their work through a computer terminal connected to their firm's main-frame. Women are particulary interested in this new form of work as it enables them to stay at home and look after their children. This system bids fair to spread in service industries, which unions view unfavourably as it proves difficult to tout telecommuters for membership.

■ The very achievements of trade unions. They have come a long way since the pioneering days, and the younger generations can now enjoy the benefits of victories won by their elders by a hard-fought, relentless struggle. Paradoxically, they are apt to wonder what on earth they could now campaign for, considering the present circumstances and future prospects.

Peculiar to some countries

■ Great Britain. The influence of trade unions was at its peak in 1979, when " the British disease " - a propensity for striking - reached a climax after holding sway over social relations throughout the Seventies. That inordinate militancy was to backfire on the Labour Party : infuriated voters brought the Conservative Party into office, and Mrs Thatcher became Prime Minister.

From the very beginning, she evinced her distrust of trade unions, and undertook to clip their wings. The last significant showdown between organized labour and the Government was won by the latter after a 51-week strike called by the National Union of Mineworkers and its leader Arthur Cargill. It resulted in 14 deaths, a matter of 1,000 arrests, numberless injured strikers and policemen, enormous losses in output, and dire repercussions throughout the British economy.

Since the Conservatives hold that " unions fuel inflation and shackle productivity ", a few laws have been enacted to whittle away their power.

- Legal picketing is limited to the place where an employee has a job.

- Protection of employees against closed-shops. A closed-shop is an industrial or a business concern in which only trade-unionists are employed. The law lays down that no one can be compelled to join a union if he/she objects to it. Moreover, a new closed-shop will be set up only if 80 % of the staff are favourable to the proposal.

- Political and sympathy strikes (sympathetic strikes) are illegal. A sympathy strike (a form of " secondary action ") consists in exerting pressure on an employer who is not the strikers'.

- Secret ballots are imposed for union elections and important issues, such as strikes.

- Blacking is illegal. It is another form of sympathy strike which consists in refusing to handle goods from a firm whose workers are on strike, or to provide that firm with services of any kind.

- Unions are liable for damages when the law is not respected.

■ France. Because they are individualists who are not partial to clubs and associations, the French have always been less unionized than other European workers.

Moreover, workers have been gradually losing interest in trade unions which they find too much politicized.

Ultimately the grass-roots are apt to ignore union leaders and deal directly with management, or the Government in the public sector.

■ Germany. German industries have been moving from the heavily industrialized Northern part of the country towards the South, which traditionally used to be less unionized.

■ Spain and Portugal. These countries do not post a decline in union membership because of the drift from the land, farmhands thronging to towns in the hope of getting more substantial wages in industry.

■ Sweden. The majority of Swedish workers are union members, and consensus had always prevailed in labour relations until the country was hit by recession. In exchange for moderate wage increases, Prime Minister Olof Palme and his Government granted the unions more economic and political power by obtaining from the Parliament in 1983 a law creating in their favour five wage-earner funds, and entitling them to buy stock in Swedish companies.

The funds derive their money from new taxes on profits and payrolls. Since each fund is allowed to buy up to 8 % of a company's shares, the five funds together can own up to 40 % of that company's equity. The accruing profits are paid into Swedish pension funds. Each fund is administered by worker representatives appointed by the Government in agreement with union leaders.

The Confederation of Swedish Employers was of course opposed to the scheme. Employers pointed out that the new taxes would entail less profit, that jobs would be favoured to the detriment of profitability, that the Government and the unions would control industry and that the latter would thus be socialized.

The Government argued on the contrary that the funds would funnel new capital into the economy, which would thus improve production, create jobs and raise profits.

(to be continued)

38 - TO DIG-DUG-DUG

creuser, bêcher
Cf. to plough : *labourer*
- They have dug a tunnel **through** the cliff (*: falaise*)
- He is digging **up** his carrots : *il arrache ses carottes.*
- Archaeologists dig **up** the remains of ancient civilizations :
Les archéologues mettent au jour les vestiges des anciennes civilisations.

Substantifs composés :
The gold-digger hides his nuggets in an old dug-out.
Le chercheur d'or cache ses pépites dans une vieille pirogue.

39 - TO DO-DID-DONE

faire (sens abstrait)

Avec prépositions :
We cannot **do away with** (to suppress) so many jobs at one go : we will phase them out.
Nous ne pouvons pas supprimer autant d'emplois en une seule fois : nous les supprimerons progressivement (graduellement).
(≠ to phase in : *introduire progressivement*)
Europe cannot **do without** (dispense with) the Third World and its vast outlets.
L'Europe ne peut se passer du Tiers Monde et de ses vastes débouchés.
Our competitors boast up-to-date machinery ; **we** still have **to make do with** antiquated machine tools (we must content ourselves with ; we must be satisfied with).
Nos concurrents se flattent de posséder des machines ultra-modernes ; nous, nous devons encore nous contenter de machines-outils vétustes (nous satisfaire de).

Substantifs :
There are moral standards in business, but one is not always rewarded by tremendous profits for one's good **deeds**, or punished by severe losses for one's **misdeeds** !
Il existe une morale dans les affaires, mais on n'est pas toujours récompensé pour ses bonnes actions par des bénéfices fantastiques, ou puni pour ses mauvaises actions (méfaits) par des pertes sévères !
- The boss is sick and tired of (is fed up with) all those thefts ; he is seeking a radical means to do away with (get rid of) all wrong-doers (evil-doers) !
Le patron en a assez de tous ces vols ; il recherche un moyen radical pour se débarrasser de tous les malfaiteurs !
- You are making much **ado** about nothing ! Your protest is irrelevant : it has nothing **to do** with the matter in hand !
Vous faites beaucoup de bruit pour rien ! Votre protestation est hors de propos : cela n'a rien ***à voir*** *avec l'affaire en question (en cours).*
- Gambling has been his **undoing** ; he has embezzled the firm's money to settle his debts.
Le jeu l'a conduit à sa perte ; il a détourné l'argent de la firme pour régler ses dettes.

Adjectif :
Well-to-do (well-off) people able to live on their private means are few and far between.
Les gens aisés capables de vivre de leurs rentes sont rares. (scarce - seldom met with)

Proverbe :
What is done cannot be undone !
Ce qui est fait est fait !

40 - TO DRAW-DREW-DRAWN

- Electric or diesel engines draw (pull) goo**ds** or passeng**er** trains ; tugs tow (tug) cargo boats (freighters) out of harbours.
Des locomotives à moteurs électriques ou diesel tirent les trains de marchandises ou de voyageurs ; des remorqueurs halent les cargos pour les faire sortir des ports.
- When I have a steady job and I draw a regular wage, I'll propose to her.
Quand j'aurai un emploi stable et que je toucherai un salaire régulier je la demanderai en mariage.
- You write out a cheque to draw (withdraw) money from a bank account.
On rédige un chèque pour retirer de l'argent d'un compte bancaire.
- May I draw your attention to the fact that prosperity in agribusiness is to a large extent dependent on the weather ?
*Puis-je attirer votre attention sur le fait que la prospérité dans le secteur de l'agr**o**alimentaire est, dans une grande mesure, tributaire des intempéries ?* (aussi : agro-food Sector)

- The Chancellor of the Exchequer has drawn a dismal (gloomy) picture of the present economic circumstances, and future prospects are anything but bright (the outlook is rather grim - bleak).
Le ministre des Finances (GB ; US : the Secretary of the Treasury ; ailleurs : the Finance Minister) *a tracé un sombre tableau de la conjoncture économique actuelle, et les perspectives d'avenir sont loin d'être brillantes (les perspectives d'avenir sont assez sombres - maussades).*
- As no volunteer had stepped forward, they drew lots to appoint the delegate who would inform the boss that they were willing to accept a compromise in order to break up the deadlock in the pay neg**ot**iations.
*Comme aucun volontaire ne s'était présenté, ils ont tiré au sort pour désigner le délégué qui informerait le patron de ce qu'ils voulaient bien accepter un compromis afin de sortir de l'impasse dans les négo**ci**ations salariales.*
+ up : *dresser, rédiger, établir* : a list, a contract, a plan, a scheme, etc.

Substantifs :

- You will find a treasure in his **chest of drawers** : the old miser has hidden there the jewels and other valuable**s** that he has been hoarding up all his life.
Vous trouverez un trésor dans sa commode : le vieil avare y a caché les bijoux et autres objets de valeur qu'il a amassés (accumulés, mis en réserve) durant toute sa vie.
- There are advantages and **drawbacks** in all the trades that you can carry on (follow), in all the professions that you can exercise (practise).
Il y a des avantages et des inconvénients dans tous les métiers que l'on peut pratiquer, dans toutes les professions que l'on peut exercer.

Draught (GB) - Draft (US)

- The modernization of the works will be phased over two years ; to enhance the well-being of our workers, we will suppress the draughts in the shops... (adjectif : a draughty (drafty) shop).
La modernisation de l'usine se fera progressivement sur deux ans ; pour accroître le bien-être de nos ouvriers, nous supprimerons les courants d'air dans les ateliers (adjectif : *un atelier rempli de courants d'air*).

5 - STRUCTURES

FOR, SINCE, AGO

1 - VERBE PRINCIPAL FRANÇAIS AU PASSÉ COMPOSÉ

- Nous avons acheté cette maison il y a 10 ans.
(cela fait..., il y a..., voici, voilà... 10 ans que nous avons acheté...)

Preterite + temps écoulé + ago It is + temps écoulé + since + preterite

- We bought this house 10 years ago.
- It is 10 years since we bought this house.

Question : How long ago + preterite interrogatif
How long is it since + preterite

2 - VERBE PRINCIPAL FRANÇAIS AU PRÉSENT

Nous habitons cette maison depuis 10 ans.
(cela fait..., il y a..., voici, voilà... 10 ans que nous habitons)

Present perfect	- progressif : l'action se poursuivra - simple : l'action ne se poursuivra pas

Le complément est introduit par " for " : durée
ou " since " : point de départ

- We have lived in this house for 10 years (since 1970).
- We have been living in this house for 10 years (since 1970).

Question :How long + Present perfect interrogatif, simple ou progressif

3 - VERBE PRINCIPAL FRANÇAIS À L'IMPARFAIT

- Nous habitions cette maison depuis 10 ans quand...
(Il y avait, cela faisait... que nous habitions...)

Plus-que-parfait, progressif ou non + for ou since

- We had been living in this house for 10 years (since 1970) when...

Question :How long + Plus-que-parfait, progressif ou non

THÈME D'APPLICATION NUMÉRO 5

1 - Voilà des mois que le patron cherche un moyen radical de se débarrasser des malfaiteurs !
2 - Cela fait des années qu'il détourne l'argent de la firme pour régler ses dettes : le jeu le conduira à sa perte.
3 - Le vieux chercheur d'or cachait ses pépites dans une vieille pirogue depuis (des) mois quand elle a coulé (to sink, preterit).
4 - Cela fait six mois que le Ministre des Finances a tracé un sombre tableau de notre économie et aujourd'hui les perspectives d'avenir sont encore loin d'être brillantes !
5 - « Il a retiré cinq cents dollars de son compte il y a un mois pour régler ses dettes. » - « S'il n'arrête pas de jouer, cela le conduira à sa perte ! »
6 - L'agroalimentaire est cinquante fois plus tributaire des intempéries que l'industrie.
7 - Cela fait des années qu'il a été décidé que la modernisation de l'usine se ferait sur deux ans mais vous n'avez pas encore amélioré le bien-être de nos ouvriers.
8 - L'Europe se passe de la Chine (China) et de ses vastes débouchés depuis trop longtemps (too long).
9 - Grâce à nos machines ultra-modernes, nous avons depuis quelque temps cinq fois moins de concurrents que par le passé (in the past).
10 - Cela fait quelque temps qu'on a commencé à creuser le Tunnel sous la Manche (= the Chunnel) ; les ouvriers mettront peut-être au jour les restes d'une civilisation ?
11 - Cela fait trois mois que j'ai un emploi stable et que je touche un salaire régulier : je vais la demander en mariage !
12 - Depuis des années le vieil avare accumulait des objets de valeur dans sa commode ; quand il est mort, en 1965, nous y avons trouvé un trésor !
13 - Je sais, cela fait vingt ans que vous devez vous contenter de machines-outils vétustes mais nous ne pouvons pas les supprimer en une seule fois.
14 - J'exerce ce métier depuis Septembre 1951 : rares sont les gens aisés qui peuvent vivre de leurs rentes dans notre pays !
15 - L'agriculture est tributaire des intempéries depuis que l'homme est agriculteur (farmer) !

6 - TRADE-UNIONS : EVOLUTION

(Deuxième partie)

CAUSES OF THE DECLINE, PECULIAR TO SOME COUNTRIES (continuation)

THE UNITED STATES

- Firms have been moving from the " rust bowl " in the North to the " sunbelt states ", traditionally less unionized, or even abroad.
- Public support has been declining, as was demonstrated when President Reagan in 1981 dismissed several thousand air-controllers for striking illegally.
- Corporate ploys causing disillusionment with unions :
  - A number of companies resort to bankruptcy courts to be allowed wage reductions without being sued for breach of contract with unions.
  - Some companies practise " double-breasting " : they farm out their work to non-unionized subsidiaries.
  - Others hire the services of professional " union busters " (union-busting law firms and consultants).
  - Some companies brandish the bugbear of lower production and the lay-offs consequent upon it. Workers resign themselves to " give-backs " in exchange for their jobs : cutbacks in wages, rollbacks in fringe benefits, higher productivity for the same pay.
- Owing to the deregulation of transport industries (airlines, trucking companies), smaller non-unionized companies, because their employees are more accomodating, undercut the bigger ones. If demand shrivels, bigger companies are reduced to slimming down.
- E.S.O.P.s : Employee Stock Ownership Plans. Trade Unions look askance at them since they enable workers to become the owners of their company. The mechanism is simple. Employees set up a trust which borrows money to buy newly issued shares from the company. To repay the loan, the latter makes contributions to the trust which are tax deductible.
- More and more workers ignore collective action to clamour for their rights ; they appeal directly to federal or state laws against unfair dismissal, sex discrimination, unsatisfactory working conditions, etc. These " whistleblowers ", as they are called, sue their employers whenever they consider that their rights have been flouted, and states respond favourably to the trend.
- Asiatic countries. When trade unions are not purely and simply banned, as in China and other numerous countries, they are kept under strict control by the state, or even their members simply regard themselves as their employers' partners : they work together for the company's sake !

THE FUTURE

Trade unions are probably here to stay provided they adjust to a changing world. Most of them are gradually doing away with ideologies and becoming more pragmatic : they pay more heed to the demands of the market and try not to run counter to firms' prosperity.

CONCESSIONS

They now consent to practices which would have seemed heretical to their founders :

- Local bargaining instead of negotiations on a national scale.
- No-strike agreements or waiving (forgoing) wage increases in exchange for job continuity.
- In the United States, they even went the length of reaching two-tier agreements in the car industry, consenting to newly-hired workers' drawing lower wages.
- In France, it is now easier for ailing firms to trim their workforce. The amount of working hours per week for a person is no longer strictly limited. Women are allowed to work at night if they want to. In the public sector, a day's pay is deducted from salaries even for a few minutes' strike, etc.

Everywhere, the spectre of unemployment has compelled unions to curb their demands.

New strategies

Trade unions cannot be satisfied with merely putting a brake on their decline. They are bent on becoming powerful again by recruiting new members.

Campaigns are being led in Great Britain and the United States to make membership more attractive by offering discounts on insurance policies, on the purchase of cars, on holiday packages ; special terms for mortgages and loans ; free legal and financial advice ; information on re-training opportunities, new openings on the job market, etc.

In the United States, trade-unions launch out into buyouts in the wake of the spate of managers who have thus become the owners of their firms. They deny being nothing else but downright capitalists intent on high returns. They assert that their aim is to shield employees from unemployment in ailing companies, or even from unfair treatment in thriving ones.

CONCLUSION

All trade-unions of course are pinning their hopes on the economic recovery : the fear of unemployment will recede, and they will be again in a position to secure pay hikes and other benefits for their members. But no one knows what the future has in store, and the recovery may well be short-lived ! Only fools rush where angels fear to tread...

TEST YOUR KNOWLEDGE

1 - Why does a decline in smokestack industries also entail a drop in union membership ?

2 - Are the public hostile to unions ?

3 - Which new forms of work make it difficult for unions to recruit members ? Why ?

4 - What is telecommuting ? To whom does it prove attractive and why ?

5 - What used to be called " the British disease " ? Why did it lead up to a political upheaval ?

6 - Which criticism do the Conservatives level at unions ?

7 - What do the Americans call " double-breasting " ?

8 - What is an E.S.O.P. ?

9 - Which benefits and services do unions offer their members today in Great Britain and the United States ?

10 - Do American unions resort to buyouts for profit ? How do they account for that practice ?

40 - TO DRAW-DREW-DRAWN (suite)

- One of the claims that workers keep putting in (putting forward) as regards the redeployment of our staff is that they do not want to be looked upon (regarded) as pawns on a draughtboard or a chessboard.
L'une des revendications que les travailleurs ne cessent de présenter en ce qui concerne la réorganisation de notre personnel est qu'ils ne veulent pas être considérés comme des pions sur un damier ou un échiquier.
Cf. to play draught**s** (chess) : *jouer aux dames (aux échecs)*
- Draughtsmen pin blueprints to their drawing-boards with drawing-pins.
Les dessinateurs industriels fixent les bleus sur leurs planches à dessin avec des punaises.
(au figuré, blueprint : plan, scheme, project)
- The draft of a letter ≠ the fair copy of a letter.
Le brouillon d'une lettre ≠ une lettre au propre.
- A draft contract : *un projet de contrat* - A draft agreement : *projet d'accord.*
- A draft : a bill (of exchange) - *une traite, une lettre de change.*
- The draft falls due ont September 15th.
La traite échoit (arrive à échéance) le 15 septembre.

Composés :

Your account is overdrawn - is in the red : *à découvert.*
To withdraw - withdrew - withdrawn - *(se) retirer.*
- To withdraw a sum of money **from** an account ≠ to pay a sum of money **into** an account.
Retirer d'un compte une somme d'argent ≠ verser une somme sur un compte.
- The shop-stewards withdrew to an adjacent room to deliberate over (upon) the issue.
Les délégués syndicaux se retirèrent dans une pièce adjacente pour délibérer sur cette question.
Mais : You retire from business.
On se retire des affaires.
- The goods have arrived : we will collect them (pick them up : take delivery of them) from the warehouse.
Les marchandises sont arrivées. Nous les retirerons à l'entrepôt (nous en prendrons livraison).

Substantif :

Withdrawal ≠ payment : *le retrait ≠ le versement*

41 - TO DREAM-DREAMT-DREAMT

rêver
- All heads of states dream **of** mopping up (**absorbing**) unemployment in their respective countries, but there are a good number of hurdles to clear (to get over) before that economic nightmare comes to an end !
*Tous les chefs d'états rêvent de **résorber** le chômage dans leurs pays respectifs mais il y a de nombreux obstacles à franchir avant que ce cauchemar économique ne se termine !*

Substantif :

- He has realized his dream : his dream has come true (has materialized).
Il a réalisé son rêve : son rêve s'est réalisé.

42 - TO DRINK-DRANK-DRUNK

boire
To be drunk : saoul (intoxicated = *ivre*)
Mais : He was poisoned by carbon dioxide.
Il a été intoxiqué par l'oxyde de carbone.
- Food poisoning : *l'intoxication alimentaire.*
- The future of the firm is in jeopardy because the boss has taken to drinking !
L'avenir de la firme est menacé parce que le patron s'est mis à boire !

43 - TO DRIVE-DROVE-DRIVEN

conduire ; rouler, transporter (en voiture).
Aussi :
- One of the catch-phrases of the temperance league is : " Each glass of spirits drives a nail into your coffin ".
L'un des slogans de la ligue antialcoolique est : " Chaque verre d'alcool enfonce un clou dans votre cercueil " !
Cf. a screwdriver : *un tournevis.*

- Constant refusals from employers can drive job-seekers (job-hunters) to despair !
Les refus constants de la part des employeurs peuvent réduire au désespoir les demandeurs d'emploi.
- That shorthand typist will drive me mad !
Cette sténo-dactylo me rendra fou !
- A propeller-driven aircraft : *un avion à hélices*, ***mais*** jet-propelled : *à réaction.*

Substantifs :

- I want my collaborators to have plenty of drive and initiative and be forward-looking.
Je veux que mes collaborateurs aient beaucoup d'allant (de dynamisme) et d'esprit d'initiative, et soient tournés vers l'avenir.
- A sales drive - a sales campaign - a marketing campaign : *une campagne commerciale.*

Mots proches :

- The drift from the land : *l'exode rural*, ***mais*** the brain drain : *l'exode des cerveaux.*

44 - TO DWELL-DWELT-DWELT

dans le sens de " *demeurer, habiter* ", *préférer* " to live "

Substantifs :

city dwellers - townsfolk : *les citadins.*
country people - country folk : *les ruraux.*
NB. Folk, singulier d'apparence, veut le verbe au pluriel.
- Cave-dwellers had no money (currency) : they bartered (swapped), for instance, game for flint tools or furs.
Les habitants des cavernes n'avaient pas de monnaie d'échange : ils troquaient, par exemple, du gibier contre des outils de silex ou des fourrures.
To dwell upon - to insist on - to lay stress on (laid - laid) : to stress - to emphasize
- As usual, he wound up his conference by dwelling upon the importance and the difficulty of matching people and jobs.
Comme d'habitude il termina sa conférence en insistant sur l'importance et la difficulté de l'adéquation des gens à leur emploi.

45 - TO EAT-ATE-EATEN

manger + up - engloutir - to swallow up - to gobble up - to devour - to engulf
- Rampant inflation has eaten up my savings.
Aussi : Acids and rust eat into metals.
Les acides et la rouille rongent les métaux.
Cf. In time of dearth, of famine, people starve to death (die **of** hunger) for lack of foodstuffs.
Quand règne la disette, la famine, les gens meurent de faim par manque de denrées (alimentaires).
- Malnutrition is the scourge that plagues the Third World.
La sous-alimentation est le fléau qui afflige le Tiers Monde.

46 - TO FALL-FALL-FALLEN

tomber (propre et figuré)

Synonyme :

to tumble
- Interest rates are falling everywhere... : are tumbling.
To let something fall - to drop : *laisser tomber quelque chose.*

Expressions :

- If the crops **fall short of** our expectations (do not **come up to** our expectations) we shall certainly have to tighten our belts !
Si les récoltes ne répondent pas à notre attente, nous devrons certainement nous serrer la ceinture !
- Any country that enters the European Economic Community has **to fall into line with** the common policy of its member states.
Tout pays qui entre dans la Communauté Économique Européenne doit s'aligner sur la politique commune de ses états membres.
- To fall due : *arriver à échéance, échoir, être payable.*

6 - STRUCTURES

ADJECTIFS ET PRONOMS PARTITIFS

1 - SANS IDÉE DE QUANTITÉ

- Au sens général, sans idée de quantité, pas d'adjectif.
- The butcher sells meat, the baker sells bread and the fishmonger fish.

2 - UNE CERTAINE QUANTITÉ

- Avec une idée d'une certaine partie, d'une certaine quantité de quelque chose.

a) **Affirmations** : some

- Bring me some butter, please, waiter : ... s'il vous plaît, garçon !

Remarque : some est synonyme de " **a** little " (singulier) et " **a** few " (pluriel)

- With a little money and a few tools he can make beautiful pieces of furniture.

Mais **sans article**, little (singulier) et few (pluriel) : peu

- I have got few friends, but they are reliable : sûrs
- Very few people can understand his poems.
- He has got very little patience.
- There is little whisky left in the bottle. *Il reste peu de whisky...*

b) **Interrogations** : any

- Is there any butter left ? *Reste-t-il du beurre ?*
- Have you got any friends with whom you could stay ? ... *chez qui vous pourriez rester ?*

Remarque : Employer " some " si l'on s'attend à une réponse affirmative ou dans une offre faite avec empressement.

- Would you care for some wine ? *Voulez-vous du vin ?*

c) **Négations** : no ; mais, **beaucoup plus fréquent** : not... any.

- We can't pay you, we haven't got any money !

d) **Les mêmes règles s'appliquent aux composés.**

- Do you know anybody called X ?
- Does he understand anything in maths ?
- Will you go anywhere this Summer ?

Some, any, **none** (not... any, **plus courant**) sont également **pronoms.**
Ils traduisent le mot " en ".

- Do you want any ? No, I've got some in my pocket !
- There is not any (none, moins courant) in the drawer. *Il n'y en a pas dans le tiroir.*

Remarque : Ne pas confondre **no one** et **none.**

- He was craving for a glass of water, but there was none ! (not any)
  Il avait grande envie d'un verre d'eau, mais il n'y en avait pas !
- He shouted for help, but no one (nobody) answered !
  Il cria pour qu'on vînt à son secours, mais personne ne répondit !

Locutions :

■ - He is anything but stupid ! *Il est loin d'être stupide !*
- It is anything but funny ! *C'est loin d'être drôle !*

■ He may earn anything between ten and twenty thousand dollars a year.
Il peut gagner quelque chose comme dix à vingt mille dollards par an : ce qu'il peut gagner est de l'ordre de...
- They talked of exporting anything up to a million cars a year in 1985 !
  Ils ont parlé d'exporter quelque chose comme un million de voitures par an en 1985 : ils ont parlé d'exportations de l'ordre de...
- It will cost you anything from ten to twenty thousand francs.
  Cela vous coûtera grosso modo de dix à vingt mille francs. (en gros, ***dans les*** *10 à 20.000 F.)*

Remarque : *Un chiffre de l'ordre de dix milliards :* a figure in the region of (of the order of) ten billion.
Formes d'insistance : any, no, none + comparatifs

- He is not any better at maths than at physics ! (he is not at all...) *Il n'est pas du tout meilleur* ***en...***
- They have taken drastic measures, but the economy is not any the better for it ! (is none the better) *... mais l'économie ne s'en porte franchement pas mieux !*
- There was a time when we lacked fast means of conveyance, but we were not any the worse for it ! (we were none the worse for it). *Il y eut un temps où nous manquions de moyens de transport rapides, mais nous ne nous en portions vraiment pas plus mal !*
- The police are not any the wiser (none the wiser) for their investigation. *La police n'est pas du tout plus avancée après son enquête.*
- The economic outlook is none too bright. *Les perspectives économiques ne sont pas tellement brillantes.*
- They say that business is picking up, and none too soon ! *On dit que les affaires reprennent, et ce n'est pas trop tôt !*
- At the time, it was none too easy to find a job ! *A l'époque, ce n'était pas tellement facile de trouver un emploi !*

Composés : **Somehow**

■ Somehow (or other), I will manage to convince him.
D'une façon ou d'une autre, j'arriverai à le convaincre ! (one way or another)

■ The boss never liked me somehow !
Pour une raison ou pour une autre, le patron ne m'a jamais aimé ! (for some vague reason !)

Somewhat : *quelque peu* - rather

I was somewhat surprised to hear that he was dead.
Je fus quelque peu surpris d'apprendre qu'il était mort.

Anyhow :

She was fired because she would do her work anyhow.
On l'a mise à la porte car elle faisait son travail n'importe comment.
Anyhow - anyway - in any case - at any rate *En tout cas, de toute façon*

THÈME D'APPLICATION NUMÉRO 6

1 - Les travailleurs ne cessent de présenter des revendications : il y en a, disent-ils, que nous considérons comme des pions sur un damier !
2 - Les marchandises sont arrivées mais nous n'en avons pas retiré de l'entrepôt.
3 - Il y a quelque chose comme deux à trois millions de chômeurs et il rêve de résorber le chômage ! Il est loin (pas « far ») d'être stupide mais il y a de nombreux obstacles à franchir !
4 - Cela fait quelques mois que nous devons nous serrer la ceinture : l'été dernier les récoltes n'ont pas répondu à notre attente.
5 - De toute façon, il terminera son discours en insistant, comme d'habitude, sur l'importance de l'adéquation des gens à leur emploi.
6 - Il y a douze pays dans la CEE : y-en-a-t-il qui ne veuillent pas s'aligner sur la politique commune ?
7 - Peu de travailleurs pensent que la firme est menacée parce que le patron s'est mis à boire !
8 - Nous sommes quelque peu responsables de (responsible for) la malnutrition dans le Tiers-Monde : ce fléau l'afflige depuis des années, et les gens meurent de faim !
9 - Grâce à ces mesures, nous commençons à résorber le chômage, et ce n'est vraiment pas trop tôt !
10 - Cela faisait des années que les refus constants de la part des employeurs réduisaient au désespoir beaucoup de demandeurs d'emploi.
11 - La France connaît l'exode rural depuis la guerre ; des débouchés (an outlet) à la campagne ? Il n'y en a pas (2 traductions) !
12 - Ce n'est pas tellement facile de vivre aujourd'hui ! L'inflation galopante engloutit (3 traductions) nos économies !
13 - Il fut un temps où les hommes troquaient du gibier contre des outils de silex ou des fourrures : ils ne s'en portaient vraiment pas plus mal !
14 - Notre compte est à découvert depuis le début du mois ; il nous reste peu de temps pour y verser un peu d'argent, la traite arrive à échéance demain !
15 - Y-a-t-il quelque chose de plus stupide ? On ne se sent pas du tout mieux après quelques verres d'alcool, et chaque verre enfonce un clou dans son cercueil !

7 - RETIREMENT

THE PROBLEM

It is paradoxical that we should still abide by the decision of German Chancellor Otto von Bismark who created the first social security pension system in 1884, and laid down that people would be eligible for such a pension at the age of 65 !

Much water has been flowing under the bridge since those times : whereas life expectancy was roughly 37 then, it now exceeds 70 in our Welfare States ; the average life span is now longer thanks to better nutrition and medical breakthroughs, and it bids fair to keep lengthening. So, a host of people who are still hale and hearty have to resign themselves to retiring at 65, or 60 in certain countries, which entails a good deal of frustration for them, and a waste of professional expertise and experience for the economy.

In Bismark's time, retirees were not too heavy a burden on social security since the greater part of workers died before they reached the age of 65, or seldom lived much longer. Considering the evolution in life expectancy, it would have been logical to postpone the age of mandatory retirement ; oddly enough, the age of retirement was kept at 65 in most industrialized countries, and was even lowered to 60, even to 55 or less for certain categories of workers !

The lowering of the age of mandatory retirement delights of course those workers who have grown weary of their trade, who by being allowed to down tools can at last shake off what has become for them a drudgery ; or those who no longer feel equal to complying with the demands of their work, or those who suffer from the stress and strain of an ambitious career, who can thus ease up before they are struck down by a coronary thrombosis, a stroke or a nervous collapse.

But people do not age at the same pace ; some have gone downhill long before they have turned 50, others will keep their physical and intellectual capacities up to a ripe old age. So, it seems irrational and arbitrary to enforce retirement on people irrespective of their wishes : it should not depend on chronological age, but on how fit each individual feels - physically, intellectually and psychologically - leaving it to him/her to decide when to resign.

" Flexible retirement " seems all the more advisable as, psychologically speaking, the abrupt transition from a life of work to one of idleness may lead up to a feeling of uselessness, of utter helplessness as to the aim to be achieved in a life henceforward devoid of - admittedly - the constraints, but also of the satisfactions of a professional activity.

The disarray ensuing from that passage used to be allayed by the comfort that retired people would find in their children's homes. The latter would indeed reciprocate what their parents had done for their sake in their youth by looking after them in their old age. No longer ! For multiple reasons legitimately put forward by their children, cramped housing, two-career couples etc., or out of sheer selfishness from the latter, the elderly now live by themselves.

If national insurance cannot dispense affection and comfort, it can at least provide for pensioners' material needs. But in that respect things are not so simple, as keeping in their later years the standard of living that people used to enjoy when they were working proves more and more difficult. The causes of that evolution are expounded in the fourth chapter (The Welfare State), and policies in this matter vary from country to country.

THE UNITED STATES

Mandatory retirement got " put out to pasture " in October 1986, when Congress passed two measures to be implemented as from January 1st, 1987. One made mandatory retirement illegal at any age ; the other allowed workers to get fatter pension benefits by working after the age of 65 (the age limit for all pension schemes so far). There was one exception : public employers had seven years before they were to implement the measures for firemen and policemen.

Since then the measures have been of course much debated ! They run counter to the current trend in the United States, as retirement age has been falling for 25 years down to an average of 63 today. One reason is that employees want to enjoy life to the full when they are still comparatively young, another is that employers urge employees to retire early to pare the labour force owing to the recession in, for example, smokestack industries.

Employers remonstrate against the measures because they can no longer get rid of the " dead wood ", i.e., the employees whose capacities are on the wane. A 1978 law entitled them to give the latter the " golden handshake " (" the golden boot ") at 70, and that made it easier for employers to put up with inefficient workers. They now have to grin and bear it until the employees concerned resolve to retire on their own initiative.

Moreover, " flexible retirement " will make it more difficult to run corporate pension schemes ; no one will be able to foresee - and not even the employee himsef/herself - when he/she will retire ! It will be difficult as well to plan the staff turnover rationally since the manager of human resources will never know when a given employee will leave : uncertainty will impede the smooth running of recruitment, of training and re-training programmes ; it will be done by fits and starts !

Employers also deplore the fact that such measures are bound to increase the number of age-discrimination lawsuits, " whistleblowers " appealing to courts of justice when they estimate that they have been turned out because of their age and not for professional misconduct. Corporations will then have to keep on their payrolls people whose lack of creativity, innovation, and productivity is manifest, who will end up like those Japanese " window-gazers " whose desks are placed near a window so that they may have an occupation !

Meanwhile, junior, worthier employees will rebel and lash out against the oldsters who hamper promotion. Corporate climate stands to deteriorate as relationships among employees will become increasingly strained. Younger employees will feel thwarted in their ambitions by " old fogeys " who cling stubbornly to their jobs !

On the contrary, supporters praise the soundness of these measures as they goad employees into remaining productive as long as possible, a sure cure against boredom and carelessness, disarray, and even despair and suicide. They quote statistics to bear out their argument : the suicide rate used to be fairly high indeed among those who had been forced to retire.

Thanks to those measures, workers will no longer lose out on the extra years spent at work after 65 : their pensions will be proportional to the number of years during which they will have been working. It will thus enable retirees to enjoy a higher standard of living since social security pensions are not substantial enough : if the population of the United States has trebled since 1900, the number of old people has increased eightfold, and the trend is growing.

Corporations will stand to gain too. Supporters quote further statistics to prove that older workers are more motivated, have a better morale, and are seldom absent from work. They also contend that it will prove cheaper for corporations to pay contributions into pension funds for a few more years than pay full pensions to retirees during that time. It will even prove profitable for the economy since that extra money funnelled into the funds will be invested in it!

Europe

Mandatory retirement is still in force everywhere. The age varies according to countries and occupations, from a maximum of 65 (e.g. British male workers) down to 55 (e.g. French primary school teachers, gendarmes, etc.) and even less (e.g. 45 for airliner pilots).

If the age of forced retirement has been lowered, as in France for instance, it is not out of consideration for the workers' desire of enjoying a life of leisure earlier, or of fulfilling themselves in some creative pastime after leaving an unrewarding job, but out of solidarity for the spate of job-seekers : by creating vacancies, the Government cherished the hope of absorbing unemployment in part.

It was to achieve that aim that " solidarity contracts " had been instituted in France, under whose terms 55 year-old workers were entitled to retire before due date with 70 % of their previous earnings until they turned 60. They then qualified for a full pension. For their part, employers committed themselves to hire unemployed people. The scheme was a failure and it was scrapped in 1984.

Employers resort to other early retirement plans in order to downsize their firms. In the mining or the steel industry for instance, workers in their mid-or late fifties are granted a pension that amounts to a hefty percentage of a normal one, and they also get a severance pay, i.e. a lump-sum bonus, as compensation for the loss of their job. They draw of course a full pension when they qualify for it. This is at humane way of paring the labour force as a worker who is laid off at that age is most often doomed to go on the dole, and his redundancy payment is not nearly enough to gild the pill for him !

NEW APPROACHES

The United States

Paradoxically, there is a shortage of skilled labour in, among others, high-technology industries, and corporations try to keep older workers by offering them diverse inducements : reduced working hours, part-time work, work-sharing, attractive new activities. The schemes go under different names : " Trial retirements " or " retirement rehearsals " allow employees to take an unpaid three-months' leave of absence with full fringe benefits. " Phased down retirement " entitles them to work only 20 hours a week with full fringe benefits, but a curtailed salary.

EUROPE

Similar plans are being sporadically put into practice, but on the whole, retirement schemes remain " inflexible " as yet.

In Sweden, since 1976, workers between 60 and 64 are eligible for " partial retirement " ; the Government subsidizes 65 % of their lost earnings.

In Denmark, firms practise " decruitment ", also called " demotion " or " downgrading " : managers are allowed to stay with their firms if they wish when they turn 60, but they must accept lower-level jobs and reduced salaries.

In short, " flexible retirement ", for the reasons stated above, seems to be highly advisable in future, but it is a concept whose materialization is going to prove tremendously tricky. Governments will have to come to grips with the thorny problem of retirees' incomes !

WHENCE THE WHEREWITHAL ?

■ The majority of industrialized countries finance pensions on a **pay-as-you-go** basis : the contributions of the active population pay for the pensions of retired people. Pay-as-you-go schemes proved appropriate in the " roaring " 50s and 60s when the economy was in expansion. As the number of workers was increasing, the contributions per head would be made easier to shoulder, and pensioners would get more than they had ever paid in their working years.

Unfortunately, the expansion has been slowing down, and the contributions have been declining in proportion as the active population was shrinking. The situation is worrying as the **dependency ratio** - the relation between the number of retired people and that of workers - has been gradually levelling out, which entails that the latter, in the not so distant future, will be saddled with an unbearable financial burden. What has been humorously dubbed " the piggy-back problem " threatens rather to become a matter for grim humour !

It has indeed been reckoned that by the year 2055, there might be only two workers to provide for every pensioner in the United States. In West Germany, the ratio might be one pensioner for every worker and the prospects in all industrialized countries are ominously similar !

■ If Japan is also undergoing the woes of an ageing population and a shrinking labour force, it is spared the problem of finding out a means of paying its old people's pensions : they are financed on a **funded basis**, i.e. they depend on the returns of the capital made up of workers' contributions into the state pension fund throughout their working years. The state has thus at its disposal a huge fund which, well-administered, is able to cover all future needs.

THE FUTURE

It is impossible for states to switch over from pay-as-you-go to funded pension schemes, and they are placed in a dilemma, either raise contributions or reduce pensions. As either measure would be unpopular, most of them adopt a middle course for the time being, gently warning their populations that they might not enjoy the old age pensions that they expected, and urging them to pay contributions into a private pension scheme (e.g. P.E.R. in France) or take out a life insurance policy. A forceful incentive : contributions and premiums can be legally deducted from taxable incomes.

Be that as it may, no candidate to elections in any country can afford to play down this problem as it concerns the " quality of life " of an ever-growing host of voters. Little by little, retired people unite to found clubs and associations whose aims are to inform or defend their members, or campaign for better living conditions, better health care, etc.

The American Association of Retired Persons is a model of its kind with 28 million members. For a nominal fee, anyone over the age of 50 can sign up for membership and is offered a wide range of benefits : cheaper insurance policies, financial and tax advice, special travel and holiday offers, etc. But it mainly informs voters on the issues which concern them, their pensions, their health, their lodgings, etc., and on the solutions proposed in the platforms of candidates to elections. The elderly already wield a fairly considerable clout : if our societies persist in their choice, if the generations are no longer judiciously renewed, will not the future eventually belong to the past ?

TEST YOUR KNOWLEDGE

1 - When was the first social security pension system created, and by whom ?

2 - Why is it paradoxical to abide by its founder's decision as regards the age of mandatory retirement ?

3 - Which categories of workers are apt to rejoice over the lowering of that age ?

4 - Why should not forced retirement depend on chronological age ?

5 - Which measures did the American Congress pass in October 1986 ?

6 - Why did the measures arouse the hostility of a great many American employers ? (quote 4 reasons)

7 - Why do Europeans resort to early retirement plans ? (quote 2 reasons)

8 - What is the " dependency ratio " ?

9 - What are " pay-as-you-go " pension schemes ?

10 - What are " funded " pension schemes ?

46 - TO FALL-FALL-FALLEN (suite)

- The bill falls due on the 10th : *la traite est payable le 10, arrive à échéance le 10.*

Avec prépositions :

- Because our reserves of fossil fuels are running out (are dwindling), we have **to fall back on** alternative sources of energy.
Parce que nos réserves de combustibles fossiles s'épuisent (s'amenuisent), nous devons nous rabattre sur des sources d'énergie de remplacement.
- We have **fallen behind with** our deliveries (we are behindhand **with** our deliveries).
Nous avons pris du retard dans nos livraisons. (***aussi :*** we are in arrears **with** our deliveries).
- We had worked out an elaborate plan to give a new impetus to our flagging economy : it has **fallen through** (it has failed - it has miscarried).
Nous avions élaboré un plan minutieux pour donner un nouvel élan à notre économie languissante : il a échoué.

Substantifs :

- Those who do not approve **of** " Reaganomics " predict that the President is heading for a fall.
Ceux qui n'approuvent pas la politique économique de Reagan prédisent que le Président va au devant de l'échec (court à sa perte).
- A fall - a drop - a decline **in** prices, **in** demand, **in** the exchange rate : *une baisse, une chute des prix (des cours, à la Bourse) de la demande, du taux du change.*
- A windfall : *une aubaine.*

Attention !

Fall (US) - Autumn (GB)
- The heads of states will meet in **the** Fall (US) - will meet in Autumn (GB) to work out a common strategy as regards LDCs.
Les chefs d'état se réuniront en Automne pour élaborer une stratégie commune en ce qui concerne les PMA.
- We tap (harness : exploit) the energy of waterfalls to generate electricity.
Nous exploitons l'énergie des chutes d'eau pour produire de l'électricité.
- The fallout of nuclear weapons **is** bound to play (to wreak) havoc **with** human beings, animals and plants.
Les retombées (**toujours singulier**) *des armes nucléaires ne peuvent manquer de provoquer des ravages* (**toujours singulier)** *chez les êtres humains, la faune et la flore.*
- We are perfectly aware of the many (numerous) pitfalls of the export market : trade barriers (tariff barriers), quotas, quality control and all the mean (petty) tricks of protectionist countries.
Nous sommes parfaitement au courant des nombreux pièges (des nombreuses embûches) du marché de l'exportation : barrières commerciales (barrières douanières), quotas, contrôle de qualité et toutes les mesquineries des pays protectionnistes.
- The recession has brought about the downfall of that industrial empire.
La récession a provoqué la chute de cet empire industriel.
- Compared with last year's dividends, there is a shortfall of X dollars : *(un déficit de...)*

Attention !

To fell (R) - to cut down : *abattre un arbre.*
To feel - felt - felt : *sentir, ressentir.*

47 - TO FEED-FED-FED

(se) nourrir, alimenter
- In Winter, they feed cattle **on** hay, mangel-wurzels, fish meal, etc.
En hiver, on nourrit le bétail avec du foin, des betteraves fourragères, de la farine de poisson, etc.
- Conveyor-belts feed blast-furnaces **with** raw materials.
*Des tapis-roulants alimentent les hauts fourneaux **en*** matières premières.
- In those islands, they feed **on** fruit and fish.
Dans ces îles on se nourrit de fruits et de poisson.
- You feed data **into** a computer.
On fournit des données à un ordinateur.

Familier :

- They are fed up with (they are sick and tired of) all those shortages and privations in a country endowed **with** (≠ devoid **of** - lacking **in**) so many natural resources.

Ils en ont marre de toutes ces pénuries et privations dans un pays doté de (≠ dépourvu de) tant de ressources naturelles.
(moins familier : they are tired of ; ***plus élégant :*** they are weary of : *ils sont las de...)*

Substantifs :

Food : *la nourriture*
F**oo**dstuffs : *les denrées alimentaires*
F**ee**dstuffs : *les aliments pour animaux*
- Rice is the staple food of Asians.
Le riz est la nourriture de base des Asiatiques.

48 - TO FEEL FELT-FELT

sentir, ressentir

Expressions :

- I don't feel like being cooped up in an office, doing clerical work all my life !
Je n'ai pas envie de rester cloîtré(e) dans un bureau à faire du travail de bureau toute ma vie !
- The Chairman and Managing Director's secretary is a fierce watchdog, and I don't feel equal **to** confronting her !
La secrétaire du Président Directeur Général est un vrai Cerbère, et je ne me sens pas de taille à l'affronter !

Substantif :

a feeling : *un sentiment*

49 - TO FIGHT-FOUGHT-FOUGHT

se battre, combattre, lutter

Synonymes :

to struggle, to contend
- " We will fight a merciless war (a ruthless battle) against poverty and disease : shanty-towns and slums are to disappear ! "
" Nous livrerons une guerre sans merci (une bataille impitoyable) contre la misère et la maladie : tous les bidonvilles et les taudis doivent disparaître ! "

Substantifs :

Fight : *la lutte, le combat*

Synonyme :

the struggle for life : *(la lutte pour la vie)*
- The everlasting strife between capital and labour.
La lutte éternelle entre le capital et le travail.
- The in-fighting among the managers poison the firm's atmosphere : *les luttes intestines...*

50 - TO FIND-FOUND-FOUND

trouver

Expressions :

- He is always finding fault with my behaviour.
Il trouve toujours à redire à ma conduite.
- Wanted : farmhand - wages 300 £ and all found.
On demande : valet de ferme - salaire 300 £ logé, nourri, blanchi.

Substantif :

You can make terrific finds at antique dealers'.
On peut faire des trouvailles formidables chez les antiquaires.

Synonyme :

Major discoveries (breakthroughs) are made every year by scientists (researchers : US ; research-workers : GB).
Des découvertes importantes sont faites chaque année par les scientifiques (les chercheurs).

Attention !

to found (R) : *fonder*
- The firm was founded in... : *La firme a été fondée en...*

51 - TO FLEE-FLED-FLED

fuir, s'enfuir
plus courant : to run away (ran - run)
- How can we repatriate the funds that have fled abroad ?
Comment pouvons-nous rapatrier les capitaux qui se sont envolés à l'étranger ?

7 - STRUCTURES

LES INDÉFINIS

1 - ENCORE

■ **Quantité :** some, no + more
- Would you like any more chips ? No more, thank you !
- There is not any more petrol in the tank !

■ **Temps :** some, any, no + longer
- He is not a private any longer : he is a sergeant !
- The doctor no longer hopes to cure him.

2 - N'IMPORTE

■ Affirmations et interrogations : any
- A good salesman can sell anybody anything anywhere any time.

■ Négations : not... **just** any
- A decent girl does not go out with just any boy !
- He is very particular, he does not eat just anything.
- You can't find crude oil just anywhere (pétrole brut).

NB. *N'importe lequel (des **2**) - l'un ou l'autre - either*
- " Which bus shall I take ? N°10 or N°14 ? " - " You can take either ! "

mais : - " Shall I take N°10, 14 or 16 ? " - " You can take any one (of them) ".

FOR, SINCE, AGO + PHRASES INTERROGATIVES

voir stuctures 5

THÈME D'APPLICATION NUMÉRO 7

1 - Nos réserves de combustibles diminuent mais nous ne pouvons pas nous rabattre sur n'importe quelles sources d'énergie de remplacement.
2 - " Combien de temps cela fait-il que tous ces capitaux se sont envolés à l'étranger ? " - " Ils ont été investis il y a trois ans et nous ne pouvons plus les rapatrier. "
3 - Nous n'approuvons plus cette politique : nous sommes las de ces pénuries dans un pays doté de tant de ressources naturelles.
4 - Depuis quand le riz est-il la nourriture de base des Asiatiques ?
5 - N'importe qui peut faire des trouvailles formidables chez les antiquaires mais les découvertes importantes ne sont pas faites par n'importe quels scientifiques !
6 - Depuis combien de temps êtes-vous cloîtrée dans cette pièce à faire du travail de bureau ?
7 - Vous avez fourni ces données à l'ordinateur il y a combien de temps ? En avez-vous encore qui seraient plus précises (accurate) ?
8 - Depuis combien de temps trouvait-il à redire à votre travail quand vous vous êtes sentie (preterit) de taille à l'affronter ?
9 - Il y a combien de temps que les chefs d'état essaient d'élaborer une stratégie commune en ce qui concerne les pays moins avancés ?
10 - Depuis quand savons nous que les retombées nucléaires ne peuvent manquer de provoquer des ravages chez les êtres humains ?
11 - Et pourtant, nous n'avions pas élaboré n'importe quel plan pour donner un nouvel élan à notre économie languissante, mais il a échoué !
12 - Ce n'était pas n'importe quel empire industriel ! Cela fait combien de temps que la récession a provoqué sa chute ?
13 - N'importe quel producteur est parfaitement au courant des nombreuses embûches du marché de l'exportation.
14 - " Depuis quand ces luttes intestines entre les directeurs existent-elles ? " - " Je ne sais, mais j'en suis las ! "
15 - " Il n'y a plus de bidonvilles et de taudis ici ! " - " Depuis quand livriez-vous cette bataille impitoyable contre la misère ? "

8 - WORLD POPULATION

THE FACTS

In 1987, there were roughly 5 billion people on earth. According to recent projections, there could be more than 8 billion people in 2025, and no fewer than 12 billion in 2070 if the present trend in the growth rate is not stemmed one way or another. It is then expected that population growth might level off. Unfortunately, that increase affects the poorer part of the earth : out of 8 billion people in 2025, 7 billion will live in the Third World. A paltry billion people only will live in industrialized countries, and in many of them, the population will keep on dwindling since their birth rate does not even reach the replacement level (2.1)

THE THIRD WORLD : THE POPULATION EXPLOSION

CAUSES

- Religious beliefs and traditions.
  - Having numerous children is regarded as a blessing from heaven. Woe betide the wife who is sterile ! Not only does she feel cursed by the gods, but she is exposed to the contempt of her husband and of his family, and she is eventually repudiated.
  - Having a son is regarded as a special benediction, and a woman will keep having babies until she is delivered of a boy !
  - The Moslem and the Roman Catholic religions, - among others - which prevail in a good many Third World countries, are opposed to abortion and sterilization, and to contraceptive devices. They only favour " natural " birth-control.
- Economic necessity and non-existent old-age insurance.
  - Subsistence or commercial farming is the mainstay of developing countries' economies, and farmers need hands to till the fields, look after the livestock, fetch wood and water, etc. Children make up a cheap labour force !
  - As there is no pension system, children provide for their parents' old days : the more numerous children are, the more comfortable parents' later years will be !

    In any case, boys are preferred to girls as the former are stronger, and the latter will eventually leave their families to follow their husbands.
  - In China, the wish for more children is a side-effect of a recent economic reform : families are allotted a plot of land, and are allowed to sell homegrown produce. Children can help to increase profit !
- Infantile mortality.
  - It seems paradoxical, but as they know that few of their children will ever reach their teens, let alone adulthood, parents will multiply their offspring, hopeful that a few strong babies will survive.
- Longer life expectancy.
  - Hygiene, sanitation, medical care (mainly vaccination) have been developing and improving, and the rate of infant and child mortality has been accordingly declining. Unfortunately, the number of births has not proportionally declined yet.
- Dying tribal traditions.
  - Birth spacing used to derive naturally from the daunting presence of mothers-in-law who came to help their daughters when they had a baby ; they managed somehow to keep their husbands away from the latter for sometimes as long as a whole year. African doctors will say humorously that mothers-in-law used to be their best contraceptives !
- Early marriages.
  - Girls are married as soon as they reach childbearing age, which increases the number of possible pregnancies or, in demographers' jargon, the number of years during which they are " at risk ".
- Illiteracy and lack of information.
  - Imparting knowledge in anatomy, physiology, contraceptive methods, etc., to people who cannot read is difficult, and the medical, or paramedical staff who could do it by word of mouth do not suffice for the task ; as for the television network, it is far too limited as yet to cover the areas which are most in need of educational programmes.

■ Political options.

- When African countries became independent, most of their leaders opted for letting the populations increase freely as their burgeoning economies were going to need either hands to till new lands and work in budding industries, or brains to be trained to be teachers, physicians, engineers, etc. Africa's population was 220 million in 1950, 470 million in 1980, and is projected to be 880 million by the year 2000.

CONSEQUENCES

Human population is expanding at an exponential rate, and even if action has already been taken to check its progress, and although new - and sometimes - drastic measures are being implemented in all countries concerned, disasters have already occurred and new threats are looming ahead.

■ Famine.

Thomas Robert Malthus (1766-1834), an English economist and a priest, in his " Essay on the Principle of Population" (1798), predicted an appalling future for humanity as the population of the earth was increasing in geometrical progression whereas the supply of food was increasing in arithmetical progression. To ward off starvation, he recommended late marriage and sexual abstinence ; as a priest, he did not approve of birth control.

His predictions were belied by industrial and agricultural development in Europe, but they are coming true today in a number of Third World countries. The FAO (the Food and Agriculture Organization of the United Nations) states in a recent survey that 65 countries, most of them in Africa, will not be able to live on their own food production by the turn of the century, and their revenues will not be substantial enough to enable them to buy from abroad all the food that they will need.

For centuries, African populations lived on produce from their livestock (cattle, sheep and goats), from slash-and-burn cultivation, and from hunting, and it has proved difficult for the hunter-warriors of old to settle down as farmers. In that type of subsistence economy, farming would be left to women, men being in charge of cash income : it explains why an increasing number of them are to be found in towns today, trying in vain to find a steady job.

Moreover, most African countries have embarked upon the production of cash-crops (e.g. cocoa, coffee, groundnuts) as a main source of revenue ; unfortunately they depend on the erratic prices of commodities which are often so low as to make that type of crops unprofitable.

The cultivation of staple foodstuffs has been given up by disheartened farmers because American and European grain surpluses depress the market so much that they cannot recoup their production costs. Populations subsist only thanks to international aid, which compounds the problem, as it makes it all the more unprofitable for farmers to produce grain that can be obtained free from International Relief Organizations.

■ Environmental damage.

Natural resources are being depleted to meet the needs of increasing populations.

- Agricultural lands are overcultivated and are on the way to becoming barren : fertilizers are too expensive.
- Overgrazing exhausts pasture land.
- Deforestation is spreading because people need wood for cooking and heating, or more arable land. It speeds up erosion (e.g. in the Sahel) or prevents flood control (e.g. in India, in Tanzania).
- Water is squandered for irrigation purposes, and especially for seasonal crops : the reserves are petering out.

Nightmare cities.

The drift from the land is gathering momentum because there is an increasing number of mouths to feed on shrinking resources, because Governments invest in agricultural machinery - agrimation supplants manpower -, because people are simply lured by the mirage of economic opportunities in big towns : as more and more people will throng to them, they keep on encroaching on the fields around. It has been calculated that by the year 2000, more than half the population of the earth would live in cities. By that date, Mexico City will number 35 million inhabitants. Cairo, Jakarta, Sao Paulo, Shangai, Nairobi, Bombay will likewise become monster cities ! Their inhabitants are already undergoing ghastly living conditions ; the ceaseless influx of people will make them disastrous !

1. Housing. The open-sewer slums and shantytowns will spread uncontrollably : Ciudades Perdidas (Mexico City), Favelas (Rio), Vilas Miseras (Buenos Aires), bidonvilles (West Africa), Barong-barong (Manila), etc.
2. Sewage and garbage disposal is already inefficient. Hovels, gutters, rubbish tips are swarming with rats. Sanitary conditions being deplorable, serious diseases are common : dysentery, diphtheria, hepatitis. The ever-increasing flood of incomers cannot but multiply the risks of epidemics.
3. Drinking water : tanker lorries cannot even meet today's needs.
4. Public transport : there are no highways ! When it exists, it cannot cope with the demand !
5. Schooling : there are not enough schools ; there are too few school-bus services, and for good reason !

Checking school attendance is difficult. Bands of waifs and strays roam about, and spend the day in petty crime. In the early Eighties, it was estimated that one-third of Brazilian children - 16 million boys and girls - would remain outcasts for life.

6. Unemployment is rife. People stay alive by shining shoes in richer districts, by selling laces, trinkets, etc., by scavenging in dustbins or refuse dumps, by begging, by stealing...
7. Crime indeed, delinquency, drug-trafficking, prostitution are already widespread scourges.

All that augurs ill for the future, and the paradox is that all the measures that are taken to improve living conditions in those sprawling cities will only succeed in attracting more migrants !

■ Illiteracy - especially among women - and unemployment are bound to worsen.

■ The degeneration of races is to be feared. The harmful effects of malnutrition are already being denounced, but the lack of proteins, of iron and other minerals, and too many pregnancies at close intervals make expectant mothers anaemic and their babies hardly viable. Surviving children will in turn give birth to yet weaker babies...

■ Unprecedented levels of abortion and infanticide, especially of female babies : today's practices can give a good idea of what tomorrow's may be like !

- Girls are discriminated against in a number of Asiatic countries (India, China, Korea, etc.), and for economic reasons ! An old Chinese proverb says that " A boy can shoulder the roof beam, while a girl cannot even prop a door frame ". It means of course that a boy is stronger than a girl, and a better worker in the fields. Furthermore, a boy will be the staff of his parents' old age, whereas his sister will help her in-laws.
- In India, it has proved impossible to enforce the 1961 law that banned the dowry system. A bride's family must give to her parents-in-law a certain amount of cash, or such consumer goods as transistor-radio sets, mopeds, sewing-machines, refrigerators, etc. It ensues that the birth of a daughter is greeted as a misfortune. Several daughters spell ruin for parents : the dowries devour their savings, and the poorer ones are often reduced to borrowing money ! On the contrary, sons can be a veritable gold mine ! In Bombay and other big cities, or Seoul (South Korea), an expectant mother will more often than not resort to abortion if a scan reveals to her that her baby is a girl.

  If the child is born, she will often be left to die through neglect ; if she survives, she will suffer from malnutrition : children fight for food in poor families, and boys are given preference.
- In China, for the reasons quoted above, small farmers are apt to reserve for boys the " one child quota " imposed by the Government. The 800 million Chinese living in rural areas cannot yet bank on ultrasonography, but if a man happens to be told by a soothsayer that his wife might well be expecting a girl baby, he will fairly often make her have an abortion.

  A good many girls come into the world though, but heinous as it is, and however severely punished it may be, a certain number of them are abandoned, are drowned in wells or rivers, or smothered in their sleep !

■ Increased dependence on industrialized nations. Developing countries are already compelled today to try and secure new loans from the International Monetary Fund, and from Western banks, to merely service their debts. Their economic growth cannot keep up with a further increase in their populations : it will fuel even more the global debt crisis !

■ The demographic imbalance between the Third World and industrialized countries will eventually trigger an evolution in political attitudes.

- The surge of racialism will lead up to stricter immigration laws.
- The cost of labour tending to become cheaper in developing countries, Western nations will adopt harsh protectionist measures.

■ Overpopulation threatens to give rise to authoritarianism in such countries as are not stable democracies yet. Governments can be tempted to infringe upon human rights and restrict personal freedom in order to stave off an impending catastrophe.

(to be continued)

TEST YOUR KNOWLEDGE

1 - It is assumed that there will be 8 billion people on earth by 2025. Will difficulties arise merely from the sheer size of the population ?

2 - What does having children mean for most parents in developing countries ?

3 - How did the authorities in newly independent countries justify their demographic laissez-faire ?

4 - Were Malthus' fears concerning the future of humanity thoroughly unwarranted ?

5 - What are the two reasons why it is not profitable for African farmers to grow cereals ?

6 - Why does overpopulation lead up to environmental damage ?

7 - Why do people flock to cities ?

8 - Why is a race bound to degenerate owing to malnutrition ?

9 - Why are girls discriminated against in Asiatic countries ?

10 - Why is overpopulation in developing countries a growing concern for industrialized nations ?

52 - TO FLING-FLUNG-FLUNG *lancer violemment*

Synonymes : to hurl, to throw violently (threw - thrown), to sling (slung - slung)
- Empress Victoria reigned over a far-flung empire *(un vaste empire).*

53 - TO FLY-FLEW-FLOWN *voler - transporter (par avion)*
- The aircraft that was flying holiday-makers to Japan has been hijacked by five hijackers...
L'appareil qui transportait des vacanciers au Japon a été détourné par cinq pirates de l'air...
- How time flies !
Comme le temps passe vite !
- He flew into a rage (into a passion, into a temper) when he knew that they had turned down his application.
Il s'emporta quand il sut qu'ils avaient refusé sa candidature.

Substantif : - They sometimes cancel flights because of bad weather.
On annule parfois les vols à cause du mauvais temps.
- The flight of capital can worsen the crisis.
La fuite des capitaux peut aggraver la crise. (dans ce sens, " flight " est le substantif de " to flee ")

Attention ! to flow : *couler, est régulier*
- Money flows **in** at the moment. It flows **into** our coffers.
L'argent rentre en ce moment. Il rentre dans nos coffres.
- They fear gold will flow **out of** the country.
Ils ont peur que l'or ne sorte massivement du pays.

Substantifs : inflow : *l'afflux, la rentrée massive*
≠ outflow : *la sortie massive, l'hémorragie*

54 - TO FORBID-FORBAD(E)-FORBIDDEN *interdire, défendre de (≠ to allow, to permit).*

Synonymes : to prohibit... from, to ban... from
- The law **forbids** industrialists **to** employ children or to make women work at night (the law **prohibits** industrialists **from** employing... **from** making...), but unfortunately sweat shops have not thoroughly disappeared.
La loi interdit aux industriels d'employer des enfants ou de faire travailler les femmes la nuit, mais malheureusement les ateliers où l'on exploite la main d'œuvre n'ont pas complètement disparu (sweat : *la sueur*).
- Civil servants are banned from holding two offices concurrently.
Il est interdit aux fonctionnaires de cumuler deux emplois.
- They have staged a ban-the-bomb demonstration : " the H-bomb is not a deterrent ", they say.
Ils ont organisé une manifestation contre la bombe atomique : " la bombe H n'est pas une force de dissuasion ", disent-ils.
- God forbid !
A Dieu ne plaise ! - J'espère bien que non !

Substantif : *une interdiction* : a ban
- The Government have imposed a ban **on** our importing more than X TV sets from Japan, and they do not seem in a hurry to lift it !
Le Gouvernement nous a imposé l'interdiction d'importer plus de X téléviseurs du Japon, et il ne semble pas près de la lever !

Adjectif : forbidding : *rébarbatif* (≠ attractive)

Remarque : To forbid est la forme négative de to bid - **bade - bidden** : *ordonner* ; désuet dans ce sens, employer : **to order**
Par contre, to bid - **bid - bid** est encore en usage :
- At an auction-sale, you bid a certain sum for an object (you make a bid for an object).
Dans une vente aux enchères, on offre une certaine somme (on fait une enchère) pour un objet.

Expression : Solar energy **bids fair to** supersede other alternative sources of energy in sun-drenched countries.

L'énergie solaire promet de supplanter les autres sources d'énergie de remplacement dans les pays inondés de soleil.

Substantifs :

- A bid : an effort, an attempt
- In a last bid to reach an agreement... *Dans un dernier effort pour arriver à un accord.*
- Before you make a bid, let me tell you the reserve price !
Avant que vous ne fassiez une offre (une enchère), permettez-moi de vous dire la mise à prix !
- It will be sold to the highest bidder.
Ce sera adjugé au dernier enchérisseur : au plus offrant.
- A takeover bid : *une offre publique d'achat (O.P.A.)*

55 - TO FORECAST-FORECAST-FORECAST

prévoir
- It is difficult to forecast the weather with accuracy more than three days in advance.
Il est difficile de prévoir le temps avec exactitude (avec précision) plus de trois jours à l'avance.
- We must acknowledge that experts had forecast that the number of unemployed workers would pass the 2 million mark.
Nous devons reconnaître que les experts avaient prévu que le nombre de chômeurs franchirait (dépasserait) le cap des 2 millions.

Substantifs :

the weather forecast (singulier) : *les prévisions météorologiques.*
- The racing forecast never proves accurate : he gambles all his savings away.
Les pronostics hippiques ne s'avèrent jamais justes : il pert toutes ses économies au jeu.
- The star forecast sways his decisions !
L'horoscope exerce une influence déterminante sur ses décisions !

56 - TO FORESEE-FORESAW-FORESEEN

prévoir
- Who could have foreseen that Europe would bolster (support) the greenback one day ?
Qui aurait pu prévoir que l'Europe soutiendrait un jour le dollar ? (a bolster : *un traversin ;* cf. a cushion : *un coussin.* To cushion a shock : *amortir un choc*).
NB. The symposium is scheduled to take place on March 3rd.
Le colloque est prévu pour le 3 mars.
- Nothing foreshadowed (heralded) that sharp fall in prices.
Rien ne laissait prévoir cette brusque chute des prix.

Substantif :

The present slump can be ascribed to the authorities' lack of foresight.
La crise actuelle peut être imputée au manque de prévoyance (à l'imprévoyance) de nos dirigeants.

Adjectifs :

provident ≠ improvident : *prévoyant ≠ imprévoyant*

57 - TO FORETELL-FORETOLD-FORETOLD

prédire (to predict)
- That shrewd observer had foretold in his warning address that a few LDCs would not survive the erratic fluctuations in prices if buffer stocks of raw materials were not built up before long.
Cet observateur perspicace avait prédit dans son allocution d'avertissement que quelques PMA ne survivraient pas aux fluctuations capricieuses des prix si des stocks régulateurs de matières premières n'étaient pas constitués à brève échéance.

Substantif :

une prédiction : a prediction

58 - TO FORGET-FORGOT-FORGOTTEN

oublier

Attention !

to remind somebody **of** something : *rappeler quelque chose à quelqu'un.*
- Can you remind me of the seasonally adjusted unemployment figure that was released last week ?
Pouvez-vous me rappeler le chiffre des chômeurs publié la semaine dernière en fonction des données corrigées des variations saisonnières ?
To remember (**transitif**) : *se rappeler quelque chose, se souvenir de quelque chose (sans effort)*
mais : to recollect (to recall) impliquent un effort de recherche
- " Can you recollect the days when the demand outstripped the supply ? " - " They have fallen into oblivion ! "
" Pouvez-vous vous rappeler l'époque où la demande dépassait l'offre ? " - " Elle est tombée dans l'oubli ! "

3 - AUCUN

■ En tête de phrase - No (adjectif), none (pronom) ≠ all
Pour deux : neither (adjectif ou pronom) ≠ both

- According to believers, no power in this world can match God's.
  Selon les croyants, aucun pouvoir en ce monde ne peut rivaliser avec celui de Dieu.
- None of these pupils (none of them) is likely to pass.
  Aucun de ces élèves (aucun d'entre eux) n'est susceptible de réussir.
- Neither of my children will follow in my footsteps (≠ both my children).
  Aucun de mes (deux) enfants ne suivra mon exemple.
- Neither prisoner can give an alibi (≠ both prisoners can give).
  Aucun des (deux) prévenus ne peut donner d'alibi

Attention ! None of my pupil**s** : No pupi**l** of mine
None of our teacher**s** : No teache**r** of ours

■ Au sein d'une phrase : not... any (adjectif ou pronom) et not... either (2)

- The teacher is unbiassed and does not favor **any** pupil in particular.
  Le professeur est impartial et ne favorise aucun élève en particulier.
- The 2 boys will perhaps pass their Baccalauréat, but I cannot imagine either of them at College !
  Les 2 jeunes gens réussiront peut-être leur Bac, mais je ne puis en imaginer aucun (imaginer ni l'un ni l'autre) à l'Université. (≠ I can easily imagine both of them at College.)

4 - PRESQUE

■ Plus affirmations : nearly (almost) - all but

- I nearly always follow my wife's advice : *je suis presque toujours...*
- He was all but dead when the police found him... *Il était presque mort...*
- You can see advertisements nearly everywhere.
- Nearly everyone has a weapon hidden somewhere !

■ Plus négations : hardly ever, hardly anyone, thing, where + construction spéciale

- We **hardly ever** go to the cinema. *Nous n'allons presque jamais...*
- I **hardly** know **anyone** in this town.
- You have **hardly** eaten **anything.**

5 - BEAUCOUP

■ **Colloquial :** " a lot " (of + complément) ou " lots of " - " plein de "

- He earns a lot of money

■ **Plain English :** plenty (of + complément) : *bien assez ou plus qu'il n'en faut*

- They say that teachers have got plenty of free time !
- Why hurry ? We've got plenty of time : *nous avons bien le temps !*

■ **Refined English :** a good (great) deal of + singulier
a good (great) many + pluriel

Bringing up children requires a good deal of patience !
L'éducation des enfants requiert beaucoup de patience !

Remarque : much + singulier et many + pluriel ne s'emploient plus guère dans les affirmations

THÈME D'APPLICATION NUMÉRO 8

1 - Il est presque toujours difficile de prévoir le temps avec exactitude plus de trois jours à l'avance.
2 - L'horoscope ne s'avère presque jamais juste mais il exerce une influence déterminante sur mes décisions.
3 - Il paraissait presque (3 traductions) improbable que l'Europe soutienne (for + infinitif) le dollar un jour !
4 - Aucun de leurs experts (3 constructions) n'est capable de nous rappeler le chiffre des chômeurs en fonction des données corrigées des variations saisonnières !
5 - Beaucoup (a) colloquial ; b) refined ; c) bien assez) d'industriels emploient des femmes ou des enfants bien que cela soit interdit dans presque tous les pays.
6 - Il n'y a aucune source d'énergie de remplacement qui promette de supplanter le pétrole dans l'immédiat (pour le moment).
7 - Nos dirigeants n'avaient presque rien prévu et la crise actuelle peut être imputée à leur manque de prévoyance !
8 - A cause de la situation politique, beaucoup (plus qu'il n'en faut) d'or va sortir massivement du pays, et la fuite des capitaux aggrave presque toujours une crise économique.
9 - Je pensais qu'il n'y avait plus d'ateliers où l'on exploite la main d'œuvre, mais la police en découvre de temps en temps.
10 - Aucun des cinq pirates de l'air ne s'est emporté quand ils ont appris que les autorités refusaient leurs exigences (a demand)...
11 - Il écoute presque toujours les pronostics hippiques, mais il ne gagne presque rien !
12 - Ce colloque ne peut avoir lieu n'importe quand car tous ces experts sont très occupés (busy).
13 - Le temps passe vite, je le reconnais, mais pas n'importe où ! En prison, par exemple !
14 - Il n'y avait presque aucun indicateur (indicator) économique qui laissât (preterit) prévoir cette brusque chute des prix.
15 - Aucun de ces deux pays ne survivra aux fluctuations capricieuses des prix des matières premières.

9 - WORLD POPULATION

(Deuxième partie)

REMEDIES

The problem for Governments is to choose between authoritarian measures which impinge upon individual liberty, and liberal ones which respect it and rely on people's sense and motivation.

■ Coercive measures.

- India

When Indira Ghandi's Government realized that there could be one billion Indians by the year 2000, they issued the Emergency Rule which enforced sterilization upon all Indian males that had fathered two or more children. 7.8 million men underwent a vasectomy between April 76 and January 77, but the programme was carried out in so ruthless a manner that it roused people to indignation and cost Indira Ghandi the 1977 elections. When she came back to power, made wiser by that unfortunate experience, she declared that she was still favourable to birth control, but that it would henceforward be voluntary.

- China

It was decreed in 1980 that the one-child family would now be a civic duty, that girls would marry at 23, men at 25 in the country and at 26 in towns, and that couples would get a bonus for every childless year after they had got married.

The couples who undertake to have only one child, and who honour that pledge, are rewarded : they can choose between a monthly allowance or free education for the child, they are given priorities as regards housing, medical treatment and vacations, they are allotted a larger plot of private land, they will draw better pensions, and their child is guaranteed regular employment. If unfortunately they happen to have a second child, all those benefits must be returned, and a third pregnancy brings about sanctions : the authorities put pressure on the mother to abort, and she may be sterilized ; they dock parents' wages, deny them larger lodgings or free medical care, levy a " large family fee " until the child is 16, suppress their patch of land, etc.

In spite of those penalties, the authorities stand to undershoot their targets. The programme has been more successful in cities - lodgings are so small ! - than in the country : farmers are still determined on having several children for they will work in the fields and take care of them when they retire !

■ Liberal measures.

If the outcome of a liberal policy is not likely to be dramatic in the short term, the trend that it will set will endure and strengthen ; its greatest merit lies in the fact that it does not flout the freedom of the individual.

It should ideally translate into the following steps :

- Legalization of abortion.

Surgical and medical care is given free, but on no account is either operation to be forced on people : they resort to either, or even to both, if it does not run counter to their convictions. It is worth pointing out that legal abortion puts an end to the sordid activities of backstreet abortionists with the hazards that they may spell for women's health.

- Improved diffusion of knowledge.

1. Schooling must be free and open to all children, especially to girls ; they must be encouraged to go beyond the three R's standard, to carry on with secondary and even, for the most gifted, with higher education.
   - School attendance is indeed apt to thwart early marriages, hence early pregnancies.
   - Studies will give girls a better insight into their nature, and into the part that they are called upon to play in this world.
   - Studies will enable them to think on their own, to leave off taking traditions at their face value, to challenge their fathers' and later their husbands' views on their condition.

   Believing that the first generation of literate women will be able to fulfil themselves is probably wishful thinking, but their experience can undoubtedly serve as a springboard for their daughters and grand-daughters.
2. The number of family-planning centres must be increased in towns and cities to provide free information on birth-control, and free contraceptive devices.
3. The same mission must be entrusted to paramedical assistants (" paramedics ") ; they will carry it out in the remotest parts of rural areas. An increasing number of them must consequently be recruited and properly trained as family-planning advisers.

4. The radio and the television networks must be extended, and a fair number of documentary and educational films or talks must be slotted into their programmes.

- A suitable number of clinics must be set up here and there in the country where volunteers can be operated on by highly qualified personnel. Travelling units of surgeons and physicians will be available to go to the places that are lacking in public means of transport.
- Infantile mortality must be reduced thanks in particular to vaccination and improved hygiene. For example, mothers are to be shown how dangerous it is not to boil the water that they mix with formula to bottle-feed their babies. Healthy babies will eventually contribute to phasing out frequent pregnancies.
- The motivation of parents must be enhanced by information campaigns in the media extolling the merits of a reduced offspring : smaller families, in contrast to larger ones, are shown in films, strip cartoons or posters, to be enjoying better health, education and living standards.
- Financial incentives are advisable to round off these measures. Small families will be " rewarded " with tax rebates, additional family allowances, a week's extra holidays, free stays in holiday camps, etc. It shows how materialistic our society is since these ploys can be used to increase the birth rate in less prolific nations !
- To avert impending disasters in already overcrowded cities, the following steps should be taken without delay :
  - Demolition of slums and shantytowns.
  - Creation of satellite towns to accomodate cities' overspill.
  - Improvement of living conditions in revamped cities.
  - Voluntary transmigration to magnet development zones.
  - Offer of free land, free fertilizers ; purchase of crops at a fair price, loans at nominal rates of interest, etc, to put a brake on the drift from the land, and possibly to reverse the trend.

It is of course obvious that such measures require an enormous investment, and that no developing country is able as yet to finance such tremendous public expenditure. But for once, " the game is well worth the candle " because the future of the earth is at stake. Not only should developing nations exert themselves to implement the required policies by making sacrifices in certain sectors, but all industrialized countries should also do their utmost to aid them.

INDUSTRIALIZED NATIONS : THE BABY BUST

THE FACTS

A matter of 320 million people are living today in the countries of the European Economic Community, which represents roughly 7 % of the world's population. As the birth rate is steadily declining, it is estimated that only 5.4 % of the global population will be living in those countries by the year 2000.

The birth rate has been plummeting everywhere. In Europe, the lowest figure is to be found in West Germany with only 1.3 children per woman : within 50 years, the population will have dropped from 62 million to 38 million inhabitants. No other European country is faring much better, except Ireland where the birth rate is 70 % above the EEC average.

The average American woman's fertility rate has sunk from 3.77 in 1957 to 1.8 in 1987. In Japan, the birth rate fell from 4.5 to 2.0 between 1945 and 1960 ; it was 1.8 in the early 80s, and it has not improved !

If nothing alters today's downward trend, it is reckoned that the Third World will be 10 times as populated as the Western World in 50 years.

CAUSES

- Industrial development.

It seems to be a necessary but not a sufficient condition to account for the slide in the birth rate. As nations are becoming more affluent, their citizens' standard of living is improving. Higher salaries and wages, a better protection against illness and unemployment, the assurance of a comfortable old age, in short all the benefits that Welfare States bestow on their citizens, might lead one to believe that the latter would be inclined to procreate more children. Nothing of the kind ! Concurrently with industrial development, there has been an evolution in mentalities.

- The self-centred philosophy.

The upbringing of children is both time-consuming and costly. And these are probably the major faults with which today's potential parents are apt to reproach them : children would deprive hedonistic couples, prone by definition to self-indulgence, from too generous a share of their leisure time and income.

People from all walks of life are to varying degrees imbued

with the same conception of happiness, but it is best epitomized by " Yuppies " - young, upwardly mobile professionals - and " Dinks " - double-income no-kids couples. Children would definitely be a burden for people whose ideal is to live in a stylish flat in a smart district, to go skiing in Winter, and/or fly to exotic countries in Summer, to drive up-market cars, to indulge in tailor - or designer made clothes, to lead a busy social life - entertaining a lot and attending numerous parties - etc. Yuppies were born in America, but their counterparts are to be found everywhere : " Yaps " in Great Britain : young aspiring professionals ; " Naps ", in France for Neuilly-Auteuil-Passy, the places for which they have a liking ; " Die Aufsteiger ", in Germany ; the " Three S Generation " in Italy for soldi, successo e sport ; " los Jovenes Lobos " in Spain, etc.

■ Motherhood : a challenged vocation.

Gone are the days when a woman's calling used to be defined by what the Germans would tersely call the " three Ks " : Kinder, Küche, Kirche ! Most women have a job today, either out of necessity - one breadwinner's pay is not substantial enough - or from inclination : an increasing number of girls are educated, and the studies that they have chosen to pursue lead on naturally to an occupation : they achieve self-fulfilment through dedication to their work. In the couples who can barely make both ends meet on husbands' earnings, women will forgo motherhood for money ; they often do it willingly as they prefer commuting to being cooped up in their homes, and the company of their fellow workers to that of their saucepans !

■ A shift in the pattern of family life.

- Late marriages. They are generally ascribed to longer studies, the fear of unemployment, the lack of housing, which often compels children to live with their parents, or simply to a wish for independence.
- The spread of cohabitation. People simply set up house together because they feel that in so doing they are not giving up their freedom.
- Divorces and re-marriages. They are more and more numerous as divorce has been legalized in most countries, and is made easier by women's economic independence : they no longer have to rely on an uncertain alimony from an ex-husband !

■ Contraception and abortion have also been legalized in all industrialized countries, except in Ireland, which still bans divorce as well.

■ The dearth of child-minding services. There are not enough day nurseries (GB), day-care centers (US), creches and kindergartens. " Latchkey children " are left to themselves, especially in the countries with short school-days (West Germany).

■ The cost of housing.

■ The fear of the future.

There was a time when people were reluctant to have children because they were afraid of war, and of their sons' becoming cannon fodder ! Younger people perhaps apprehend a Third World war and the nuclear holocaust that it would entail.

Even in peace time, accidents in nuclear power stations or chemical plants can trigger environmental disasters. People remember Three Mile Island, Chernobyl, Seveso, Bhopal, Bâle, etc., and may dread similar or worse catastrophes !

Consequences

■ Pessimistic considerations : it has been said that refusing to have more babies in developed nations is tantamount to committing national suicide !

- The baby bust will give rise to unemployment in the branches where demand is bound to tail off : it will start with firms producing formula, jars of baby food, baby clothes, items like cradles, cots, perambulators, playpens, toys, nappies, etc ; the layoffs will snowball in the firms that cater for teenagers, and make clothes, books, records, walkmans, bicycles, mopeds, etc.
- Nursery, primary, secondary school teachers will in turn be thrown out into the street, and all the public funds that had been invested in school buildings and equipment will purely and simply result in a write-off.
- The labour force will shrink gradually. Skilled workers will become scarcer and firms will either invest in labour-saving machinery to boost productivity, or fall back on foreign hands, compounding the problem of immigration.
- The baby bust imperils the protection of nations. In West Germany, the Bundeswehr is already lacking in men and it has been decreed that as from 1989, conscripts would have to serve 18 instead of 15 months. It gives the Government 2 or 3 years' respite, but it does not solve the problem.

  By the mid-90s, it will prove difficult for the European members of NATO - except Turkey, and for good reason - to fulfil their commitments.
- The graying population will overstrain welfare programmes by worsening the dependency ratio (the " piggyback problem "). See Retirement and The Welfare State.
- The drop in the birth rate will impair the population balance :

  1. Geographically. In France, for example, whole regions are dying out whereas the Paris, the

Marseille or the Lyons areas, the Côte d'Azur are overcrowded.

2. Ethnically. The fertility of migrant workers' wives and the influx of new arrivals may very well jeopardize a country's national identity. 26 % of Luxembourg's population is foreign today. It is expected to be 34 % in the year 2000, and its birth-rate is among the lowest in the world !

   There are roughly 4.5 million guest workers in West Germany, especially Turks. Each Turkish woman has an average of 3.5 children, almost 3 times as many as a German woman.

   50 % of the Soviet population is made up of Slavs, but the birth rate in Moslem Central Asia and Caucasus is 5 times as high as theirs, and they stand to lose their numerical superiority within the next decade.

   For the same reason in Belgium, the Flemish exceed the Walloons in number. The Indians and the Malays threaten to outnumber the Chinese in Singapore, etc.

   In the United States, the proportion of the European-descended share of the population has declined from 80 % to 60 % because of the increasing number of births among Blacks and Hispanics : it may alter in the long run the values that W.A.S.P.S. have traditionally championed.

   And of course such an imbalance within a country's population may well bring about an upsurge in racialism, and complex political problems.

■ Optimistic views : having fewer children is not a bane, but a boon !

- It enhances the quality of their life. Parents are able to devote more attention to them ; they get better health care, and better education since the ratio teachers/pupils is improved. They are later more likely to get a good job.
- Public expenditure is lowered since the state no longer has to build and maintain so many schools, no longer has to train and pay so many teachers.
- It will solve in part the housing problem, and it will even enable young people to get married earlier, to start a home and possibly a family !
- The ageing population is going to provide the economy with new outlets. Manufacturers will simply turn over to the making of clothes for the elderly ; more homes, more retirement villages will have to be built, and outfitted, and staffed ! Tourism will enjoy a new boom, which will do nicely for travel agencies, tour operators, hotel and restaurant keepers, shipping companies operating cruise liners, etc.
- As the labour force is shrinking, minorities will no longer be discriminated against because of their race or sex (e.g. Blacks, Hispanics, women, in the United States ; immigrants elsewhere).
- Delinquency will be on the wane since unemployment will have ebbed away.

Remedies

Considering the difficulties that are looming ahead, it is urgent that the developed world should succeed in sparking a new - but not transient - baby boom. The miracle solution is yet to be found, and even if it dawned today upon the authorities concerned, it would take a long time before the point at which deaths and births balance out (Z.P.G. : zero population growth) is reached again. It entails having at least three children for a good many families since the replacement level has been calculated to be 2.1 children per woman (couples then just replace themselves).

Of course, people cannot be compelled to have children, but they should at least be given every opportunity to do so if they want to.

■ Negative measures.

- Abortion, available on demand and at no cost, could be made either more difficult to obtain, or at least more expensive. Some Russian young women have up to six or more abortions before they turn 25 !
- Immigrants could be repatriated on their own accord, their departure being encouraged by a substantial premium.
- Immigration could be checked, or at least reduced to a mere trickle.
- Higher taxes could be levied on childless couples, but that smacks too much of coercion !

■ Positive measures.

Most of them have already been or are still being resorted to, more or less successfully :

- Pro-birth campaigns in the media.
- Improved housing facilities. Cheaper rents, loans and mortgages ; rent allowances (housing benefits), proportional to the number of children. East Germany grants mortgages without interest, a portion of which is forgiven with each new child.
- Substantial reductions in public means of transport.
- Generalization of part-time work, temporary work, flextime, telecommuting. Women are thus given the opportunity of fulfilling themselves thoroughly by reconciling their occupational activities and motherhood.
- Extended maternity leaves. Parenthood leave in

Sweden grants 180 days to mothers or fathers at 90 % of their salaries.

- Guarantee of returning to one's job after a leave, even a protracted one, e.g. a sabbatical.
- Earlier retirement for mothers who have had 3 children or more.
- Financial incentives
  1. Generous family allowances, particulary for the third child. Some countries contemplate paying housebound mothers with three children a state salary.
  2. Generous tax relief proportional to the number of children.
  3. Fatter grants and scholarships, subsidies for clothes, school books, bags and stationery at the start of each new school year. Free studies and a guaranteed minimum wage for single or widowed mothers ; free day-care services for their child or children.
- Multiplication of child-minding services, free or at a reasonable cost.

TEST YOUR KNOWLEDGE

1 - Why are Chinese farmers determined on having several children in spite of the Government's penalties for doing so ?

2 - How can girls' education lead up to a lower birth rate ?

3 - Why is it paradoxical that the birth rate should be so low in industrialized countries ?

4 - Which are the two major faults that potential parents reproach children with ?

5 - Why are marriages usually late in developed countries ?

6 - Which is in your opinion the worst consequence of the baby bust ?

7 - What may arise from the disproportion in the birth rates of the United States' racial communities ?

8 - Which is in your opinion the best consequence of the baby bust ?

9 - Which new work patterns can help women to be mothers and still keep their jobs ? Why ?

10 - In your opinion, are financial incentives strong enough to entice couples into having children ?

59 - TO FORGIVE-FORGAVE-FORGIVEN

pardonner
- She implored his forgiveness, but he was adamant : she was laid off, without the usual redundancy payment.
Elle implora son pardon mais il fut inflexible : elle fut licenciée, sans l'indemnité de licenciement habituelle.

60 - TO FORSAKE-FORSOOK-FORSAKEN

abandonner (refined)
- Affluent countries cannot forsake those starving populations !
Les pays nantis ne peuvent abandonner ces populations affamées !

61 - TO FREEZE-FROZE-FROZEN

geler (≠ to thaw)
- Traffic is disrupted both when it is freezing or thawing.
La circulation est perturbée à la fois quand il gèle ou qu'il dégèle.
A deep-freeze : *un congélateur*
deep-frozen foods : *les produits congelés*
a price freeze, a wage freeze : *le blocage des prix, des salaires*

62 - TO GET-GOT-GOT

innumerable - countless - numberless meanings : *innombrables sens !*

63 - TO GIVE-GAVE-GIVEN

donner

Mots proches :

- I **will** not hand in (tender-give **in**) my resignation.
Je ne veux pas donner ma démission.
- He was awarded X pounds as damage**s.**
On lui a accordé X livres à titre de dommages et intérêts (mais : " damag**e** " *les dommages, les dégats :* toujours singulier).
- She was granted permission to retire early.
On lui a accordé la permission de prendre une retraite anticipée (de partir en pré-retraite).
- That country provides us **with** - supplies us **with** the nitrate fertilizers (nitrates) and phosphates that are essential to our impoverished soil.
Ce pays-là nous fournit les engrais azotés (les nitrates) et les phosphates qui sont indispensables à notre sol appauvri.
- A fairly large sum is allocated **to** (earmarked **for**) the training and re-training of workers.
Une somme assez importante est attributée (affectée) à la formation et au recyclage des ouvriers.
- On a collective farm beyond the Iron Curtain each family is allotted a small patch of land (plot of land) that they may till to provide **for** their own needs.
Dans une ferme collective, au delà du Rideau de fer, chaque famille se voit attribuer un petit lopin de terre qu'elle peut cultiver pour subvenir à ses propres besoins.
- Every morning, the foreman assigns us our daily stint.
Chaque matin, le contremaître nous assigne notre tâche quotidienne.

Expressions :

- No matter how alluring (enticing) that publicity is, he will not give way to temptation (he will not yield to temptation).
Quelque alléchante que soit cette publicité, il ne cède pas à la tentation.
- Although the future is all gloom and down, do not give way (do not yield) to despair, and take the Japanese as a model (pattern yourselves upon the Japanese) : they **set** a good example **to** us.
Bien que l'avenir se présente sous les couleurs les plus sombres, ne cédez pas au désespoir, et prenez modèle sur les Japonais : ils nous donnent le bon exemple !
+ up : *abandonner, cesser, renoncer à*
- He has given up his studio.
- You would not cough so much if you gave up smoking : *vous ne tousseriez pas tant...*
- They agree to give **up** a pay rise (to waive : to forgo a pay rise) to hold down costs and prevent further layoffs.
Ils sont d'accord pour renoncer à une augmentation pour maintenir les coûts et empêcher de nouveaux licenciements. (to forgo - forwent - forgone)

Substantif :

A gift : *un don, un cadeau*
- She has a gift for languages : *elle est douée pour les langues.*

- Nature has bestowed its gifts munificently upon our country (has lavished its gifts on our country) : it is endowed with boundless natural re**s**ources.
La nature a généreusement dispensé ses dons à notre pays (a prodigué ses dons à notre pays) : il est doté de ressources naturelles illimitées.

64 - TO GNAW-GNAWED-GNAWN

ronger, grignoter [n ɔ :]
- Dogs love gnawing big marrow bones.
Les chiens adorent ronger de gros os à mœlle.
- Inflation gnaws away at our savings (erodes our savings).
L'inflation grignote nos économies (chips away at - nibbles away at - eats away at - whittles down our savings).

65 - TO GO-WENT-GONE ou BEEN

aller, partir

Attention !

■ He has **gone** to Paris to give a new impetus to the negotiations : they are losing momentum.
*Il est **parti** à Paris pour redonner de l'élan aux négociations : elles sont en perte de vitesse (elles s'enlisent).*
■ He has **been** to Paris, but to no avail : the negotiations have reached total deadlock. How can we break the stalemate ?
*Il est **allé** à Paris, mais sans résultat : les négociations sont complètement dans l'impasse. Comment pouvons-nous sortir de cette impasse ?*

Rappel :

■ To be going to - to be about to - futur immédiat
- They are going to build up a stockpile of foodstuffs as a cushion against unavoidable restrictions.
Ils vonts se constituer un stock de denrées alimentaires pour amortir les effets de restrictions inévitables.
Cf. They are on the verge of (on the brink of) undergoing (going through = experiencing) the worst restrictions a country has ever had to endure.
Ils sont sur le point (à deux doigts) de subir les pires restrictions qu'un pays ait jamais eues à endurer.
■ Comme tous les verbes de mouvement ainsi que " to try ", " to go " peut se conjuguer avec " and ", à condition que les deux verbes conservent la forme de l'infinitif.
- We will **go and tell** the Minister that we want to bring our returns into line with those of other EEC farmers.
Nous irons dire au Ministre que nous voulons aligner nos bénéfices sur ceux des autres agriculteurs de la CEE.
Mais : they **went to tell** the Minister... *Ils sont allés dire...*
Try and focus your attention on... *Essayez de concentrer votre attention sur...*
Mais : He has **tried to focus** his attention on...
Il a essayé de concentrer son attention sur...
■ To go on - to keep on - to carry on + gérondif : *continuer à*
devant un C.O.D. ajouter " with " : Go on with your work.

Expressions :

- Things have started to go wrong (to deteriorate) : we are on the threshold of a serious crisis.
Les choses ont commencé à mal tourner (à se dégrader) nous sommes au seuil d'une crise grave.
- The firm has gone bankrupt : *la société a fait faillite.*
- I do not think that they will **go the length of** making a foray (an inroad) into the wine market : it would be unfair competition !
Je ne pense pas qu'ils iront jusqu'à faire une incursion (tenter une percée) sur le marché du vin : ce serait de la concurrence déloyale ! (Cf. to break into a market : *faire la conquête d'un marché)*
- The government gave the go-ahead yesterday to an ambitious plan (*le feu vert*).

9 - STRUCTURES

LES INDÉFINIS (suite)

6 - PEU

little + singulier - Few + pluriel

- They showed little gratitude towards their benefactor.
  Ils ont montré peu de gratitude envers leur bienfaiteur.
- Few girls like violence !
  Peu de filles aiment la violence !

7 - TROP ET TROP PEU

too much ≠ too little (singulier)
too many ≠ too few (pluriel)

- Pupils always complain of having too much work !
- We have got too few opportunities of practising English.
  Beaucoup trop ; far too much (+ singulier), far too many (+ pluriel)

Remarque :

■ " Assez " : adjectif + enough
enough + substantif

- I am strong enough to lift that stone : I've got enough strength.

■ " De trop " : un (2, 3, etc.) de trop ; one (2, 3, etc.) too many

- Have we got enough tickets ? We've got three too many... *nous en avons trois de trop.*

8 - LA PLUPART

most + substantif
most of + article ou adjectif possessif

- Most boys love football

Mais :

- Most **of** the boys in our school love football.
- Most **of** the boys that I know love football.
- Most **of** them love it.

9 - TRADUCTION DE "AUTRE"

■ **Other** adjectif ou pronom - An + other : another

- Have you read these books ? I've read this one, but not the others : the other ones.
- Can you give me another example ? All right, I'll give you another (one).

■ **Else** après : what, where, who et les composés de some, any, no

- What else do you need for the expedition ?
- I won't drink anything else, thank you.
- Couldn't you go somewhere else (elsewhere) to clean your bike ?
- Nobody else **but** my father is allowed to drive the car.
  Personne d'autre ***que*** *mon père...*

FUTUR ET CONDITIONNEL AVEC LES CONJONCTIONS DE TEMPS

Après : when - while - as soon as - everytime (whenever) : chaque fois que - once : une fois que - as long as : tant que - after : après
futur français : présent anglais
conditionnel français : preterit anglais

- When you **come** to Manchester, I'll show you round the town.
- He said that when I **came** to Manchester, he would show me round the town.

Exceptions :

■ La subordonnée sert de c.o.d. à la principale (après : to say, to tell, to ask, to know, to wonder).
- I wonder when **he will stop** behaving like a child.
- Did he tell you when **he would come** ?

■ Dans les indépendantes
- When **will this war come** to an end ?

Quand cette guerre se terminera-t-elle ?

THÈME D'APPLICATION NUMÉRO 9

1 - Nous sommes au seuil d'une crise grave, et bien des gens pensent que l'avenir se présente sous les couleurs les plus sombres.

2 - Ce pays-là ne nous fournit rien d'autre que des engrais qui sont indispensables à notre sol appauvri.

3 - Pas un franc de trop n'a été attribué (2 traductions) à la formation des ouvriers ; le patron a été inflexible !

4 - La nature a dispensé trop peu de dons à ces pays-là ; les pays nantis ne peuvent pas abandonner leurs populations affamées.

5 - Nous sommes sur le point (2 traductions) de subir des restrictions draconiennes (drastic) mais nous avons trop peu de temps pour nous constituer un stock de denrées alimentaires.

6 - Je ne cède pas à n'importe quelle publicité, quelque alléchante qu'elle soit !

7 - On ne lui a presque rien accordé à titre de dommages et intérêts et beaucoup d'hommes cèderaient au désespoir, mais il nous donne le bon exemple !

8 - Il n'essaie plus de concentrer son attention sur une solution car les négociations sont complètement dans l'impasse.

9 - Chaque fois que nous essaierons de faire une incursion sur leur marché, iront-ils jusqu'à dire que c'est de la concurrence déloyale ?

10 - Nous nous demandons quand le Gouvernement donnera le feu vert à un projet que la plupart d'entre nous considèrent comme très ambitieux.

11 - Presque tous leurs ouvriers sont d'accord : lorsque les choses commenceront à mal tourner, ils renonceront aux augmentations de salaire pour éviter les licenciements.

12 - Il a promis qu'il cesserait de fumer dès qu'il tousserait trop.

13 - Tant qu'une somme assez importante sera affectée au recyclage des ouvriers, aucun d'entre eux ne touchera l'indemnité de licenciement.

14 - Trop peu d'épargnants (a saver) ont prévu que l'inflation grignoterait (3 traductions) leurs économies.

15 - Nos agriculteurs seront satisfaits une fois que leurs bénéfices seront alignés sur ceux des autres agriculteurs de la CEE.

10 - UNEMPLOYMENT

A FEW FIGURES

There are some 31.5 million unemployed people in the OECD countries in 1988, that is to say, 8.25 % of the active population.

In Europe, double-digit unemployment rates still plague Spain (20.1 %), Italy (15.7 %), Holland (14 %), Belgium (10.9 %), France (10.3 %). Other countries are faring better : the United Kingdom (9 %), West Germany (8.9 %), Sweden (1.8 %), the prize going to Switzerland with a trifling 0.8 % !

In the United States, the unemployment rate has been declining since 1985 and has fallen to 5.4 % ; Japan's is a mere 2.6 % !

The young unfortunately have been bearing the brunt of the job shortage and the unemployed among them represent the following percentages of the working population : in Italy 37 %, in France 23 %, in Great Britain 17.70 %, but only 7.70 % in West Germany. It is still 11.2 % in the United States, but only 5.7 % in Japan.

CONSEQUENCES

They are painful for all, and tragical for some, especially for the long-term unemployed who stand to remain for ever the wards of the state : the longer they have to wait, the poorer the chance is of their ever finding a job.

Despair drives some of them to suicide, others take to drinking or to drugs ; some will give themselves up to delinquency probably under the impression that in so doing they get their revenge on society for failing to help them.

The more destitute can no longer pay a rent, and they are to be found sleeping under pitiful pieces of cardboard in public parks, in the streets, in the nooks and crannies of railway or Underground (US : Subway) stations, or they seek shelter in the hostels of the Salvation Army, the Red Cross, or other charitable organizations. They queue up for food at soup kitchens. A host of unemployed people now swell the ranks of all big cities' inevitable vagrants and beggars to constitute what has been named the Fourth World or the New Poor.

Unemployment also perturbs family life. A jobless father is apt to be ashamed of himself for no longer providing for his family, hence a feeling of guilt, a profound anguish as regards the future which may lead to depression and nervous collapse. He may lose his authority over his children, or his wife's respect, as they perhaps despise him for his incompetence.

One can rightly wonder why unemployment on such a scale does not spark off more desperate reactions, more outburts of violence, tumultuous marches and demonstrations, and ultimately riots with a trail of burnt cars, looted shops, and severe clashes with the police.

- One must bear in mind that the unemployed do not make up a permanent body : there is a constant turnover in their ranks, as the more fortunate among them manage - more or less rapidly - to find employment.
- Moreover, there is an increasing number of salaried women, and consequently fewer and fewer single bread-earners in families : it makes it easier to weather a spell of unemployment, one paypacket helping to make ends meet in the meantime.
- Redundancy payments and unemployment benefits are also instrumental in tiding people over until they obtain another job.
- In accordance with most Governments' schemes, school-leavers and redundant people are entitled to go on paid training or retraining courses meant to lead on to jobs, which enables them to wait and see.
- The more resourceful - or the less scrupulous - resort to moonlighting, while scroungers are quite satisfied with sponging upon the Welfare State !

THE WORLD'S DEPRESSION AND ITS REPERCUSSIONS

After a 30 years' boom (1946-1976), economic growth in industrialized countries went into a tail-spin. The annual growth rate tumbled to 2 % in the United States and Europe ; Japan weathered the storm better with 4 %.

It was due in part to the three oil price shocks (1973-1979-1984) and subsequent rises which sent the price of energy soaring. The prices of raw materials followed suit if only because the extraction and the transport of ores, for instance, proved more expensive.

As a consequence, the prices of domestic products kept rising : inflation made imports comparatively cheaper and exports went on the downswing. As the demand for foreign goods increased, domestic production slowed down : nations had to grapple with slumpflation (slump+inflation) and stagflation (economic stagnation+inflation). To remain competitive, industrialists had to reduce production costs. One way to do it was to improve productivity by investing in new machinery and new technology (automation, computerization), which of course resulted in thinning out the workforce. High-technology industries (electronics, data-processing, robotics, fiber-optics, etc.) were still too young to soak up the sudden spate of jobless workers.

Smokestack industries (sunset industries) : coal-mines, steel-works, car factories, textiles, shipbuilding, etc., were to suffer most from the recession. They used to be labour-intensive, and their streamlining entailed slashing hundreds of thousands of unskilled workers : they were obviously the more liable ones to be replaced by " steel-collar workers " (robots) or other " job-killers " (computerized equipment).

TRADE-UNIONS

- They used to be powerful, and by wielding their favourite weapon - strikes - or through collective bargaining, they would obtain pay rises everytime they considered that workers' purchasing power had sagged. That was to lead up to the inflationary spiral (the wage-price spiral). Cost-of-living adjustments would increase production costs, which would result in higher prices, and consequently in further claims for rises ! We have seen the relationship that exists between inflation and unemployment. Paradoxically, the measures taken by some Governments to curb inflation contributed to raising unemployment by jeopardizing economic expansion : a wage-freeze would lower purchasing-power, and so would credit-squeeze by fixing a ceiling to bank-loans and tightening hire-purchase ; a reduction in public expenditure would obviously deprive firms of orders.
- Unions used to be adamant as regards any innovation in working practices. They would not hear of employers' laying off workers in a recession, even if the latter undertook to take them on again when business revived. With the economy in the doldrums, employers were understandably wary of recruiting new workers ! Unions were also unyielding as concerns part-time and temporary work, flexitime, telecommuting, the five-day working week, etc.

WELFARE BENEFITS

cf. Welfare and the unemployment trap.

The dole has often been charged with being a disincentive to work. It used to be true in the heyday of Welfare States when benefits were so generous that unemployed people refused jobs whose wages would not have made them much better off. Furthermore mentalities had evolved : it was no longer disreputable to draw unemployment benefits : relief was no longer regarded as a stain on one's reputation.

BABY BOOM

The baby boom in the late 50s and early 60s (1955-1964) caused the number of job-seekers to reach an all-time peak on the labour-market in the 70s and afterwards.

WOMEN'S INFLUX INTO THE LABOUR MARKET

From 1870 to 1983, the number of salaried women in the seven largest countries of the OECD zoomed from 14 to 56 %, and it is still rising !

THE DRIFT FROM THE LAND

The Western world is suffering from an overproduction of foodstuffs. It is due to agrimation, high-yield crops resulting from breakthroughs in genetics (new hybrids), from the intensive use of fertilizers, pesticides, weed-killers, etc. It makes the selling of those goods more and more difficult ; and they are more often than not cleared off at a loss : the EEC imposes production quotas, governments are compelled everywhere to subsidize farming heavily to make the prices of their crops competitive on global markets.

The outlook is grim as stricter measures are in the offing : thousands of hectares will have to be left fallow, millions of vines will be uprooted, quotas will yet again be cut down ; furthermore GATT (General Agreement on Tariffs and Trade) demands that all subsidies be suppressed. That evolution spells death for small and medium-sized farms to the advantage of the larger, capital-intensive agricultural estates.

EUROSCLEROSIS : RIGIDITY OF THE EUROPEAN LABOUR-MARKET

- Government regulations - originating in the satisfaction of trade-unions' claims :
  1 - Prevent employers from adjusting wages to the fluctuations of the economy : a drop in demand is not to be followed by a cut in wages.
  2 - Enforce wage indexation : wages are geared to the cost-of-living.
  3 - Enforce minimum wages even when production is faltering for lack of demand.
  4 - Enforce a rigid working-time. There is no getting away from the conventional 5-day working week.
  5 - Forbid employers to axe the workforce when production has stalled, etc.
- Hurdles hinder job-creation :
  1 - Red tape and stingy Government financial support make startups uncertain. Moreover, too little venture capital is available (one tenth as much as in the United States), otherwise a greater number of enterprising people would set up on their own.
  2 - A lack of financial backup also hampers the expansion of small- and medium-sized concerns.
- Bankruptcy laws are too severe in Europe.

  A bankrupt is guilty of an offence, even if his insolvency does not arise from fraudulent schemes. His honour is for ever sullied. As for his business, the official receivers are more concerned with satisfying creditors by selling its assets than with keeping it going in order not to lay off its employees.

  In the United States, bankruptcy is not shameful ; the law urges the bankrupt to take heart and start again !

LACK OF MOBILITY

For different reasons, workers jib at moving to where jobs are being offered ; relocation raises problems :

- Owner-occupiers find it difficult to sell their houses in depressed areas, and they need the money to settle in more prosperous places.
- Housing is either lacking or outrageously expensive where jobs are to be found.
- Some people are simply loath to sever the emotional bonds that unite them or the members of their families to a place, to a school, to people or to particular activities.

EDUCATION

Our education system falls obviously short of the economic requirements of the modern world. For centuries, it has aimed at the cultural enrichment of students, passing on to them the knowledge and the wisdom of our philosophers, of our historians, of our best writers, at developing in them a taste for the beautiful and the righteous, but it has thoroughly failed in giving them the skills which they needed to find a job and earn their daily bread !

IMMIGRANTS (SEE NEXT CHAPTER)

When factories were working at full capacity, migrant workers flocked to industrialized countries ; at the outset of the recession, they often were the first to become unemployed.

(to be continued)

TEST YOUR KNOWLEDGE

1 - What are the dire consequences of unemployment for some unfortunate jobless people ?

2 - Why are not the consequences of unemployment far worse than they actually are ?

3 - What is the relationship between the oil-price shocks and unemployment ?

4 - Why did smokestack industries suffer most from the recession ?

5 - What is the inflationary spiral (the wage-price spiral) ?

6 - How can anti-inflationary measures contribute to raising unemployment ?

7 - Why is the outlook grim as regards job opportunities in agriculture ?

8 - What is " Eurosclerosis " ?

9 - Why are jobless workers reluctant to move to where there are vacancies ?

10 - Which main criticism can be levelled at the education system in most European countries ?

66 - TO GRIND-GROUND-GROUND

moudre, aiguiser, grincer
- Millers used to grind wheat into flour in windmills.
Autrefois les meuniers réduisaient (moulaient) le blé en farine dans des moulins à vent.
- A grinder grinds (sharpens) blunt knives and scissors on a grindstone.
Un rémouleur aiguise les couteaux et les ciseaux émoussés (≠ sharp*) sur une meule.*
- It is no use grinding your teeth : because of your negligence, you have forfeited your right to redundancy payment.
Cela ne sert à rien de grincer des dents : à cause de ta négligence, tu as perdu ton droit à la prime de licenciement.
- With all those strikes, production ground to a halt.
Avec toutes les grèves, la production s'arrêta peu à peu.

Attention ! to ground (R) : *baser, fonder*
- " I am sure they are going to retaliate against us for scorning (spurning-turning down) their offer ! " - " On what arguments do you ground your opinion ? "
" Je suis sûr qu'ils vont user de représailles envers nous pour avoir méprisé (repoussé-dédaigné) leur offre ! " - " Sur quels arguments fondez-vous votre opinion ? "
- My fears were well-grounded : they have ousted us from the South American market.
Mes craintes étaient bien fondées : ils nous ont évincés du marché Sud-Américain.

Substantif et adjectif :
- On what grounds do you suspect them of restrictive practices ? Your suspicions are groundless !
Pour quels motifs les soupçonnez-vous d'entraves à la libre concurrence ? Vos soupçons sont dénués de tout fondement !

67 - TO GROW-GREW-GROWN

- Cod-liver oil is prescribed by physicians for rickety children, or those who have been growing too fast.
L'huile de foie de morue est ordonnée par les médecins aux enfants rachitiques, ou à ceux qui ont grandi trop vite.
- They will soon **grow weary of** trying to grow sugar-cane on that barren (≠ fertile) soil.
Ils se lasseront vite d'essayer de faire pousser de la canne à sucre sur ce sol aride (≠ fertile).
- He wants to become an engineer when he is grown-up.
Il veut devenir ingénieur quand il sera grand.
- This project (scheme, plan) has been on the shelf (one shelf, two shel**ves**) (has been in abeyance) for years : I have a growing desire to carry it out. (un plan : **aussi** a blueprint)
Ce projet est dans les tiroirs (est en suspens) depuis des années : j'ai de plus en plus envie de le mettre à exécution.

Substantifs et adjectif :
- It is not because you are of age that you are (a) grown-up (two grown-up**s**).
Ce n'est pas parce qu'on est majeur qu'on est (un) adulte.
- Growth : *la croissance (*development).
- The growth rate : *le taux de croissance.*
- Zero economic growth : *la croissance zéro.*

68 - TO HANG-HUNG-HUNG

Ou régulier pour la *pendaison par le cou*
- Murderers used to be hanged in Great Britain.
Autrefois on pendait les meurtriers en Grande-Bretagne.
- Sausages are hanging **from** the ceiling in the butcher's shop.
*Des saucisses pendent **au** plafond dans la boucherie.*
- Filthy smog hangs permanently over the valley as scores of cooling towers and chimneys belch out (belch forth) noxious (harmful ≠ harmless) steam, smoke and fumes.
Un brouillard épais et sale plane en permanence sur la vallée car des dizaines de tours de refroidissement et de cheminées déversent (vomissent) des torrents (des flots) de vapeur, de fumée et de gaz nocifs (≠ inoffensifs).

ahead).
La vie de la firme ne tient qu'à un fil ; la faillite paraît imminente (menace dangereusement).

69 - TO HAVE-HAD-HAD

Rappel :

■ You **would rather** malinger and loaf about, but you **had** better shake yourself up and work !
Vous aimeriez mieux faire le malade et fainéanter, mais vous feriez mieux de vous secouer et de travailler !
(a malingerer : *un simulateur, un " tire-au-flanc ", un faux malade)*
■ She thinks her husband is unfaithful to her, and she **has** him follow**ed**.
Elle pense que son mari la trompe (lui est infidèle) et elle le fait suivre.
Mais : She **made** him **confess** his unfaithfulness.
Elle lui fit avouer son indifélité.
The have-nots - the underprivileged ≠ the affluent - the well-to-do : *les déshérités, les sous-prolétaires ≠ les nantis.*
The haves and the have-nots : *les riches et les pauvres.*

70 - TO HEAR-HEARD-HEARD

entendre
" When she **gave birth** to that illegitimate child, it **gave rise** to a scandal " - " I have never heard **of** it ".
" Quand elle a donné naissance à cet enfant illégitime, cela a donné naissance à un scandale " - " Je n'en ai jamais entendu parler ".
- As my husband is a sales representative (a travelling salesman - a commercial traveller - " a rep "), he is always on the move, but I hear **from** him everyday, no matter where he is.
Comme mon mari est représentant de commerce, il est toujours par monts et par vaux, mais il me donne de ses nouvelles tous les jours, où qu'il soit.
- He remains deaf to our entreaties : he will not hear of a workers' cooperative and prefers to close down the factory !
Il demeure sourd à nos prières : il ne veut pas entendre parler d'une coopérative ouvrière et préfère fermer l'usine !
(to entreat - to implore : *supplier, implorer).*
- We know from hearsay that you intend to invite tenders for the development of the industrial estate.
Nous savons par ouï-dire que vous avez l'intention de lancer un appel d'offres pour l'aménagement de la zone industrielle.
NB. The Chairman and Managing Director in on very good terms with everyone - get on very well with everyone.
Le Président Directeur Général s'entend très bien avec tout le monde.

71 - TO HEAVE

R - parfois : hove - hove
- In view of the glut on the market, I shall heave a sigh of relief if we manage to dispose of our surpluses (singulier : a surplus).
*Au vu de l'engorgement du marché, je pousserai un soupir de soulagement si nous arrivons à écouler nos excédents (*to relieve = *soulager).*

Substantif :

Computerization has triggered (off) (sparked off = touched off) tremendous technological and social upheavals in industry.
L'information a provoqué dans l'industrie de formidables bouleversements technologiques et sociaux.

10 - STRUCTURES

TRADUCTION DE L'IMPARFAIT FRANCAIS

Ne pas traduire d'emblée par un preterit simple.

1 - LE PLUS COURAMMENT : PRETERIT PROGRESSIF

- When the Headmaster entered, the pupils were playing cards.

2 - PLUS-QUE-PARFAIT DANS LES TEMPORELLES + SINCE OU FOR

- He had been swimming for 6 hours when he reached the shore (*le rivage*).

3 - FORME FRÉQUENTATIVE

a) used to [ju:st] : **contraste** entre ce qui était et ce qui n'est plus.
- I used to smoke a lot, but I've given it up.

b) would : **répétition fréquente** ou **tendance naturelle**
- An obliging old man, he would help anyone in trouble.
  Vieil homme serviable, il aidait quiconque se trouvait en difficulté.
- Before I gave up smoking, I would smoke three packets of cigarettes a day.

THÈME D'APPLICATION NUMÉRO 10

1 - Cela ne servira à rien de grincer des dents quand tu auras perdu ton droit à la prime de licenciement !
2 - Il a dit qu'ils useraient de représailles envers nous chaque fois que nous refuserions leurs offres !
3 - Je me demande quand ils lanceront un appel d'offres pour l'aménagement de la zone industrielle.
4 - Mes craintes étaient bien fondées, mais ils ne nous ont pas dit quand ils essaieraient de nous évincer du marché Sud-Américain. Nous ferions mieux de nous secouer !
5 - Tant que mon mari sera représentant de commerce, il sera toujours par monts et par vaux et me sera infidèle !
6 - Quand arriverons-nous à écouler nos excédents ? Je pousserai un soupir de soulagement quand nous mettrons notre projet à exécution !
7 - Le délégué syndical (shopsteward) a dit que tant que le Président Directeur Général ne voudrait pas entendre parler d'une coopérative ouvrière, la vie de la société ne tiendrait qu'à un fil !
8 - " Je me demande quand l'informatisation déclenchera (3 traductions) un bouleversement dans cette usine. " - " Tant que le projet sera dans les tiroirs, le brouillard sale et épais planera sur la vallée ! "
9 - Autrefois, les médecins prescrivaient de l'huile de foie de morue aux enfants rachitiques.
10 - Nous ne regrettons pas l'usine qui a fait faillite : ses cheminées vomissaient tous les jours des torrents de gaz nocifs.
11 - Dans le temps, ils faisaient pousser de la canne à sucre dans leurs champs mais les récoltes étaient maigres (poor) sur ce sol aride.
12 - Tous les chefs d'état se demandent quand la CEE arrivera à écouler tous ses excédents de nourriture (nom composé).
13 - " Lui as-tu demandé ce qu'il ferait quand il serait grand ? " - " Autrefois, il voulait être ingénieur ; aujourd'hui il rêve de devenir Président Directeur Général ! "
14 - Cela faisait des mois que nous le suppliions de monter (to set up) une coopérative mais il a préféré fermer l'usine.
15 - La faillite menaçait dangereusement depuis quelques mois, mais pendant tout ce temps, le Directeur faisait le malade et fainéantait.

11 - UNEMPLOYMENT

(Deuxième partie)

REMEDIES

If there were a sovereign remedy against it, unemployment would no longer hold sway over the industrialized world since it would have been administered ages ago. The disease has put a good many governments to the test, and varied treatments have been, and are still being, more or less felicitously, applied to it.

WORK SHARING

Trade-unions advocated it at one time as a way of " sharing the cake " more equitably. The number of working hours was accordingly pared down to 39 hours per week in France, to 36 hours in Belgium. It was hoped that employers would take on more employees to maintain the same output, but they preferred either to ask their work-force to work overtime, or at the very most to hire temporary workers. It was to be expected since a cut in working hours without a cut in wages was actually tantamount to a pay rise !

EARLY RETIREMENT SCHEMES

e. g. French " solidarity contracts ".

They were inspired by the same generous idea, but they were to meet with the same fate. Job-seekers were to have taken the place of early retirees - employers being helped to that end by government subsidies - but it proved in most cases to be nothing more than wishful thinking.

SUBSIDIES TO " LAME DUCKS "

Governments strove to bail out such ailing industries as, for instance, coal-mining and steel, by injecting public funds into them, but to no avail : the attempt proved ineffective and swallowed up astronomical sums that could have been put to better use as investment in pace-setting sectors - electronics, robotics, biotechnology -. The Japanese knew better and favoured sunrise rather than sunset industries, with the results that we know.

DEFICIT FINANCING (US : PUMP PRIMING)

If a government reduces taxes and at the same time increases public expenditure, it injects money into the economy : consumers will have more money at their disposal, demand will rise and it will encourage firms to invest and engage workers. The drawback is that it entails running a budgetary deficit that has to be made up by borrowing. This is the policy that President Reagan has been applying since he came into office : " Reaganomics ".

REFLATION

A reflationary policy consists also in increasing demand by raising consumers' purchasing power ; it is obtained this time by pushing up salaries and wages, especially the lower ones. It is then hoped that the economy will take off again. That was what the French Government attempted to do in the early 80s, and the French responded readily. Unfortunately they set their hearts on foreign goods - chiefly Japanese ones - and the upshot was a major deficit in the trade balance, and no dent whatsoever in unemployment.

FOREIGN FIRMS

To control imports better, and at the same time fuel industrial activity, the United States and European countries have been wooing foreign firms - again mainly Japanese ones - with tempting offers like capital grants, tax relief, low interest loans, etc., vaunting the climate of their respective countries, its geographical position, the skills of its workers, its gentle way of life, etc. Quite a number of them have responded to the overtures, and have set up factories in diverse host countries, among which Great Britain comes first, and Ireland is runner-up. Unfortunately they are often mere " screwdriver plants " (GB : factories), assembling component parts imported from abroad with the help of very few local workers.

TRADE UNIONS' AND LIBERAL GOVERNMENTS' CONCESSIONS

- Trade unions no longer look askance at temporary and part-time work. Working mothers appreciate it for obvious reasons, and so do school-leavers who thus can acquire the experience that they lack. Employers in the sectors where demand is irregular (in the retailing or catering trade for instance, in farming of course, but also in the toy industry, etc.) prefer to hire more " temps " than a smaller number of full-time employees : they thus avoid higher labour costs and redundancies. Temporary help agencies have mushroomed everywhere. In the United States, " disposable " or " dispensable " employees make up 25 % of the labour-force.

- Governments and trade unions have also relented as regards working hours. The rigid weekly mould has been broken, and working hours can be determined in each firm through an agreement between management and labour with a view to optimizing production. Labour costs are reduced, which rebounds on the price of finished goods : it indeed spares the employer either the extracost of overtime work or the hiring of " temps ". The number of working hours is no longer calculated on a weekly basis, but on a monthly or even a yearly one. Workers are granted in exchange a 5 % cut in the total number of hours, especially those who opt for work over week-ends or at night. If the scheme makes the business thrive, the latter cannot but expand and need more manpower.
- Salaries and wages are no longer pegged to the cost-of-living to avoid the inflationary spiral. Pay rises are obtained through collective bargaining. Fairly often in the United States, workers trade off pay hikes for job security. In certain sectors, trade unions have even accepted two-tier wage schemes provided firms hire new workers : these draw lower wages until they retire. Such schemes, it is true, contribute in part to mopping up unemployment, and to trimming labour costs, but on the other hand, employers may be tempted to entice senior workers into retiring early in order to engage new workers and economize on wages...

European governments

They are overhauling their bankruptcy laws : the firms which are in financial straits will no longer hesitate to appeal to bankruptcy courts before they are teetering on the brink of collapse. They will be granted a certain amount of leeway (e. g. a moratorium on their debts), and possibly financial backing before they set out again on a safer course.

Workfare

The dole is no longer so generous as it used to be. The tendency today is to help people in need with the proviso that they accept a job or that they train or re-train to get one.

Startups

Efforts are also being made in Europe to promote startups by simplifying the paperwork and easing up on the official financial backup. Unfortunately venture capital as yet remains difficult to hunt down, which probably also accounts for employee buyouts being still rather uncommon.

Baby bust

The baby boom started to subside in 1965 and the effects of the declining birth rate will begin to be felt in the 1990s. The demand for jobs will ease off, but it is to be feared that we shall " lose on the swings what we make on the roundabouts " : the baby bust will compel governments to come to grips with other serious problems (cf. Welfare and Retirement).

Stopgap measures

- Special schemes have been devised to help the long-term unemployed. For instance, the P. I. L. (Programmes d'insertion locaux) in France or the new Restart scheme in Great Britain. The former concerns people over 25 who have been unemployed for a long time. The latter is intended for anybody who has been unemployed for more than one year (40 % of the unemployed). He/she is summoned to an employment agency for an interview, the aim of which is to bring him/her back into contact with the labour market.
- Government sponsored job-training programmes.

  A patchwork of schemes which concern school-leavers and University dropouts has been worked out every where. They vary from country to country, and so do the details of their implementation.

  They have however a few common features :

  - They want to remedy the shortcomings of the education system by offering on-the-job training periods alternating with remedial or introductory courses.
  - They are tailored to the ages and to the aptitudes of applicants.
  - Trainees are paid.

One such scheme, the Y. T. S. (Youth Training Scheme) in Great Britain, run by the Manpower Services Commission, is intended to prepare 16-and 17-year-olds for the labour market in 2 years. Firms offer vocational training on their premises, trainees attend classes one day per week, and they are paid up to 35 pounds a week.

Undergoing such a training period is unfortunately not a guarantee of success, and people will inevitably denounce the fact that it does **not with certainty** lead on to a job.

Unlucky trainees can still fall back on such makeshift schemes as " les T. U. C. " (Travaux d'Utilité Collective) in France, or Community-Training Programmes in Great-Britain, which give them a second chance, or at least the opportunity of not being unemployed until things sort themselves out !

OVERHAUL OF THE EDUCATION SYSTEM

It is paradoxical that Europe should experience at the same time double-digit unemployment and a shortage of skilled labour, but even American, and to a much lesser degree, Japanese employers, are hunting for qualified workers.

Too many students embark upon studies irrespective of job prospects. Universities churn out batches of graduates in arts, languages, law, etc., whose degrees are thoroughly worthless on the labour market, but they will not hear of the latter swaying their choice.

Too many students again are unsuited for higher education ; 50 % of French undergraduates, for instance, give up their studies after two years at University, but they will not hear of selective entry.

Technical schools and technology institutes have too long been relegated to a position of secondary importance, too many parents wanting probably their children to have a profession in law, architecture or medicine !

Industry itself can also repent of not investing enough in vocational training : when investment of that type comes up to 3 % in the United States, it is a mere 1.1 % in France and a measly 0.15 % in Great Britain !

The reformers in charge of rethinking the whole issue will be hard put to it to streamline the system, but they will probably be inspired by the German model, which has been in existence for more than a century, and which appropriately combines academic education and vocational training. Let those who think that the proof of the pudding is in the eating consider the achievements of German industry.

Within the framework of the German " dual system ", 70 % of boys and girls, form 15 to 18 years of age, are apprenticed to firms for three years. They attend courses in vocational training schools one day per week. 20 % among them go on with their studies, and on the whole, 90 % of them become skilled craftsmen, technicians, engineers, etc. in their respective fields. Firms take on apprentices the more willingly as they know that the trainees are an asset for them in future, and as the costs involved are tax-deductible.

Reformers will however have to see further ahead, bearing in mind the quantum leaps taken by science and technology since World War II, and the giant strides with which both are bound to progress in future. Workers will have to keep abreast of those advances, and as new jobs will constantly be created, they will inevitably have to be trained and retrained throughout their working lives.

EMPLOYMENT AGENCIES, JOB CENTRES, OUTPLACEMENT FIRMS

Efforts of course are not focused only on the young since thousands of older workers are being made redundant every week with firms being closed down, streamlined or restructured. Private employment agencies, or national ones - e. g. Job Centres, in the United Kingdom, A. N. P. E. in France - are to be found in most towns and act as intermediaries between employers and job-hunters. They offer a wide range of services which generally comprise :

- a self-service department where notices about available jobs are put up to keep the unemployed posted about vacancies in the area, but also in other parts of the country, as agencies are linked to one another by computer and telex.
- departments in which job-hunters are offered :
  - occupational guidance, i. e., advice on the occupation they are best suited for (they can be subjected to tests), on how to make career changes, etc.
  - advice on how to reply to an advertisement, how to fill in an application form, how to write out a curriculum vitae (a C. V., a resume, a data sheet), how to show themselves off to best advantage in an interview with a personnel manager, etc.

Those services are always free for those who are looking for a job ; in private agencies, the firms with the vacancies are charged a fee when these are filled.

Employment agencies also run training and retraining schemes especially in the trades where supply does not meet demand for skilled labour.

Born in the United States, but spreading to other countries, outplacement firms deal specifically with the problems of dismissed or laid off executives and managers. They prepare them for interviews, put offices with telephone receivers at their disposal, as well as clerical staff to help them type or photocopy documents. The more fortunate among them may also be contacted by " head-hunters " (executive-search consultants) !

In most nations, the trend is to phase out state intervention in the economy. The number of privatizations (denationalizations) has been growing, chiefly in Great Britain. By selling off their assets, states opt for a free market in which competition is unshackled ; the hope is that it will contribute to lowering prices and increasing demand, that an economic revival will spark off the recruitment of job-seekers.

The member states of the EEC set great store by the Single European Market which is due to become operative by the end of 1992. Anyone will be allowed to go and work in any country belonging to the Community if there is a vacancy for a job whose requirements dovetail with his/her qualifications. Job opportunities are bound to increase in a huge economic zone which will encompass some 320 million people, and where competition will be fostered by the dismantling of trade barriers. Every rose has its thorn though ! Will not firms resort to new technologies in order to enhance their competitiveness ? That would mean scaling down recruitment in a bid for lower costs !

Of course, investing in new technologies makes good sense : the cost of computers, robots and numerically-controlled machine-tools has been declining, whereas that of the labour force has been skyrocketing (salaries and wages + bonuses + fringe benefits + social security contributions + contributions into pension funds + training expenditure and levies, etc.). Moreover employers emphasize the fact that electronic equipment never gets pregnant, never goes out on strike, will work round the clock, and carry out irksome, dirty or hazardous tasks without grumbling.

Pessimists contend that not only are robots already chipping away at jobs, but that they will take over factories one day, that they will ultimately become so clever that they will be able to design and make other robots, ousting all men from industry, apart from a few computer scientists !

Optimists retort first, that industrial progress has always created jobs : the steam engine, electricity, the spinning jenny and the loom touched off economic growth in their time, hence higher employment. Second, that by reducing costs and by producing goods of flawless workmanship, robots will be instrumental in increasing demand, hence employment : robots and electronic equipment will not lower the number of workers - anyway machines need maintenance but they will require increasingly higher qualifications from their operators. Workers will have to keep step with technological progress : they will develop from hand - into brain-workers.

TEST YOUR KNOWLEDGE

1 - Why were not work-sharing and early-retirement schemes effective cures against unemployment ?

2 - How can " pump priming " reduce unemployment ?

3 - Why did not reflation work in France in the early 80s.

4 - What are " two-tier wage schemes " ?

5 - To which flaws in the education system can a shortage of skilled labour be ascribed ?

6 - What does the German " dual-system " consist in ?

7 - How can the privatization of a public-sector firm foster employment ?

8 - Why does investing in new technologies make good sense for employers ?

9 - What are the gloomy predictions of prophets of doom as regards new technologies ?

10 - Which optimistic vision of the future can be opposed to those prophecies ?

72 - TO HIDE-HID-HIDDEN

cacher, dissimuler (to conceal)
- However ingenious their hiding-places may be, customs officers will eventually find out the dru**gs** or the smuggled goods that drug-traffickers or smugglers have hidden in them.
*Quelque ingénieuses que soient leurs cachettes, les douaniers finiront par trouver **la** drogue ou la contrebande que les **trafi**quants de drogue ou les contrebandiers y ont cachée.*

73 - TO HIT-HIT-HIT

To strike - struck - struck
NB. stricken, forme adjectivale, souvent employée en composés
- Our industry was working at full capacity when it was hit by the recession.
Notre industrie, marchait à plein rendement quand elle a été frappée (atteinte-touchée) par la récession.
- The further rise in the price of crude oil decided **on** by OPEC has woefully hit the poverty-stricken countries in the THIRD World.
La nouvelle augmentation du prix du pétrole brut décidée par l'OPEP a cruellement affecté les pays misérables du TIERS Monde.
- That importer's trade was hard hit by the fixing of quotas on goods imported from Japan.
Le négoce de cet importateur a été durement touché par le contingentement des marchandises importées du Japon.
- The dollar has hit an all-time high (≠ has sank to an all-time low) : *n'a jamais été aussi haut ≠ bas.*

74 - TO HOLD-HELD-HELD

tenir, détenir
- That shareholder holds the majority of shares in that limited liability company. (Cf. He has a vested interest in (a stake in) the concern)
Cet actionnaire détient la majorité des actions dans cette société anonyme à responsabilité limitée (Cf. Il a des intérêts dans l'entreprise).
- The boss holds strange views about the profitability of capital investments ; they are at variance with mine !
Le patron professe des idées étranges sur la rentabilité des investissements ; elles s'opposent aux miennes !
- It is a widely-held view.
C'est une considération très répandue.
- Trains cannot run on schedule : they are held up (delayed) by snow drifts.
Les trains ne peuvent pas respecter l'horaire : ils sont retardés par les congères.
- A stronghold : *une forteresse.*

75 - TO HURT-HURT-HURT

blesser, faire mal
Unhurt - unharmed - unscathed : *indemne*

76 - TO KEEP-KEPT-KEPT

garder, conserver
Aussi :
- They keep an inn in Brittany.
Ils tiennent une auberge en Bretagne.
Cf. an inn-keeper, a hotel-keeper, a shopkeeper : *un aubergiste, un hôtelier, un commerçant.*
- The eldest brother keeps the family (provides for the needs of ther family) ; he is their only bread-winner (wage earner).
L'aîné entretient la famille (subvient aux besoins de la famille) ; il est son seul soutien.
- I can't keep from (I can't help - I can't resist) being optimistic : business is looking up (is picking up).
Je ne puis m'empêcher d'être optimiste : les affaires reprennent.
- The trade unions keep plaguing (pestering-badgering) the Government **with** claims (demands).
Les syndicats n'arrêtent pas de harceler le Gouvernement de leurs revendications.
- We cannot keep them waiting until they are 65 !
Nous ne pouvons les faire attendre jusqu'à ce qu'ils aient 65 ans !
- We keep in touch with our agents abroad by telex.

Nous gardons le contact avec nos concessionnaires à l'étranger par telex.
- He cannot keep pace with (keep up with) his fellow trainees.
Il n'arrive pas à se maintenir au niveau de ses camarades stagiaires.
- The boss keeps abreast of the times (keeps up with the times) ; he wants the offices to be equipped with word processors !
Le patron est de son temps ; il veut que tous les bureaux soient équipés de machines à traiter les textes !
- A book-keeper keeps accounts ; a chartered accountant audits them.
Un comptable tient les comptes ; un expert comptable les apure.
- In keeping with my promises, I grant you permission to...
Conformément à mes promesses...

77 - TO KNEEL-KNELT-KNELT *être agenouillé.* + down : *s'agenouiller.* a knee : *un genou*

78 - TO KNIT R : *tricoter.* knitting-needles : *aiguilles à tricoter*

79 - TO KNOW-KNEW-KNOWN *savoir, connaître*

Synonyme : I am perfectly acquainted with the situation.
Je connais parfaitement la situation.

Rappel : ■ " How to " avant l'infinitif (comme to teach et to learn)
- I don't know **how to** operate the word processor.
Je ne sais pas me servir de la machine à traiter les textes.
■ Si = whether après to know, to tell, to ask, to wonder, etc.
- I do not know whether he is trustworthy or not.
Je ne sais pas s'il est digne de confiance ou non.

Attention ! " Shall we make up the deficit ? " - " I don't know "
" Comblerons-nous le déficit ? " - " ***Je l'ignore*** *".*
Mais : " to ignore " : *ne pas prêter attention à* (not to take notice of).
- We work in the same office, but he **ignores** me.
Nous travaillons dans le même bureau mais il ne fait pas attention à moi !
- *Connaître-subir :* to undergo, to experience, to go through.
We are going through hard times.

Substantifs : - I made his acquaintance (I got acquainted with him) in Sydney ; he had been appointed to the post on account of his excellent knowledge of English.
J'ai fait sa connaissance à Sydney ; il avait été nommé à ce poste en raison de son excellente connaissance de l'anglais.
(knowledge : *les connaissances,* toujours singulier).

11 - STRUCTURES

HABITUDE DANS LE PRÉSENT

1 - SIMPLE ADVERBE :

Usually, generally, traditionally
- We usually spend our holidays in Brighton.

2 - PÉRIPHRASE AVEC " CUSTOM " OU " TRADITION " OU " PRACTICE "

- It is a custom in our family to have a cold meal in the evening.
- It is a tradition in France to serve a red wine with cheese.
- It is the practice of our firm to do : Our firm makes it a practice to do : Our firm makes it a practice of doing...

3 - MANIE DÉPLAISANTE :

I have **a** habit of...
- He has **a** habit of spitting everywhere, which is exasperating.

NB. To be in **the** habit of n'a pas de nuance péjorative.

4 - " WILL " À TOUTES LES PERSONNES

(synonyme : to be apt to) : tendance naturelle, trait de caractère
- When the cat is away, mice **will** play.
- Daddy **will** grumble (is apt to grumble) at meals !

  Il faut toujours que Papa ronchonne aux repas !

NE PAS CONFONDRE

" Used to " et " to be used to " (to be accustomed to)
- " Do you mind sleeping so little ? " - " No, I am used to getting up early ".

  " Cela vous dérange-t-il de dormir si peu ? " - " Non, je suis habitué au fait de me lever tôt ".
- " I used to mind staying indoors for long, but I am now accustomed (used) to working in an office.

  Autrefois, je trouvais à redire au fait de rester longtemps enfermé, mais je suis maintenant habitué au travail dans un bureau. "

D'où : " to get used to, to get accustomed to " : *s'habituer à*
- He will never get used to obeying orders blindly.

  Il ne s'habituera jamais à obéir aveuglément aux ordres.
- After his amputation, he soon got accustomed to doing everything with his left hand.

TRADUCTION DE L'IMPARFAIT

voir structures 10

THÈME D'APPLICATION NUMÉRO 11

1 - Hier les trains ne pouvaient pas respecter l'horaire, ils étaient retardés par les congères !
2 - Quelques ingénieuses que fussent les cachettes des contrebandiers, les douaniers finissaient (toujours) par trouver la drogue ou la contrebande !
3 - Autrefois, il détenait la majorité des actions dans cette société à responsabilité limitée ; il professait des idées étranges sur la rentabilité des investissements.
4 - Les syndicats harcelaient le Gouvernement depuis cinq semaines quand le Ministre a satisfait (preterit) leurs revendications.
5 - Jadis, le patron était de son temps ; il se maintenait constamment au niveau de ses concurrents.
6 - Quand je suis arrivé (preterit), elle était agenouillée devant la machine à traiter les textes et essayait de s'en servir.
7 - Cela faisait cinq ans que nous travaillions dans le même bureau quand il a été nommé (preterit) à Sydney en raison de son excellente connaissance de l'anglais.
8 - Autrefois, notre industrie marchait à plein rendement ; nous oubliions la récession qui frappait cruellement d'autres secteurs.
9 - L'OPEP a l'habitude d'augmenter le prix du pétrole brut sans se soucier des (to bother about) pays misérables du Tiers Monde.
10 - Il faut toujours qu'il nous fasse attendre, il ne fait pas attention à nous !
11 - Elle a l'habitude de tricoter en regardant la télévision, elle ne peut s'en empêcher !
12 - Je n'arrive pas à m'habituer aux idées étranges que professe le patron, elles s'opposent aux miennes.
13 - Cet importateur ne peut pas s'habituer au contingentement des marchandises importées du Japon : le bénéfice de son négoce n'a jamais été aussi bas.
14 - Nous avons l'habitude de garder le contact avec nos concessionnaires par des messages telex quotidiens (daily).
15 - Il avait des intérêts dans cette société quand elle a été durement touchée par la récession.

12 - IMMIGRATION

CAUSES

History shows that in order to survive men have often had to move to other regions or countries. They flee from natural catastrophes – droughts, volcanic eruptions, floods, etc – from such evils as wars, religious, political or racial persecutions inflicted upon them by their fellow men, or simply move away when local resources have become insufficient.
History being a process of constant renewal, we are witnesses today to the same types of migration. Desertification – e. g. in the Sahel or in Northern Brazil – compels populations to leave their villages and resettle where less barren land is still to be found ; unemployment and extreme poverty in developing countries reduce men to emigrating to industrialized countries, and unfortunately mankind has not yet made a clean sweep of war or persecution, and refugees are seeking asylum in the countries which champion human rights.

CONFLICTS OF OPINIONS : REFUGEES

Examples abound. In the not too distant past, French Huguenots went into exile (to Holland and Prussia) after the revocation of the Edict of Nantes in 1683, a good many nobles and clergymen went to Britain after the 1789 Revolution, 17th century English Puritans emigrated to America, Russian nobles left their country when the Bolsheviks took over in 1917, antifascists left Italy in the 20s, Hitler's opponents took flight in the 30s after he had come into power, and today the Afghans have taken refuge in Pakistan and Iran rather than submit to the Soviet yoke, Ethiopians leave a country which is torn by civil war, so do Iranians whose country has been waging war for years against Iraq, Tamils escape from Sri Lanka, boat people from Viet Nam, etc.

The Western World grants political asylum to those people in the name of human rights. They are entitled to it provided they can prove, in accordance with the definition of the United Nations, that they are persecuted " on grounds of race, religion, nationality or politics ". But it is difficult to screen all the applicants in order to sort out the genuine refugees : most of them are destitute people who are lured by Western affluence, or who want to be reunited with their families when they have already reached safety.

The influx of refugees compounds the problem of immigration since sham refugees are only illegal immigrants who manage to bypass immigration laws with forged documents and made up stories of imprisonment, political harassment, etc.

UNEMPLOYMENT AND POVERTY IN DEVELOPING COUNTRIES

Statistics are deceptive. In the 50s and 60s, figures showed that income per capita was growing – on an average – in developing countries, but unfortunately all sectors were not sharing equally in the economic growth. Industrialization had not been launched with a view to providing as many people as possible with jobs. When priority should have been given to the creation and the development of labour-intensive industries, capital-intensive ones had been set up with the financial aid of Western countries, and according of course to Western patterns : they offered too few job opportunities.

Prestige projects had been carried out that swallowed up fortunes. The authorities of newly independent countries wanted probably to show former colonial powers that they were now on a par with them, that they had no cause to be jealous of them.

Money – most often lent by wealthier nations – had been invested in public works which were not urgently needed. The only sector able to make a sizeable dent in unemployment and poverty – agriculture – remained more or less ignored.

Agriculture was indeed the only sector which enabled the population to subsist, and today 80 % of the unemployed are still to be found in rural areas.

Population growth in those countries was a long way from being stemmed. Education had improved, but it was more and more difficult for young people who held diplomas to find a suitable job. They were reduced to accepting employment which was inconsistent with their studies or for which they were overqualified. The brightest students were lured by better opportunities abroad, which worsened the brain-drain when they yielded to temptation.

Lastly, developing nations were still too young to have set up some sort of relief institution to take in charge their needy citizens. There was no Social Security, and unemployed people were left to fend for themselves as best they could without unemployment benefits of course, or compensation of any kind. Emigration was really the only resort left.

Unemployment, or less lucrative employment in a few European Countries

It was logical especially for Spaniards, Italians, Yugoslavs, Greeks, Portuguese and Irish people to avail themselves of the employment opportunities offered by their more affluent neighbours. In the mid-80s, some 3.6 million Europeans would live and work in EEC countries other than their own, mainly in France, Germany and Great Britain ; roughly 1.9 million of them were to be found in France.

The economic boom in developed countries

It was naturally to be expected that jobless people in developing countries, deprived accordingly of the bare necessities of life, should look towards Western nations which at the time – from roughly the early 50s to the early 70s – were undergoing an unprecedented economic expansion. Entire European cities had to be rebuilt, as well as roads, bridges, railway networks. Industry had risen from its ashes and was hard put to it to meet the demand for goods that had been rationed or could not be obtained during the war.

The economy needed an ever-increasing number of workers and especially unskilled and cheap ones, and as Europeans found it demeaning to perform certain tasks, the labour shortage had to be made up one way or another. Developing countries had a huge pool of labour to draw on. Not only were immigrants readily engaged when they applied for jobs, but they were coaxed into joining European mines, factories, construction sites, etc. French steel and car companies had even opened employment offices in North Africa !

HOST COUNTRIES AND THEIR GUESTS

In the mid-80s

In the mid-80s, it was estimated that there lived nearly 8 m immigrants in the EEC. They were divided up in the following way :

- In France, more than 1.5 million North Africans (from Algeria, Morocco, Tunisia) ; 135,000 Turks, 35,000 Senegalese and 85,000 Yugoslavs.
- In Britain, 700,000 Indians, 500,000 people from the West Indies and Guyana, 280,000 Pakistanese, 65,000 Africans and 52,000 Bangladeshis.
- In West Germany, 1.5 million Turks, 70,000 North Africans (from Tunisia and Morocco), 25,000 Indians and 16,000 Pakistanese.
- In the Netherlands, 180,000 people from Surinam, 150,000 Turks, 100,000 Moroccans, 35,000 people from Moluccas and 35,000 from the Dutch Antilles.
- In Belgium, 60,000 Turks, and 120,000 North Africans, chiefly Moroccans, etc.

The situation overseas

The situation was different in the United States and Australia since those countries are countries of immigration.

- Since 1965, the United States had been admitting up to 500,000 immigrants per year, with a ceiling of 20,000 people per country, priority being given to skilled professionals, scientists, engineers, etc, and artists, composers, writers, painters, etc.

  A good many people yet could not be bothered to submit to the administrative procedures in order to reside and work legally in the United States. Crossing the Rio Grande proved less troublesome ! In the mid-80s, estimates as to the number of illegal residents in the country ranged from a conservative 2 million to a high of 10 million, and it was considered that this population was still increasing by up to 500,000 people a year !

In Australia

- Australia is also a nation of immigrants but it had cold-shouldered its Asian neighbours up to 1973. The immigration laws enforced one principle : whites only ! Then the authorities, aware for some time of the dramatic expansion of their neighbours' economies, decided that they might as well jump on to the bandwagon to avail themselves of the boom. Since then, some 60,000 Asians have been entering Australia each year (nearly half the total number of immigrants), giving a fillip to business in such sectors as the catering industry, banking, international trade, etc. Wealthy companies invest their liquidities in real estate, etc.

The Middle East

In the heyday of OPEC, the Arab producers of the Persian Gulf – Kuwait, Saudi Arabia and the United Arab Emirates – would welcome workers from North and South Yemen, Pakistan, Egypt, Jordan, Yugoslavia, Bangladesh, India, Sri Lanka, Turkey and Syria. In the 70s and early 80s, there were probably 4 million guest workers in those countries.

Asia

- Japan has always been averse to engaging foreigners unless they possess certain skills that are not to be found in its own labour-force : English, French or German language teachers for instance ! When numerous illegal workers tried to enter Japan in the 60s when there were labour shortages, the authorities turned them back, asserting that they would remedy the situation by hiring women and retired people, or by resorting to high technology (computerization, robots, etc.).
- Taiwan, Hong Kong, Singapore. As those NICs (Newly industrialized countries) were developing rapidly, people from poorer neighbouring countries wanted to make the most of the opportunity, and tens of thousands of immigrants thronged there from Malaysia, Thailand and the Philippines, the greater part illegally, to perform the menial tasks that the now fastidious nationals would shun.

FROM THE BOOM TIMES TO THE SLUMP

Europe : EEC countries

As long as industry worked at full capacity, immigrants were welcome since they met a demand for unskilled labour that European workers could not or would not satisfy : they turned up their noses at jobs that guest workers were only too glad to accept, even if they drew meagre wages : they were still far higher than those that they would have got at home !

They would perform arduous tasks in collieries, construction sites, steelworks, etc, hazardous ones in chemical plants, irksome and mind-numbing ones on assembly lines in car factories or textile mills, noisy ones operating stamping presses, dirty ones collecting refuse, clearing out drains, sewers, etc.

Clandestine immigration was rife : the authorities would close their eyes to it as everyone could make a niche for themselves.

With the 1973 oil crisis, the economic upswing came to an end. Smokestack industries started shedding workers by the thousand ; immigrants fell victims to plant shutdowns, to automation, to all the technological improvements that were to enable ailing industries – " lame ducks " – to cut back on labour costs and enhance productivity. Migrant workers bore the brunt of those massive layoffs : they belonged obviously to the " last hired, first fired " category of workers.

Governments however did not want to be mean. After all they had wooed those people into joining the undermanned sectors of their industries, and they could not purely and simply expel them, without granting them at least some compensation.

Immigrants were offered generous repatriation grants (bonuses), or the possibility of taking early retirement on condition that they returned to their own countries. Few of them availed themselves of those opportunities.

As modernization entailed technological competence, they were offered re-training periods, but most of them were illiterate, not only in European languages, but even in their mother tongues : they were thoroughly unsuited to the new patterns of work in industry. They were in consequence humanely allowed to stay and enjoy the same rights as the citizens of their host countries, qualifying for unemployment benefits, family allowances, etc.

Europe : Switzerland

The Swiss never burdened themselves with so many scruples, and today they have not reached the deadlock that confronts other European nations. When the economy is flagging, Swiss workers are put on short time ; when it picks up, they resume full time work. Since 1965, it has not fared so well with migrant workers as the Swiss since then have had a system of labour permits that enables their citizens not to suffer too much from unemployment by getting rid in lean years of up to 11 % of the total labour force, viz. foreign workers who hold temporary permits valid only for 9 or 12 months.

Other countries : the Middle East

Oil revenues have been tumbling since the mid-80s, and since then more than 25 % of the 4 million foreign workers that had got on the gravy train have gone back home. Those who stay there earn only half as much as they used to. It helps the oil producers in the Gulf to compensate for their loss of profit.

Things have now come to a head, especially in Europe.

From the economic point of view, immigrants had been welcomed everywhere since they contributed to boosting production without encroaching upon the privileges of European workers : they were eager to do the work that the latter would scorn ! To think that in 1962, an official in West Germany had presented the millionth Gastarbeiter (guest worker) to arrive in Cologne with a moped !

From the social point of view, they had been tolerated, first because originally they had been unaccompanied men who had left their wives and children behind, and secondly because they intended to go back home as soon as they had put aside enough money. People had thought that the inconvenience would be temporary.

Little by little however the immigrant community had grown. As soon as they had been able to afford it, the once solitary workers had arranged for their wives and children to rejoin them, others had got married, and the birth rate in those families outpaced that of European ones.

Immigrants – especially those from North Africa in France, from Turkey in West Germany, as well as Britain's blacks, who include in common parlance Pakistanis and Indians – had been relegated to the poorest parts of big cities, to slums that were doomed to demolition, or at best, to jerry-built blocks of council flats that were gradually falling into disrepair. As they had never become integrated into the rest of the host society, they had withdrawn into themselves, had stubbornly remained faithful to the old country, to their beliefs and to their traditions, which had widened even more the gap between them and the rest of the population.

The relationship with the latter began to deteriorate when the recession became more acute and thousands of European workers were made redundant. They blamed the immigrants who had not been laid off for despoiling them of their jobs, and those who were unemployed for getting unemployment benefits, family allowances, rent subsidies, etc., in the same way as fully-fledged citizens.

The children who were born to them have been torn since their births between two civilizations, without identifying themselves with either of them – cf. les Beurs, in France, back slang for " Arabs ", or the West Indians of the second generation in Great Britain. They have rejected their forbears' values, are now regarded as foreigners in their parents' countries of origin, but are not acknowledged in their countries of adoption. Their condition bears a resemblance to that of young blacks in the ghettos of American inner cities.

They play truant more often than not, soon drop out of school, and are faced as a consequence with bleak job prospects. The rate of unemployment among them reaches up to twice that of whites. They sink into delinquency, drug-addiction and prostitution at a rate which is far above average. The odds against which they have to fight are so heavy that few of them contrive somehow to get on in life.

At first, the authorities tried to play down the situation, laying all the blame for it on the economic downturn. Things would work themselves out unaided as soon as there were signs of a recovery. After all, it was understandable that native workers should feel bitter about those foreigners' taking their jobs from them ! Yet the authorities had to face facts. There were actually two labour markets, one for " the brains ", the other one for " the brawn ". It would have been demeaning for Europeans to accept the menial jobs that had been disdainfully allotted to migrants for years.

One has to bow to the evidence. Immigrants in European societies are subjected to segregation, and although most countries have passed laws against discrimination, landlords discriminate against North Africans or blacks – they are not racialists, but the neighbours are ! – white applicants for jobs are engaged in preference to immigrants with even better qualifications, certain cafés or discos reject their children, etc.

They are given insulting nicknames, " Kanaken ", " nignogs ", " bougnouls ", etc. ; they endure hostile stares, threats, abuse ; graffiti urge them coarsely to leave the country ; they can be assaulted, and in extreme cases, murdered. Violence begetting violence, it all ends up in riots : cars are burnt in the streets, shops and stores are looted, houses are set on fire, and unfortunately, there are casualties amont the rioters and the police (cf. the 1985 riots in Birmingham, Liverpool and London)

Refugees

A good many claims of political asylum are rejected today as most Western governments are afraid of too considerable an influx of destitute people from the Third World asserting to be political refugees.

- West Germany, for instance, allows asylum-seekers to find work in the country five years after they have been admitted – instead of two years previously. Those who have spent a minimum of 3 months in another European country are denied admittance.
- Hong Kong closed its doors to the Boat People from Viet Nam in June 1988 : 16,500 of them were already living in camps there, hoping to emigrate to a Western country. Newcomers will be strictly screened, and it is estimated that only 10 % of them will be accepted as genuine refugees. Thailand took similar measures a little earlier and Malaysia is expected to follow suit shortly.
- Austria prides itself on being the haven of Europe, and rightly so : since 1945 it has received some 2 million refugees in transit from the East bloc. Australia, Canada and the United States admit a matter of 4,000 asylum-seekers a year, and it takes 2 years to ascertain whether a person is entitled to the status of political refugee. As Austria has still 10,000 applicants in its camps, and providing for them proves expensive, it has decided no longer to admit Polish and Hungarian refugees into the country, putting forward the fact that political repression has eased off in those countries. The authorities are actually afraid of too many Poles and Hungarians flocking to the country for purely economic reasons after the loosening of travel restrictions by their governments.

Immigrants

There comes a time when a lifeboat is so full of shipwrecked people that taking one more aboard would capsize the boat and jeopardize everyone's chances of survival. Governments in most industrialized countries think that immigration has reached a critical threshold, and in their concern to safeguard their countries' stability, they have been tightening their regulations, and they now clamp down especially on illegal immigrants. That is why so many poor wretches from the Third World try to pass themselves off as political refugees ; it has given rise to a veritable traffic in forged documents for which they pathetically sacrifice their savings.

- Great Britain. When Queen Victoria, Empress of India, reigned over a quarter of the world's population, nearly one million people – most of them non-white – were regarded as British subjects, and a majority of them were legally entitled to come to Great Britain to reside and work there.

  As an increasingly large number of those former subjects were availing themselves of that opportunity, and for fear too large an influx of arrivals should aggravate the rise in racialism, a law was passed in 1981 that curtailed the number of those who could lay claim to British citizenship.

  There are now three classes of citizens in Britain :

  1. Those who were born in the United Kingdom, of a British citizen or a legal resident, as well as the children of Britons living or working in a foreign country, are people with full British citizenship.
  2. Those who live for instance in Hong Kong, Gibraltar and Bermuda are " citizens of the British dependent territories ". They are not allowed to reside in Britain.
  3. Those who live mostly in India, Malaysia and East Africa are " British overseas citizens ". They are not allowed to come to Britain, and their descendants will no longer be British citizens.

     Furthermore, in September 1986, the Government demanded that visitors from India, Pakistan, Bangladesh, Ghana and Nigeria should obtain visas from British embassies to be admitted into the country.

     The average Briton applauded the measures ; the " non-whites " denounced them as being aimed at them, and downright racialist.

     Undeterred, the Government put through a new law in March 1987 imposing a fine upon airlines if they flew visitors to Britain without the required entry visas, and compelling them to fly them back home in that case.

- The United States. The immigration Reform and Control Act – known as the Simpson-Rodino bill – became operative on May 5th 1987, and the Immigration and Naturalization Service (I.N.S.) opened 108 offices throughout the country to receive the applications of illegal immigrants up to May 4th 1988.

  – Illegal aliens who had lived and worked in the country for five years – since January 1st 1982 – were eligible for temporary resident status, and after 18 months for citizenship.

– Seasonal workers who had worked on farms for 90 days every year since 1984 were given the same right (that was to humour Californian farmers, in need of seasonal labour).

– Employers were prohibited from hiring illegal workers. They were given a year's grace – up to May 31st 1988 – before they were liable to very heavy fines or even jail sentences if they contravened the law.

It is estimated that 1.4 million aliens applied for legal-residence status under the amnesty program. 500,000 preferred to remain hidden. Since May 5th 1988, " La Migra " – the I.N.S. – has been cracking down on " wetbacks " again, but as usual, this will prove ineffective. The authorities pin their hopes on the fact that the law will act as a deterrent : because of the stiff penalties meted out to recalcitrant employers, the demand for cheap foreign labour is expected to tail off, and Mexicans will be less tempted to ford the Rio Grande.

■ Other countries. All countries in Europe have tightened their regulations. Germany for instance now issues tourist visas that are valid for only one month.

Italy is an exception in Europe. Denied admittance into other countries, migrant workers have been thronging to the only one whose doors have been open to them for a matter of 10 years now. Although there are occasional outbursts of racialism, resulting chiefly from the high – and still rising – unemployment rate (11 %), Italian people seem to put up with migrant workers, remembering perhaps the times when **they** were in the same situation in foreign countries, exposed to the unfriendliness and the prejudice of part of the native population.

In Asia, reactions vary according to countries. Japan will not hear of unskilled illegal workers on its soil. In 1987, it deported 13,726 foreigners, most of them for that reason. Immigrants from Bangladesh meet with the same fate as soon as they are caught. Not to have a guilty conscience though, but also not to be bothered with immigrants, the Japanese prefer to invest and create jobs abroad !

The Governments of the N.I.C.s – newly industrialized countries –, Taiwan, Hong Kong and Singapore, are at a loss for the right solution. Their countries, thriving economies require thousands of workers, both skilled and unskilled, but they are wary of letting in too many foreign workers as the economic expansion might slow down suddenly : Europe and its problems gives them food for thought ! Moreover, they would like their industries to pattern themselves upon the Japanese ones and become " technology-intensive " instead of labour-intensive.

In the meantime, and for years to come, the N.I.C.s will suffer from a labour shortage, the more considerable as, to complicate matters, their birth-rates are declining !

THE FUTURE

Thinking that immigrants are going to leave " en masse " and go back home is illusory. Making scapegoats of them by laying all the blame upon their shoulders for the economic woes of industrialized countries, and the frustrations of their populations, is unfair and vain. Visiting upon the children the " sins " that are imputed to the fathers is unjustified. Our societies have become multi-racial and multicultural. If assimilation is an ambitious and distant dream – the United States are not a real melting-pot yet – we might, even so, learn how to live together !

It is however indispensable that illegal immigration should be stemmed for nations not to lose their identities. Third World nations should step up their efforts in order to lower their birth rates, and create as many jobs as possible by furthering the development of labour-intensive industries. Wealthier nations should invest abroad in order to set up firms likely to absorb local unemployment. " Returnees " should be encouraged to start up their own businesses thanks to the skills that they have acquired abroad, to their savings, repatriation bonuses or severance (redundancy) pay, and with the help of their governments. Lastly, the nations concerned should reach diplomatic agreements to staunch the outflow of refugees.

TEST YOUR KNOWLEDGE

1 - How can you account for the presence of so many migrant workers in industrialized countries ?

2 - Why has not industrial development absorbed unemployment in Third World nations ?

3 - What incited Australia to allow Asian immigrants into the country ?

4 - How does Japan intend to make up its labour shortage ?

5 - Why would European workers tolerate foreigners when economic activity was in full swing ?

6 - Why are not migrant workers a problem for Switzerland ?

7 - Why are the children of migrant workers often in a plight in their countries of adoption ?

8 - Why are British immigration laws regarded as racialist ?

9 - Why is the American immigration law expected to stop the influx of undocumented aliens ?

10 - What can be done in future to solve the problem of immigration ?

80 - TO LAY-LAID-LAID

poser, pondre (eggs)

Expressions :

- During the interview, he laid stress on the non-negligible part (role) that I should be called on to play in the firm.
Au cours de l'entrevue, il a mis l'accent sur le rôle non négligeable que je serais appelé(e) à jouer dans la société.
- If you assume (take on) that responsibility, you will lay yourself open to criticism and if prices collapse (plummet-nosedive) they will lay all the blame on you for it.
Si vous assumez cette responsabilité, vous prêterez le flanc à la critique et si les prix s'effondrent, ils en rejetteront sur vous toute la faute.
- The extent of the damage is tragical : locusts have laid waste (have wreaked havoc. have played havoc with) all the crops.
L'ampleur des dégâts est dramatique : les sauterelles ont dévasté toutes les récoltes.
(***NB.*** dramatical : *spectaculaire*).
+ off
- The company has laid off half its workforce : *la société a licencié la moitié de son personnel.*
+ out
- The new factory has been cleverly laid out (designed) : I like its layout.
La nouvelle usine a été astucieusement conçue ; j'aime sa disposition (son agencement).
- It is incumbent upon the Government to lay out the necessary funds to set up vocational training courses for school-leavers : it will entail a sizeable outlay !
Il incombe au Gouvernement de débourser les fonds nécessaires pour mettre sur pied des cours de formation professionnelle pour les lycéens qui arrêtent leurs études : cela entraînera une mise de fonds conséquente !

Substantifs :

- The oil slick has reached the beach, which is now coated with a thick layer of sticky oil !
La marée noire (la nappe de pétrole) a atteint la plage, qui est maintenant recouverte d'une épaisse couche de mazout gluant !
A bricklayer : *un maçon* (a mason)
NB. I am a layman as regards robot technology.
Je suis un profane en ce qui concerne la robotique.

81 - TO LEAD-LED-LED

mener, conduire
- The fear of nationalizations has **led up to** (brought about) a massive outflow of capital.
La crainte des nationalisations a entraîné une hémorragie de capitaux.

Substantifs et adjectif :

A leader : *un meneur, un chef*
- Our competitors have fallen behind : we have taken over the lead (≠ we have lost the lead) as regards ship building.
Nos concurrents se sont laissés distancer : nous avons pris la tête (≠ nous avons perdu la première place) en ce qui concerne la construction navale.
- The new President has restored the country's confidence ; under his leadership, the recovery is gathering momentum.
Le nouveau Président a redonné confiance au pays ; sous sa direction, la reprise s'amplifie (se confirme).
A leading industry : *une industrie de pointe.*

Attention !

Lead [led] : *le plomb*

82 - TO LEAN

R - (leant-leant) *(se) pencher, (s') appuyer*

Substantifs :

- He has a leaning towards credit relaxation, tax exemptions and tax incentives.
Il a un penchant pour l'assouplissement du crédit, l'exonération d'impôts et les aides fiscales.
Mais : he has a liking (a weakness) for good food.
Il a un penchant pour la bonne chère.

Adjectif :

Lean : *maigre* ≠ fat
- We are going to go through lean times, and we shall have to dip into our reserves...
Nous allons connaître des temps difficiles, et nous devrons puiser dans nos

83 - TO LEAP-LEAPT-LEAPT

sauter, bondir - to jump, to spring (sprang-sprung) - to bound (R)
- When restraints on credit slackened off (eased out-relaxed), people went on a shopping spree, and prices leapt up (shot up-soared-rocketed).
Lorsque les restrictions de crédit se sont assouplies, les gens ont acheté sans retenue (spree : *orgie, débauche*) *et les prix ont fait un bond.*
- Unemployment has leapt forward.
Le chômage a fait un bond en avant.

Substantif :

(to make) a great leap forward - (to make) a great advance
(faire) un grand bond en avant - un grand progrès
A leap-year : *une année bissextile*
By leaps and bounds : very rapidly

84 - TO LEARN-LEARNT-LEARNT

R : *apprendre*
to learn **how to** do something (Cf. to teach et to know)

Substantif et adjectif :

- A learned (' L :nid] man is a man of great learning !
Un érudit est un homme d'une grande érudition !

85 - TO LEAVE-LEFT-LEFT

quitter, laisser, abandonner, partir
- The labelling of these tins leaves much to be desired : it is deceptive ; the producer cheats over the quality and the quantity of the content**s**.
*L'étiquetage de ces boîtes (de conserves) laisse beaucoup à désirer : il est trompeur ; le producteur triche sur la qualité et la quantité du conten**u**.*
(" deceptive " de : to deceive - *tromper* mais : to disappoint - *décevoir*)
NB. To leave off - to give up - to stop + gérondif

Traduction de " rester " :

être de reste
- Think of the very few days there are left to meet your commitments.
Pensez au très petit nombre de jours qu'il reste pour faire face à vos engagements.
- If the drift from the land is not checked, we shall not have enough people left on farms to look after (to take care of - to attend to) the fields.
Si l'exode rural n'est pas enrayé, il ne nous restera pas assez de monde dans les fermes pour veiller aux champs.

Substantifs :

To be on leave : *être en permission, être en congé*
- I wish I could take a few weeks' leave - a few weeks' holiday - a few weeks off !
Si seulement je pouvais prendre quelques semaines de congé !
- She is on sick leave, on maternity leave.
Elle est en congé de maladie, de maternité.
Mais : school holidays (GB) - school vacation (US) : *les congés scolaires.*
- They fatten pigs with the left-overs from the canteen.
On engraisse des porcs avec les restes de la cantine.
NB. Généralement, laisser + C.O.D. : to leave
laisser + verbe : to let
- Let me drive the car... leave me the ignition keys
Laisse-moi conduire la voiture... laisse-moi les clefs de contact.

86 - TO LEND-LENT-LENT

prêter
To lend somebody something ≠ to borrow something **from** somebody.

Substantif :

A loan : *un prêt, un emprunt*
- Within the framework of the recovery plan, they will float a loan to pump money into the economy.
Dans le cadre du plan de relance, on va lancer un emprunt pour injecter de l'argent dans l'économie.
- You will not be able to secure a loan without collateral security.
Vous ne pourrez pas obtenir un prêt sans nantissement.

12 - STRUCTURES

L'HABITUDE DANS LE PRÉSENT

voir structures 11

THÈME D'APPLICATION NUMÉRO 12

1 - Chaque fois que je le vois, il a l'habitude de mettre l'accent sur le rôle non négligeable que je joue dans la société.
2 - Ces populations sont habituées à ce que les sauterelles dévastent toutes les récoltes.
3 - Ils ont l'habitude de rejeter sur moi toute la faute lorsque les prix s'effondrent (3 traductions).
4 - Nous avons l'habitude d'acheter sans retenue lorsque les restrictions de crédit s'assouplissent.
5 - Les banques ont l'habitude d'exiger un nantissement quand une personne veut obtenir un prêt !
6 - Je sais qu'il ne reste qu'un petit nombre de jours, mais dans notre famille, Monsieur, nous avons l'habitude de faire face à nos engagements.
7 - Ils n'arrivent pas à s'habituer à ce que leurs plages soient recouvertes d'une épaisse couche de mazout gluant chaque fois qu'une marée noire les atteint.
8 - Dans tous ses discours, il a l'habitude de dire que nous allons connaître des temps difficiles.
9 - Autrefois, nous étions considérés comme une industrie de pointe mais nous nous sommes laissés distancer.
10 - Certains producteurs ont l'habitude de tricher sur la qualité et la quantité du contenu des boîtes de conserves.
11- Dans le cadre de tous les plans de relance, les gouvernements ont l'habitude de lancer des emprunts pour injecter de l'argent dans l'économie de leurs pays.
12 - Cela faisait des mois que nous puisions dans nos réserves quand le Président a redonné (preterit) confiance au pays.
13 - Les nationalisations ont l'habitude d'entraîner une hémorragie de capitaux.
14 - Le patron était un profane en ce qui concerne la robotique mais il est de son temps : à cause des robots la Société a licencié la moitié de son personnel !
15 - Pendant la guerre, la viande était rare, mais comme il avait un penchant pour la bonne chère, il engraissait des porcs avec les restes de la cantine !

13 - THE SUBMERGED ECONOMY

DEFINITION, EXTENT AND CAUSES

The submerged economy is also called the concealed or the hidden economy, the black economy, the informal or the parallel economy, the underground, the secret, the shadow economy.

It encompasses all the money-making activities that are not declared to the taxation authorities (to the taxing authorities : US). This is made possible by the fact that the people who are engaged in those activities are paid in cash for the goods or the services that they produce, or that they do not pay for the goods or the services of which they take advantage.

It is by definition difficult to gauge the size of that economy, and because scanty figures are available, it is usually guesstimated. Its existence though is undeniable. Otherwise, how could one account for people and companies spending more than what they declare on their tax-returns ? Or, paradoxically, why is the cash demand increasing when a majority of people are paying by cheque or credit cards ? Or why are so many high-denomination bank notes (US : bills) to be found in circulation ?

The submerged economy has been assessed at 10 % of GDP – on an average – in Europe, but it varies markedly from one country to another. The " champions " are Italy : 25 to 30 % of GDP, Spain : 23 %, Belgium : 21 % and Sweden : 13 %. They are followed by France, Germany and Great Britain : in the region of 10 %. It is 10 to 12 % in the United States, 20 % in India, 30 % in Taiwan, but only in the neighbourhood of 4 % in Japan and Switzerland.

NB. GDP : Gross domestic product (*Produit intérieur brut*) : the total value of goods and services produced within the country in one year.

GNP : Gross national product = GDP + income from abroad (earned by nationals abroad). *(Produit national brut)*

The birth and rapid development of the submerged economy can be ascribed to multiple causes, among which :

- Unemployment. Some people, who are no longer entitled to the dole, or who cannot find work because of their age, are reduced to doing odd jobs to scrape a living.
- Cheating. Some people who are on the dole eke out welfare benefits by working on the side.
- Low wages. It concerns for instance unskilled or part time workers, very often in the service sector. Women, in the United States, who often get only 60 % of men's earnings, supplement their incomes by typing, child-minding, telephone canvassing for banks or other financial institutions, telephone selling, etc, in the evening, especially when they are divorced, widowed or separated with children to support.
- High rates and taxes, and social security contributions. People think that the inroads of the state into their incomes are not justified by what they get in return.
- V.A.T. (Value added tax) which inflates craftsmen's bills tremendously ; it proves cheaper to pay in cash the neighbour's son who does some plumbing " on the sly " !
- Illegal immigrants who by force of circumstances must remain " underground " even if they are shamelessly exploited.
- Longer holidays, part-time work, shift work, flextime, privileged work schedules (in Italy, civil servants do not work in the afternoon) generate plenty of free time.
- Cheap and efficient DIY (do-it-yourself) equipment.
- Rigid regulations which ban employers from laying off workers when business is at a low ebb : they hire instead illegal migrant workers, or temporary ones.
- Red tape which discourages young entrepreneurs from starting up their own firms.
- In East-bloc countries, some goods or services are not always available on the official market.
- Swindling the state is no longer disreputable, but people will still look askance at scroungers who top up welfare benefits by moonlighting. Etc.

The activities and practices which make up the submerged economy are multitudinous and fall into two categories.

■ The first one concerns the undeclared production of legal goods and services.

1. Moonlighting (black labour). The moonlighter has two jobs (even three sometimes !). The first one is declared and liable to income tax ; the second one is undeclared ; it may be regular or casual, it is done during the moonlighter's spare time, but it is paid in cash, without receipt, to avoid taxes. It is common practice with craftsmen (plumbers, joiners, bricklayers, mechanics, electricians), but also with accountants, business or tax consultants, etc. The nature of the second job can be thoroughly different from the registered one : a turner can very well dabble in gardening, a policeman in interior decoration, etc.
2. " Ghosts ". They are people who are unknown to the Registrar of Companies, let alone to the Inland Revenue (US : Internal Revenue). For instance, the owners of sweat shops in the garment industry in which seamstresses are illegal immigrants.
3. Barter. No less common is the exchange of services, or the payment of services in kind. A dentist or a physician can treat a mathematics teacher, the latter giving private tuition to their children in lieu of fees. The owner of a villa at the sea-side can rent it free to a craftsman's family if he repairs the bathroom plumbing, redoes the paintwork or the wallpaper. A wine grower will have his car repaired in exchange for a few bottles of a good vintage, etc.
4. Some economists consider that such domestic activities as cooking, cleaning, washing, gardening and DIY (do-it-yourself) ones are part and parcel of the submerged economy. The value of such home production has been estimated at 40 % of GDP in the United States, Great Britain and France, at 70 % in West Germany !

■ Production, acquisition or use of illegal goods and services : it covers the whole gamut of crime !

1. Unscrupulous use of services.
   On the bottom rung, there are for instance the none too highly-principled employees who make use of the firm's car, telephone, franking machine, computer or photocopier for private purposes ; the commercial travellers who pad out their expense accounts, the fare dodgers on public means of transport, the victims of thefts, fires, crashes, etc, who put in inflated claims for damages, the crafty odd-job men who wangle sick leaves out of the National Health Service in order to complete their neighbour's central-heating installation, etc.
2. Illegal income in kind.
   There are employees who dip casually into their firm's stationery, who occasionally pilfer a few items of whatever their factory manufactures ; poachers trap game on reserves (e. g salmon in Scottish, Welsh, Irish rivers), shops, stores and supermarkets are plagued with shrinkage and shoplifting ; building materials – copper pipes, electric wire, etc. – disappear from building sites, etc.
3. Traffics of all types.
   On the upper rungs of crime, we find gambling, smuggling – e. g rare animal species, works of art, antiques, treasures spirited out of ancient temples, tombs and even museums ; pharmaceuticals like hormones used for cattle rearing ; the pirating of books, tapes, films, computer software, video games, etc. – and worse, drug-trafficking, prostitution, the sale of babies from Latin America to sterile North Americans or European couples who are yearning for a child of their own ; the theft of goods from docks and warehouses, the hijacking of lorries loaded with word processors, hi-fi systems, cameras, etc.

■ Tax evasion (colloquial : tax dodging).

It is not to be mistaken with tax avoidance. Companies and individuals are apt to declare that they are overburdened with taxes. That is why they try, with the help sometimes of tax consultants, to take advantage of loopholes in tax laws to get more or less substantial reductions.

For instance, employers manage to lighten pay-roll taxes by granting untaxed perquisites (fringe benefits), " perks " in colloquial English, to their staff : company cars, rent-free flats or houses, free subscriptions to sports clubs, private health-insurance policies, etc. It also proves entirely to the staff's advantage since " perks " do not have to appear on tax returns !

Industrialists also set up factories in tax havens (tax shelters), i. e countries which offer very low tax rates, like for instance the Republic of Ireland. Shipping companies register their ships in Panama, Liberia, Honduras or Costa Rica : whole merchant fleets sail under flags of convenience. Successful artists, wealthy businessmen, well-to-do pensioners take up residence in such havens for instance in Switzerland, to avoid too drastic a cut in their incomes !

This is all above board, although it deprives a country of sizeable revenues, but there are also illegal means of avoiding taxation.

Tax evasion (tax dodging) consists for instance in bypassing pay-roll taxes entirely, and social security contributions as well, by hiring illegal foreign hands. The poor fellows are paid starvation wages, but they are not in a position to inform against their employers !

The self-employed and professional people can overstate their general expenses (overheads), and understate their incomes : it is easy if some of their services are paid in cash or in kind, or if they swap (swop) them for other services. Customers cannot complain as there is no charge for VAT in that case !

Salaried employees find it difficult to practise that kind of legerdemain because it is easy for tax auditors to check whether the figures on their returns coincide with those on their employers' ledgers. It is really impossible with P.A.Y.E. (Pay-as-you-earn ; US : Pay-as-you-go), the tax system where income tax is deducted from employees' salaries before they get them ! In that case, moonlighting only can bring in tax-free additional earnings !

Plenty of families employ daily helps, window cleaners or gardeners, without declaring them, thus economizing on social security contributions ; everyone is satisfied since the workers themselves take home tax-free pay packets !

ADVANTAGES

- The submerged economy is often regarded as a shock-absorber, and Governments will turn a blind eye to it when the official one is ailing : it wards off labour unrest and starvation by mopping up unemployment, and it helps exports to remain competitive on international markets. It saved Italy's and Spain's economies when they were crippled by the recession in the 70s.
- It testifies to the merits of free enterprise : unshackled by rigid regulations, it encourages initiative and develops creativity.
- It makes life bearable in the countries whose economies are in the grip of state control by making up for shortages in goods and services.

DRAWBACKS

- The submerged economy entails an astronomical loss in tax revenues which could otherwise be allotted to welfare, to job creation, and would eventually make it possible to lower tax rates. Law-abiding firms and individuals must pay, and offenders escape scot-free !
- Honest companies are undercut by competitors which subcontract work to sweatshops, and are tempted to follow suit in order to survive.
- The submerged economy favours corruption (bribery). Deals are clinched, bargains are struck, privileges obtained, tenders accepted thanks to bribes, kickbacks, under-the-counter payments.
- No insurance whatever covers either employers or workers against accidents.
- In case of labour disputes, there is no possible appeal to a trade union or to an industrial tribunal.
- Customers can turn to no one if work is badly done, if an article is faulty.

REMEDIES ?

The submerged economy is probably here to stay, but it is hoped that its size will shrink in proportion as the revival of the " above-ground " economy is gaining momentum, and Governments' efforts are bearing fruit.

The latter have all cracked down on illegal immigration ; they have increased the number of tax inspectors (US : tax ferrets) in order to track down (ferret out) tax evaders ; they have contemplated granting an amnesty to offenders with the proviso that their activities were straightforward in future ; some governments have even relaxed so far pro-labour employment regulations.

Trade unions are in an awkward position. They do not condone moonlighting, but they do not criticize offenders too virulently since plenty of their members indulge in that blamevorthy activity !

As for tax evasion, it seems as if it had become a kind of national sport in most countries, as if " fiddling " one's tax returns were a good trick that one played on the state, a way of shielding a fair part of one's earnings from that ruthless, money-grubbing octopus !

TEST YOUR KNOWLEDGE

1 - How is it possible for tax-payers to conceal part of their income from the taxation authorities ?

2 - How do economists prove the existence of the submerged economy ?

3 - What is the difference between GDP and GNP ?

4 - Quote a few factors that can account for the existence of the submerged economy.

5 - Why can DIY activities be regarded as part of the submerged economy ?

6 - What is the difference between tax avoidance and tax evasion ?

7 - What is P.A.Y.E. ?

8 - Why is the submerged economy regarded as a shock-absorber ?

9 - Quote three major drawbacks of the submerged economy.

10 - What is the position of trade unions as concerns moonlighting ?

87 - TO LET-LET-LET

laisser, autoriser, permettre (to allow) ; *louer*
- The landlord **lets** his flat, his house ; the tenant **rents** it.
Le propriétaire loue son appartement, sa maison ; le locataire le (la) loue.
Supplée aux personnes manquantes de l'impératif.
- Do not let him bank on (reckon on, count on) reflation.
Qu'il ne table pas (ne mise pas, ne compte pas) sur la relance.
NB. The rent is high but the location of the flat is excellent.
Le loyer est élevé mais la situation (l'emplacement) de l'appartement est excellente.
NB. *Permettre - rendre capable* = to enable + complément de personne ; to make it possible sans complément.
- This package of measures will enable the Government (will make it possible) to stamp out inflation (to rein in inflation - to check inflation ; to curb - to bridle inflation).
Ce train de mesures permettra au Gouvernement (permettra) de juguler l'inflation (de la maîtriser-de l'enrayer, de la freiner).

Substantif :
- Sport is an excellent outlet for the people who are cooped up (confined-shut up) in an office all day long : thus they give vent to their surplus energy.
Le sport est un excellent exutoire pour les gens qui restent enfermés (cloîtrés-confinés) dans un bureau toute la journée : ils donnent ainsi libre cours à leur trop plein d'énergie.
- All right ! we are in a depressed area, but let us not (do not let us) accept defeat : let us look for new outlets !
D'accord, nous sommes dans une zone touchée par la crise, mais n'acceptons pas la défaite : cherchons de nouveaux débouchés !
- A let-up : *un répit* (a respite)
- They plan no let-up in the austerity programme.

88 - TO LIE-LAY-LAIN

être couché, étendu + down : *s'étendre, se coucher*
- Hundreds of casualties were **lying** about in the galleries.
Des centaines de victimes gisaient éparses dans les galeries.
Ne pas confondre : to lie (R) : *mentir* - a lie : *un mensonge* - a liar : *un menteur*

89 - TO LIGHT-R-LIT-LIT

allumer, éclairer, illuminer
- To light (to kindle) a fire.
- You light a candle with a match or a lighter.
On allume une bougie avec une allumette ou un briquet.
- During Christmas, they do not care about energy conservation : the streets are lit up with myriads of electric bulbs.
A l'époque de Noël, on ne se soucie pas des économies d'énergie : les rues sont illuminées par des myriades d'ampoules électriques.
- Moonlighting : *le travail (au) noir* (black labour)
- Wage increases will rekindle inflation : *rallumer, raviver*

Substantif :
- If there were no traffic-lights at crossroads, there would be more traffic jams !
S'il n'y avait pas de feux aux carrefours, il y aurait davantage de bouchons !

90 - TO LOSE-LOST-LOST

perdre (propre et figuré)
- If you lose your job, you can go on the dole.
Si on perd son emploi, on peut s'inscrire pour toucher les allocations de chômage.
- " They have lost their lawsuit, their fortune, everything. They are on welfare now ! " - " I should say they are sponging on the community ! "
" Ils ont perdu leur procès, leur fortune, tout ! Ils vivent maintenant des prestations sociales ! " - " Je dirais qu'ils vivent aux crochets de la collectivité ! "
- If they clamp down on private enterprise, if they disproportionately (immoderately-inordinately) widen (broaden) the public sector, the economic revival is bound to lose momentum (to stall).
Si on restreint rigoureusement l'entreprise privée, si on élargit démesurément le secteur public, la reprise économique ne peut manquer de battre de l'aile (de perdre son élan, d'être en perte de vitesse) (to clamp down on : to crack down on)
NB. *perdre - gaspiller :* to waste, to squander

Substantif :
- Closing down the mines is a great loss for the area.
La fermeture des mines est une grande perte pour la région.

- To sell at a loss : *vendre à perte.*
- Economists are **at a loss** to explain why that currency has suddenly appreciated ≠ depreciated.
Les économistes sont bien embarrassés pour expliquer pourquoi cette devise a soudain pris de la valeur ≠ s'est soudain dépréciée.

91 - TO MAKE-MADE-MADE

- They make steel in that **works**, cars in that **factory**, cotton and wool yarn in that **mill**, chemicals in that **plant.**
*On fabrique de l'acier dans cette **usine** sidérurgique, des voitures dans cette **usine**, du fil de coton et de laine dans cette **usine**, des produits chimiques dans cette **usine** !*
- You make someone happy or famous ; you make yourself useful ; you make a scandal public, but you **drive** someone mad ; you **restore** the goods you had stolen, you **return** what you had borrowed, etc.
On rend quelqu'un heureux ou célèbre ; on se rend utile ; on rend un scandale public, mais on rend quelqu'un fou ; on rend les biens qu'on avait volés et on rend ce qu'on avait emprunté.

Rappel : *faire* + infinitif
- That unexpected economic recovery (revival of business ; resumption of industrial activity) makes us adjust our estimates upwards (≠ to adjust... downwards).
Cette reprise économique inattendue (cette reprise des affaires ; cette reprise de l'activité industrielle) nous fait réviser nos prévisions en hausse (≠ réviser... en baisse).

Expressions :
- Make an effort : make up your mind ; make a decision ; make an appointment with the tax inspector.
Faites un effort : décidez-vous ; prenez une décision ; prenez rendez-vous avec le contrôleur des contributions.
- They are making headway (they are making progress - they are advancing) in their research work.
Ils font des progrès dans leurs recherches.
- If you have any complaints to make, make a report !
Si vous avez des plaintes à formuler, faites un rapport !
- Do not make light of his advice (don't scorn his advice - don't spurn his advice), he has made his way in the world of finance.
Ne méprisez pas ses conseils : il a fait son chemin dans le monde de la finance.
- Our operators cannot make do with (content themselves with-be satisfied with) that switchboard in the age of electronics !
Nos standardistes ne peuvent se satisfaire de ce standard à l'âge de l'électronique.
- That is how he makes a living ! He does not make a great profit, but he manages to make ends meet !
Voilà comment il gagne sa vie ! Il ne fait pas grand bénéfice mais il arrive à joindre les deux bouts !
- That multinational is made up of (is composed of, consists of, comprises) the parent company (the head office is in N. Y.) and a matter of twenty subsidiaries that are scattered all over the world.
Cette multinationale se compose de la maison mère (le siège social est à N. Y.) et de quelque vingt filiales éparpillées dans le monde entier.
- How can we make up the deficit ?
Comment pouvons nous combler le déficit ?
- It is no use trying to make up for lost time : you ought to have availed yourself of that opportunity.
Cela ne sert à rien d'essayer de rattraper le temps perdu : vous auriez dû profiter de cette occasion !
- Experience can make up for (compensate for-offset) lack of vocational training.
L'expérience peut compenser le manque de formation professionnelle.

Substantifs :
- I always buy cars of French make, **out of** chauvinism, but also **out of** self-interest !
J'achète toujours des voitures de marque (de fabrication) française, par chauvinisme mais aussi par intérêt.
- You have the making**s** of an excellent secretary !
Vous avez l'étoffe d'une excellente secrétaire !

13 - STRUCTURES

INFINITIF SANS " TO "

1 - APRES LES DÉFECTIFS :

can, may, must, should mais pas ought **to**, synonyme de should

- You shou**ld w**ork more - you ought **to** work more.
  Tu devrais travailler davantage.

2 - APRES TO DARE :

oser et to need : avoir besoin, falloir qui peuvent être considérés comme défectifs ; le verbe to help : aider, peut-être suivi de l'infinitif sans " to ". On peut dire au choix :

- He dar**e** n**ot pr**opose to her - he do**es** not dare **to** propose to her.
  Il n'ose pas la demander en mariage.
- He ne**ed not t**ake an examination to obtain that job - he do**es** not ne**ed t**o take an examination...
  Il n'a pas besoin de passer un examen pour obtenir cet emploi (Il ne faut pas qu'il passe...).
- Help me carry my bag, please !
  Aide-moi à porter mon sac, s'il te plaît (ou : help me **to** carry my bag).

3 - APRES TO LET :

voir Impératif (Chapitre 14)

4 - APRES LES VERBES DE PERCEPTION

si on n'insiste pas sur la longueur de l'action

- I saw him strike the boy.
  Je l'ai vu frapper l'enfant (1 coup de poing).
- I saw him beating the boy.
  Je l'ai vu battre l'enfant (plusieurs coups de poing).
- I felt the sna**ke bi**te me.
  J'ai senti le serpent me mordre (morsure rapide).

mais :

- I felt the snake **creeping** up my leg.
  J'ai senti le serpent grimper le long de ma jambe (lente reptation).

5 - APRES I WOULD RATHER :
ET I HAD BETTER :

j'aimerais mieux, je préfèrerais.
Je ferais mieux.

- Pupils would rather play all the time ; they had better work as much as possible !
  Les enfants aimeraient mieux jouer continuellement ; ils feraient mieux de travailler autant que possible !

6 - APRES TO MAKE :

voir rubrique suivante (Chapitre 14)

THÈME D'APPLICATION NUMÉRO 13

1 - Le Gouvernement ferait mieux de trouver rapidement de nouveaux débouchés pour la région car la fermeture des mines est une grande perte.

2 - Il a dit que toutes les régions qui étaient autrefois prospères seraient touchées par la crise tant que le Gouvernement ne jugulerait pas (5 traductions) l'inflation.

3 - " Il n'ose pas (2 constructions) profiter de cette occasion ! " " Il n'a pas besoin (2 constructions) de rattraper le temps perdu ! "

4 - Autrefois, les économistes tablaient (3 traductions) sur la relance ; ils sont bien embarrassés aujourd'hui !

5 - Je n'arrive pas à m'habituer à ce que tant de gens vivent aux crochets de la communauté !

6 - Il ne peut pas formuler de plaintes : chaque fois que j'essayais de lui donner des conseils, il les méprisait (3 traductions) (conseils : singulier en anglais).

7 - J'ai l'habitude de donner libre cours à mon trop plein d'énergie en jouant (au) tennis.

8 - Il a dit que tant que notre devise prendrait de la valeur, la reprise ne battrait pas de l'aile (2 traductions).

9 - " Vous ne devriez (2 traductions) pas rester cloîtré dans un bureau toute la journée ! " - " Je sais, mais il faut que je fasse des progrès dans mes recherches ! "

10 - " Je l'ai entendu raconter une triste histoire au café : il avait perdu son procès, son emploi, sa fortune, tout ! " - " Ce n'est pas vrai, il préfère vivre aux crochets de la collectivité ! "

11 - Il se peut que vous ayez des plaintes à formuler, alors faites un rapport !

12 - Vous feriez mieux de ne pas mépriser ses conseils (3 traductions) car il a fait son chemin dans le monde de la finance !

13 - Il aimerait mieux payer un loyer moins élevé mais la situation de l'appartement est excellente.

14 - Voilà comment il gagne sa vie, il arrive simplement à joindre les deux bouts. Mais il n'a pas besoin de faire grand bénéfice car il n'est pas exigeant (hard to please).

15 - Quand comprendront-ils que tant qu'ils restreindront rigoureusement l'entreprise privée, la reprise ne pourra que battre de l'aile ?

14 - COMMERCE AND THE CONSUMER SOCIETY

(Première partie)

A GOOD MATCH

Commerce and the consumer society seem to have been made for each other ! Modern society has been labelled as " the consumer society " owing to its materialistic philosophy whose tenets are that we are on earth to pursue happiness, and that happiness is directly proportional to the amount of goods and services that we are able to buy. Now commerce can be defined as the exchange of goods (merchandise) or services for money. It ensues that the more we buy, the happier we are, and the more flourishing commerce is !

Commerce also benefits from the fact that in that type of society people are no longer judged by what they are, but by what they have, and accordingly by what they earn. It is logical : the more you have, the closer you are supposed to get to happiness, and the more enviable you become ! It enhances your status in your neighbours'eyes ; a drop in your purchasing power entails a fall in status. That is why people will try to keep up with the Joneses, and even strive to outshine them by more numerous or more costly acquisitions.

In the years following the Second World War, people were eager to forget about their sufferings and privations, and they launched out into a consuming spree. Industry readily met the demand by churning out goods in very large quantities – which lowered production costs and selling prices – and people pounced **en masse** upon the goods. Mass production led up to mass consumption, and vice versa, in endless interaction. People would clamour again and again for higher salaries and wages to increase their purchasing power. It was the heyday of commerce, and the reign of " the affluent society ", in Professor J. K. Galbraith's words, in reference to the high standard of living of western countries, and their extravagant exploitation of natural resources.

That type of society, only just budding in the 50s, blossomed out in the 60s, depleting the earth of its riches, heedless of the havoc that it was wreaking on the environment, gradually turning " the affluent society " into an " effluent society " i.e. polluting the industrial world to such an extent that it would endanger life there, or at the very least make it very unpleasant. Commerce however was roaring !

When the market was glutted (saturated), customers were persuaded into buying " doubles " of as many goods as possible : radio and television sets, cars, second homes – which meant more furniture, more refrigerators, etc. – and into using " disposables " to simplify their existence : nappies, tissues, towels, table-cloths, and even underwear, made of non-woven fabric, cigarette lighters, razors, pens, etc. There were myriads of non-returnable glass, metal or plastic containers piling up in dumps, or littering the countryside...

Nations have ultimately become aware of the fact that those excesses imperilled the future, and they have wisely reacted against the squandering of their resources and the poisoning of their territories. They realized, so to say, that they were killing by inches the goose that laid the golden eggs ! It gave rise to campaigns for energy conservation and the reclaiming of materials.

It is however difficult to rapidly get out of ingrained habits, and the world is still resolutely materialistic, and wasteful – if a little cleaner – much to the advantage of commerce !

THE PROTAGONISTS ; CHANNELS OF DISTRIBUTION

We are all consumers, but apart from the parasites who live on the fringes of society – vagrants, tramps, beggars, drop-outs and the like –, we are also producers, either of goods or services. We can be engaged in three types of production, according to the economic sector in which we are working.

PRIMARY INDUSTRY

Primary industry is concerned with the exploitation of the raw materials that are to be found in nature. It includes :

- Farming, fishing, forestry.

■ The extraction of minerals :

1. Quarrying for stone, marble, slate, limestone, etc.
2. Mining for coal and ores (iron, copper, uranium, gold, etc.)
3. The exploitation of oil wells, etc.

With the exception of fish and farm produce, the greater part of the output of primary industry cannot be used as it is : it must be processed in factories, mills, works, etc.

SECONDARY INDUSTRY

Secondary industry is in charge of processing the raw materials found in nature, i.e, transforming them into semi-finished or finished goods.

TERTIARY INDUSTRY

Tertiary industry is not concerned with the production of goods, but with the provision of services : commerce (trade) is one of these, as well as banking, insurance, transport, etc.

The two following diagrams show the main channels of distribution through which goods are made to go for them to reach consumers :

CHANNELS OF DISTRIBUTION

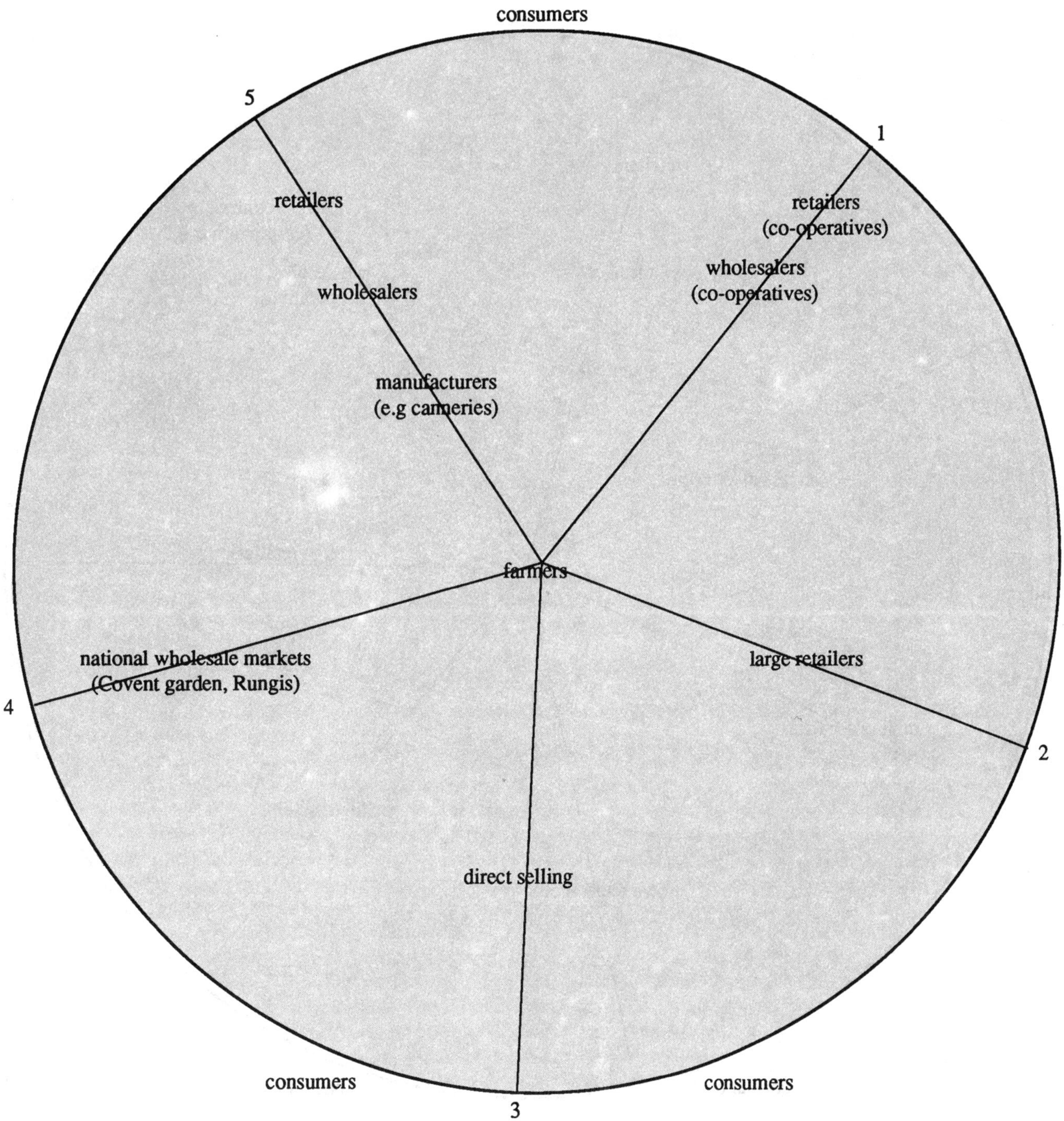

DIAGRAM A - PRIMARY INDUSTRY

CHANNELS OF DISTRIBUTION

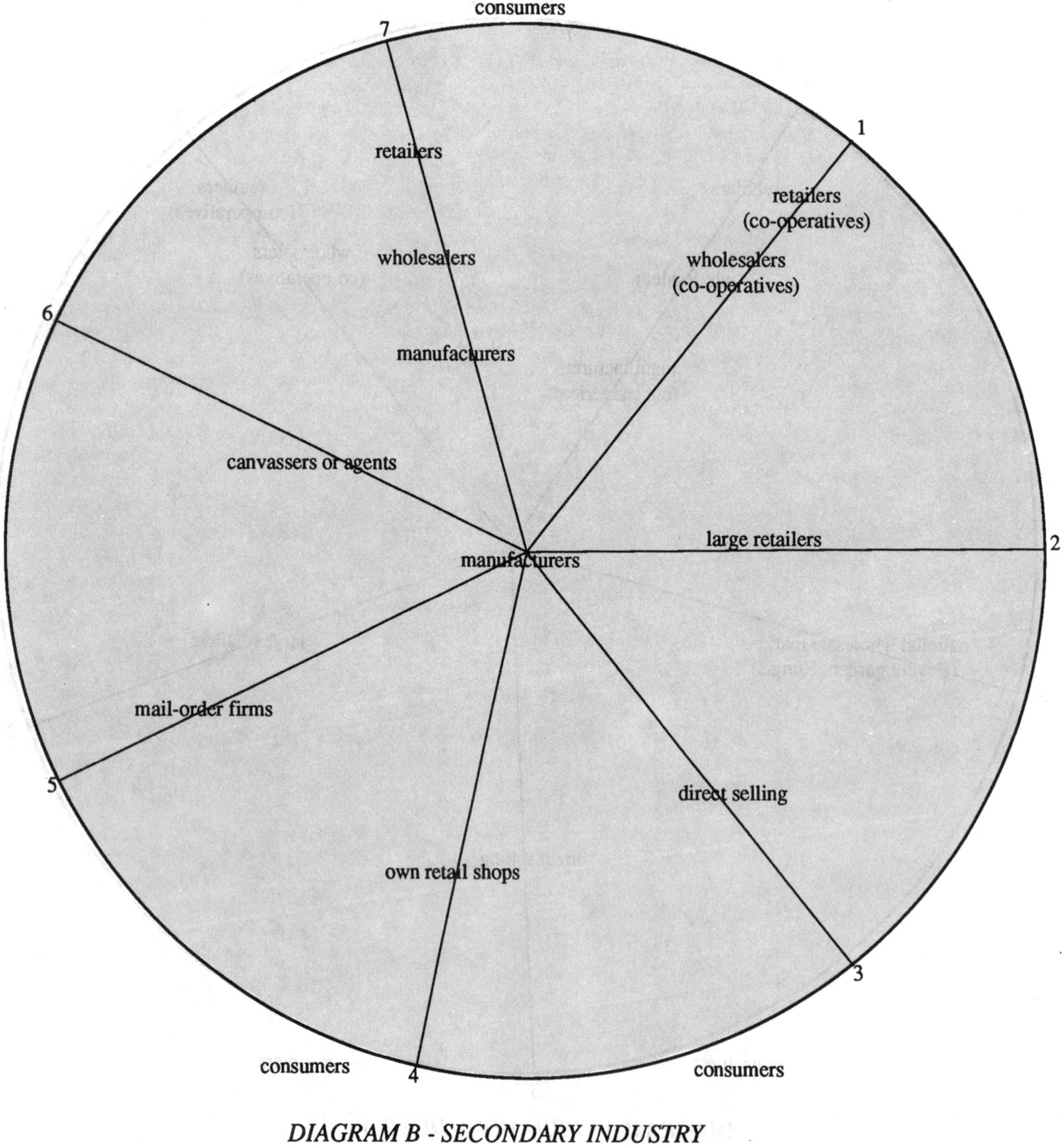

DIAGRAM B - SECONDARY INDUSTRY

CHANNEL 1

As regards primary and secondary industries, the conventional channel of distribution is N° 1 (A1 and B1). Wholesalers buy goods in bulk from manufacturers or for instance farmers, sell them to retailers who sell them to consumers. " In bulk " has two different meanings :

– First : " in large amounts ", which entails that wholesalers must have space (warehouses) to store the goods.

– Second : " loose ", i.e, not prepacked, not packed in tins, cans, boxes, bottles, crates, etc.

Very often, both meanings apply to the goods that are bought by the wholesaler. He must then break bulk, i.e, split up the large quantities that he has in stock into smaller ones that will be sold to the retailer. The latter does the same for his customers.

Goods go through channel A5 or channel B7 when they are manufactured or processed in two stages, first into semi-finished then into finished goods. It adds a link (a middleman = an intermediary) to the chain.

NB. Wholesalers and retailers can be co-operatives, i.e, organizations whose profits are shared among their members ; in retail co-operatives, customers are given dividend stamps in proportion to their purchases.

CHANNEL 2

Channel 2 is becoming more and more common in all industrialized countries, except in Japan. Small shops are gradually being replaced by large retailers (large-scale outlets) such as supermarkets (more than 400 square metres of selling space, according to EEC definitions), superstores (more than 2,500 square metres) and hypermarkets (more than 5,000 square metres).

Japan is lagging behind as regards its distribution network because Japanese consumers remain faithful to a multitude of " mom-and-pop " stores. These and their customers can legally veto the setting up of large outlets. As small wholesalers are also too numerous and inefficient, consumer prices are notoriously high in Japan, and the Government have at last begun to contemplate updating the system.

Most supermarkets, superstores and hypermarkets are also " multiples ", i.e, multiple stores or chain-stores : each one of them is part of a chain (a group) of stores owned and operated by the same organization.

Department stores – very often multiples – have been competing for a long time with small, independent retail shops. They are also large-scale outlets which sell different types of goods in separate departments ; a manager is responsible for each one of these.

The commercial success of all those organizations is due to a large extent to the fact that they all have central purchasing offices which place very large orders directly with manufacturers or producers : it enables them to enjoy very substantial discounts, and it cuts out middlemen and their profit margins.

DIRECT SELLING

Manufacturers or farmers – and other comparable producers (fruit-growers, wine-growers, bee keepers, etc.) can resort to direct selling (A3 and B3) : in that case, they do away with middlemen between themselves and consumers.

- They can try and attract customers through advertisements in newspapers and magazines (direct response advertising), or through advertising material sent by post ; people are often swamped with that unsolicited literature, and they disparagingly call it " junk mail " ! Those who are interested can order honey, wine, herbs, organic food, books or clothes, reclining chairs, terry towels, etc.
- Farmers and other producers can sell their produce at their own gates, or they have stalls in rest areas on motorways or in street markets, etc.
- Manufacturers can also have their own retail shops (B4).

HOME-SHOPPING

Mail-order firms (B5) sell a wide range of goods that customers can choose by consulting glossy, attractive catalogues, and order by mail (often by freepost) or by telephone (by dialling freephone – " freefone " – numbers ; US : toll-free numbers). It is very convenient for the people who live in remote country districts, especially as the goods are delivered to their doors.

Alternative kinds of " home-shopping " have appeared recently. Some mail-order firms have replaced their catalogues by videocassettes, and others by videodiscs. It is also possible to shop through a computer or a Minitel in France (a Videotex terminal). You can place your orders at any hour of the day or night, but on the other hand, you can only see a list of items on the screen, their prices and their references.

Teleshopping – all the rage in the United States – is far more attractive. Goods are displayed in one to two minute commercials slotted into variety shows, especially on cable television. Televiewers place their orders by telephone (free of charge of course !)

REPRESENTATIVES

Catalogues can also be replaced by representatives who go from house to house to solicit people's custom : they are door-to-door salesmen, or canvassers ; they practise door-to-door selling, or door-to-door canvassing. Usually well-groomed and well-spoken, they try to entice people into buying their wares by showing them samples and giving them " the sales talk " !

Some firms market their goods through agents who try to sell them at parties that they ask housewives to give, and to which neighbours, relatives, friends, etc., are invited (B6).

ADVANTAGES AND DRAWBACKS

There are advantages and drawbacks in each one of these distribution channels. Large-scale retailing however stands higher and higher in consumers' favour mainly because it enables them to save money, time and energy.

- Large-scale retailers offer lower prices because they buy in bulk directly from manufacturers or producers, and thus obtain sizeable discounts. They also employ a skeleton staff by using self-service : it trims costs to a minimum.
- They make " one-stop shopping " possible : housewives find all that they need on the premises.
- They put vast and free car-parks at customers' disposal, as well as trolleys to carry the goods, or give little Johny a pleasure ride !

  A good many housewives do their shopping there out of interest, or out of necessity – because of the constraints of working mothers' timetables – but not from inclination. They miss the kind welcome, the solicitude that they find in the little shop around the corner, and probably the little chat about the baby's first tooth, Jane's gorgeous boy-friend, and whatever !

(to be continued)

TEST YOUR KNOWLEDGE

1 - WHY CAN IT BE SAID THAT COMMERCE AND THE CONSUMER SOCIETY SEEM TO HAVE BEEN MADE FOR EACH OTHER ?

2 - WHAT IS MEANT BY " THE AFFLUENT SOCIETY " ?

3 - WHEN THE MARKET BECAME SATURATED, HOW WERE CONSUMERS MADE TO BUY MORE THAN WHAT THEY REALLY NEEDED ?

4 - WHAT ARE THE FIELDS OF ACTIVITY OF PRIMARY, SECONDARY AND TERTIARY INDUSTRIES ?

5 - WHAT DOES " IN BULK " MEAN ?

6 - WHY IS " BREAKING BULK " NECESSARY ?

7 - WHY IS JAPAN LAGGING BEHIND AS FAR AS DISTRIBUTION IS CONCERNED ?

8 - WHAT IS " JUNK MAIL " ? WHY THAT NAME ?

9 - WHAT ARE THE ADVANTAGES OF " HOME SHOPPING ", AND PERHAPS ITS DRAWBACKS ?

10 - DO YOU THINK THAT THE EVOLUTION IN RETAILING WILL INEXORABLY BRING ABOUT THE DEMISE OF THE SMALL SHOP ?

92 - TO MEAN-MEANT-MEANT

- What does " Giro " mean in French ?
Que signifie (veut dire) " Giro " en français ? (Giro-CCP)
NB. It does not signify - it does not matter : *cela n'a pas d'importance (peu importe ; cela importe peu)*
- Significant changes : *des changements importants*
- He means (he intends) to sensitize public opinion to that problem.
Il a l'intention de sensibiliser l'opinion publique à ce problème.
- What does increased production mean when it entails a decline in quality standards ?
Que représente une production accrue quand cela entraîne une baisse du niveau de la qualité ?

Substantifs :

- What is the meaning of " prerequisite " ?
*Quel est le sens de "*prerequisite*" (condition préalable) ?*
NB. Mean**s** : toujours un " s " sauf dans : the golden mea**n** : *le juste milieu*
- We shall soon find the mean**s** of reversing the trend.
*Nous trouverons vite **le** moye**n** de renverser la tendance.*
- They have enhanced the quality of the goods (lines) by mean**s** of Quality Circles.
Ils ont rehaussé la qualité de leurs articles au moyen de Cercles de Qualité.
- Those extra (additional) revenues provide the State with the necessary means (the wherewitha**l**) to import such staple commodities as cereals, meat and dairy produc**e**.
*Ces revenus supplémentaires fournissent à l'État les moyens (fonds) nécessaires à l'importation de denrées de base telles que les céréales, la viande et **les** produit**s** laitier**s**.*

Adjectif :

- Don't be mean (petty), grant him that permission !
Ne sois pas mesquin, accorde-lui cette permission !
- The mean temperature - the average temperature
La température moyenne.
Mais : *en moyenne* : **on** an average ;
au dessus ≠ en dessous de la moyenne : above ≠ below the average

93 - TO MEET-MET-MET

- " I don't think you've met our Chairman and Managing Director before, I'll introduce you to him right away ! " -... " How do you do ? " - " Pleased to meet you ! "
" Je ne pense pas que vous connaissiez notre Président Directeur Général, je vais vous le présenter tout de suite ! " -... " Enchanté ! " - " Très heureux de faire votre connaissance ! "
- Their attorney (proxy) is due to arrive this afternoon, you will meet him at the airport.
Leur fondé de pouvoir (mandataire) doit arriver cette après-midi, vous irez le chercher à l'aéroport.
- We have resolved (made up our minds) to meet all their claims (satisfy-comply with) merely to ward off (avert-prevent-fend off-stave off) a new bout of social unrest (social disturbances, disorders, troubles).
Nous nous sommes décidés (résolus) à satisfaire toutes leurs revendications simplement pour prévenir une nouvelle crise (accès) d'agitation sociale.
- Our appliances have been designed (devised) so as to meet all requirements (so as to meet all needs).
Nos appareils ont été conçus de façon à satisfaire toutes les exigences (de façon à satisfaire tous les besoins).
- To meet **with** : implique la fortuité
- We have cleared the hurdle this time, but we might meet **with** (encounter) other obstacles in **the** near future ; we must guard against all contingencies.
Nous avons franchi l'obstacle cette fois-ci mais nous pourrions rencontrer d'autres difficultés dans un proche avenir ; nous devons parer à toute éventualité.
- I have met with a refusal : they have turned down our proposal.
J'ai essuyé un refus : ils ont rejeté notre proposition.
- He has been drawing a disability pension ever since he met with that unexplained accident.
Il touche une pension d'invalidité depuis qu'il a été l'objet de cet accident inexpliqué.

Substantif :

a political meeting ; a sports meeting :
une réunion politique, sportive

94 - TO MELT

(R) sauf molten : *en fusion*
- When it thaws, ice and snow melt.
Quand il dégèle, la neige et la glace fondent.
- In a foundry, they make for instance truck (wagon) wheels by casting (pouring) molten steel into moulds.
Dans une fonderie, on fait par exemple des roues de wagons en coulant de l'acier en fusion dans des moules.
Cf. " The melting pot ".
Le " creuset " : les États Unis, creuset de toutes les nationalités.
NB. *Faire fondre, extraire par fusion :* to smelt (R)
An aluminium, a copper-smelting works : *une fonderie d'aluminium, de cuivre.*
Mais : They smelt iron ore in a **steelworks.**
On fond le minerai de fer dans une aciérie.

95 - TO MISLAY-LAID-LAID

- The boss keeps mislaying his glasses.
Le patron ne fait qu'égarer ses lunettes.
Mais :
- Their letter has probably got lost.
Leur lettre s'est probablement égarée.
- We cannot condone (overlook) such acts of violence, although we are convinced that the demonstrators were distraught (distracted) with worry and a deep feeling of helplessness !
Nous ne pouvons pardonner (fermer les yeux sur) de tels actes de violence bien que nous soyons convaincus que les manifestants étaient égarés par l'anxiété et un profond sentiment d'impuissance !
- Appearances are misleading (deceptive).
Les apparences sont trompeuses (de to mislead-led-led : *égarer - induire en erreur).*
Autres traductions de " tromper "
- I am disappointed, the foreman has deceived us !
Je suis déçu, le contremaître nous a trompés !
- The boss is notoriously unfaithful to his wife !
Il est de notoriété publique que le chef trompe sa femme !
- The cheque has bounced (it is a dud cheque), we have been duped by a swindler.
Le chèque a été refusé (c'est un chèque sans provision), nous avons été trompés par un escroc.
Plus élégant : the cheque has been dishonoured.

14 - STRUCTURES

FAIRE + INFINITIF

1 - MOYEN MNÉMOTECHNIQUE :

Remplacer " faire " par " faire en sorte que ".
Si la forme est active : **to make + infinitif sans to.**
Si la forme est passive : **to have (ou to get) + participe passé.**

ATTENTION À LA CONSTRUCTION :

- *Les clowns font rire les enfants - ils font en sorte que les enfants rient :* **forme active :** Clowns make children laugh.
- *Je fais couper mes cheveux tous les mois - je fais en sorte que mes cheveux soient coupés :* **forme passive :** I have (I get) my hair cut every month.
- *Fais réparer la voiture - fais en sorte que la voiture soit réparée :* **forme passive :** Have (get) the car repaired.

Mais : *le Professeur fait travailler les élèves - fait en sorte que les élèves travaillent :* **forme active :** The teacher makes pupils work.

2 - REMARQUES :

- Quand " to make " doit se mettre au passif, il gouverne l'infinitif **+ to.**
  - *On me fait travailler :* I am made **to** work ***mais*** They make **me work.**
- Dans la langue littéraire, on peut employer " to cause " dans tous les cas avec l'**infinitif complet.**
  - *Il a fait mourir sa femme :* He made his wife die ou
    He caused his wife **to** die.
  - *Il fait peindre sa maison :* He has his house paint**ed** ou
    He causes his house **to** be painted.

IMPÉRATIF

Go. Let him go. Don't let us go = Let us not go.
Pour distinguer de " laisser " employer " to allow " et l'infinitif complet.
Let him go out ! Allow him to go out !
Qu'il sorte ! Laisse-le sortir !

L'INFINITIF SANS TO

voir structures 13

THÈME D'APPLICATION NUMÉRO 14

1 - Ainsi, le chèque a été refusé ! Cela signifie que nous avons été trompés par un escroc !
2 - Le Président Directeur Général aimerait mieux rejeter leurs propositions mais nous ferions mieux de satisfaire leurs revendications pour prévenir une nouvelle crise d'agitation sociale.
3 - Ne pardonnons pas (2 constructions) de tels actes de violence car nous pourrions rencontrer d'autres difficultés dans un proche avenir.
4 - La Direction veut nous faire accroître la production mais cela entraînera une baisse du niveau de la qualité.
5 - Après la catastrophe, le Gouvernement a fait importer des denrées de base des États Unis, telles que des céréales et des produits laitiers.
6 - Dans l'industrie, on fait adopter les cercles de qualité pour rehausser la qualité des articles.
7 - On leur fait toujours concevoir les appareils de façon à satisfaire toutes les exigences : nous ne voulons pas tromper nos clients !
8 - (Le fait de) trouver (gérondif) les fonds nécessaires (2 traductions) est une condition préalable ; en outre, nous devrions sensibiliser l'opinion publique à ce problème.
9 - Renverser cette tendance entraînera des changements importants ; que les travailleurs nous aident à franchir les obstacles que nous pourrions rencontrer !
10 - Qu'il ne touche pas (2 constructions) cette pension d'invalidité si l'accident dont il a été l'objet reste inexpliqué !
11 - Notre Président Directeur Général veut vous faire faire la connaissance de son fondé de pouvoir.
12 - On nous fait satisfaire leurs exigences pour prévenir une nouvelle crise d'agitation sociale (traduction différente de phrase 2).
13 - Nous avons essuyé un refus en ce qui concerne les roues de wagon : ils ne les feront pas fabriquer dans notre fonderie !
14 - On leur fait couler de l'acier en fusion dans des moules de différentes formes.
15 - Il est vraiment mesquin, et je suis déçu : il n'a rien fait pour me faire obtenir cette permission !

15 - COMMERCE AND THE CONSUMER SOCIETY

(Deuxième partie)

MEANS OF ACTION : THE MARKETING MIX

Producers strive for optimal levels of profit – it is their ***raison d'être*** – and there is good reason to believe that they share the philosophy that pervades today's society. That is why they logically concern themselves with producing only what is likely to sell well. The opposite approach – producing goods haphazardly, and wondering afterwards whether they will sell at all – would be preposterous and suicidal !

Producers are going to :

– ascertain whether there are potential outlets for this or that product,

– assess their nature and volume,

– market the product if the information is promising so as to secure as substantial a profit as possible, and comply at the same time with wholesalers', retailers' and consumers' wishes.

The whole process is called marketing (*le marchéage, la mercatique*), and it is entrusted in big firms to a special department. Its aim is achieved by applying a combination of procedures that makes up the **marketing mix.**

A BIRD'S EYE VIEW

The marketing mix includes two main component parts :

■ The collection of information through **marketing research**, which comprises several activities :

1. Economic research. A study of the economic situation prevailing at a certain time in a country, or of the activities of a particular economic sector, or of the results of a particular type of industry, etc !
2. **Market research** *(l'étude de marché).* It is not to be mistaken for marketing research *(la recherche commerciale).* The latter tries to define the problems that confront a producer who wants to launch a product – either a market follower or a pioneer product –, whereas market research is a study of consumers' demand as regards a category of products similar to the one that our producer wants to launch. It can be carried out through a **sample survey** *(enquête par sondage)* in which case a sample section of consumers *(une section représentative de consommateurs)* are given a questionnaire, their answers providing information about the size, the location of the market, the tastes of consumers and their wishes, the price they are willing to pay, etc. Information can also be obtained from questionnaires on the use of samples, tests in shops, etc.
3. Competitor research. It consists in finding out which competitors are to be found on the market, whether it is possible to vie with them, or perhaps oust them, considering the quality of their products, their prices, etc.
4. Distribution research. It is essential if, by streamlining distribution for instance, it becomes possible to undercut competitors.

■ Direct action : advertising.

Now that his product bids fair to carve out a niche for itself on the market thanks to the information which has made its development possible, the producer will try to boost its sales – hence his profit – through advertising. The latter has three main purposes :

1. It informs consumers of the existence of a new product, or of the improvements, the lower price of an old favourite.
2. It tries to persuade consumers into buying a product by assuring them that they make a good choice.
3. It keeps the name of the product alive in consumers' minds to maintain their loyalty to the brand.

   Advertisers can choose from a wide range of media to convey their message :

1. The press : newspapers or magazines
2. The radio or television
3. Cinemas, theatres
4. Posters, on poster sites, hoardings, etc.
5. Lorries, buses, vans, cars, etc.
6. Direct mail
7. Products themselves (bags, training suits, watches, tee-shirts, etc.)

■ The case for advertising.

1. Producers

– Although advertising proves very expensive, especially commercials (advertising spots) on the radio and television at peak hours, it is the most effective way of increasing sales, and consequently profit.

– It keeps consumers informed. Otherwise, they would have to wait until goods were in the shops, or they would learn of their existence by hearsay. It would make investment in new products worthless.

2. Consumers

– If sales are booming, prices can be lowered, which makes goods more competitive, and boosts sales even more : mass-production entails another drop in prices !

– Without advertising, television licence fees and the price of newspapers and magazines would be much higher.

– It favours competition among producers. If one of them advertises goods at X pounds per unit, another will go one better, and knock a few pounds off the price. Not only does it apply to consumables, but also to durables : it keeps down the cost of living.

– It keeps up the quality standard of branded goods. Woe to the firm whose goods would belie the quality that it boasts : it would tarnish its brand image, and send its sales plummeting.

– By furthering large-scale production (mass production), advertising makes the wheels of industry turn at full speed, which can be conducive to a dent in unemployment.

■ The case against advertising.

1. Producers

– Advertising is so expensive that producers will have to recoup their investment by raising prices.

– It will be the case a fortiori when an advertising campaign proves to be a flop !

– The market is bound to become saturated, and the rise in sales will be disproportionate to the sums invested : a fall in prices will be impossible !

2. Consumers

– They stand to lose for any of the three reasons stated above : their purses will bear the brunt of the costs incurred by producers.

– Advertising is ubiquitous, i.e, present everywhere. It intrudes itself insidiously into our minds, and by dint of harping on the qualities of this or that product – repetition makes reputation –, it eventually leads us into buying it. We feel manipulated, the victims of a milder form of brainwashing.

– Not only does it often entice people into buying products that they do not need, but they are apt to do so although they really cannot afford it (impulse buying).

– Advertising does not appeal to our reason, but to our emotions, our instincts, our shortcomings. It capitalizes on our fears (for the benefit, for instance, of insurance companies), our vanity (much exploited by the fashion, the perfume or the cosmetics industries ; the car, the building, the furniture industries) – and in this respect admen (advertisers) apply Thornstein Veblen's theory on conspicuous consumption –, our propensity to take the line of least resistance (cf. the hype surrounding an impressive array of labour-saving appliances), our greed for money or food, not to mention sexual desires, etc.

THE MARKETING MIX : OTHER PLOYS

■ Branding-giving a product a brand name, i.e, a trade mark – and packaging – the containers or wrappings in which a product is sold – are excellent " baits " to attract customers : those who set great store by a particular brand will remain loyal to it, and the packaging of a product can be so attractive – because of the colours, the shape, and that clever widget at the top… – that customers will buy it preferably.

■ Public relations.

The person who is in charge of public relations sees to it that the public at large – not only customers, but also suppliers, bankers, shareholders, etc. – are informed of all that may occur in a firm that is likely to keep alive, or even enhance its reputation : its achievements, its plans, the extension to the present factory, the new machine tools, etc. He/she does it through press releases, open days, exhibitions, lunches with V.I.P.s, etc.

■ Product management.

– It consists primarily in selling as many products as possible on the existing markets, but also in trying to break into new markets, making sure all the time that the firm makes a profit in spite of such variables as costs (raw materials, labour, equipment, etc.) competition, credit squeeze, etc., and in withdrawing the products which are no longer profitable for one reason or another.

– It can entail the development of new products to give the firm an advantage over its competitors, or a modification of existing ones : this is unavoidable because of the evolution of science and technology, but also because of consumers' modernity snobbery. To keep up with the Joneses, and even have the edge on them, they will buy a state-of-the-art Hi-Fi system, or television set, or car. Producers of course respect, and even encourage the consumers' wish of purchasing only the last word in everything. Planned – or built-in – obsolescence serves that purpose. It consists either in using materials of lesser quality to manufacture products, which makes them less durable and serviceable, or in bringing them into line with current tastes by giving them nothing more than a new look.

– The problem for the producer is to strike a balance between quality, durability and price. Consumers are becoming more and more fastidious as regards quality, hence the multiplication of quality circles in industry, but if they do not put up any longer with goods of shoddy workmanship, they do not accept either to pay through the nose for those of sterling quality !

– Planned obsolescence also fosters the sales of component parts. Defective parts in appliances, for instance, are no longer repaired, they are purely and simply discarded and replaced by brand new ones, as long as these are available of course. Otherwise, the appliance itself must be replaced by its latest model...

■ Guarantees or warranties.

To overcome consumers' hesitation, goods are sold under guarantee (under warranty). The producer assures the consumer in a guarantee certificate that the article that he/she has just bought is of good quality, that it will work properly, failing which, provided a claim is made within a stated period, the producer undertakes to replace the faulty part in the article free of charge (sometimes the guarantee covers spare parts but not labour costs), or the article itself, or to refund the purchase price. Because they can stimulate demand, guarantee periods are becoming longer and longer : competition is keen !

■ After-sales service.

A reliable after-sales service is also essential for a producer to get the upper hand of his competitors. It sees that the article works properly after it has been sold by carrying out the necessary repairs if it breaks down, or simply its maintenance (checking its safety devices, cleaning and greasing it), very often under a maintenance agreement.

■ Merchandising *(le marchandisage)*.

It refers to the large variety of devices that can be resorted to in order :

1. To bring consumers into close contact with the goods that are on sale. Self-service is the appropriate method, since it enables consumers to handle goods, and so to have a foretaste of their possession. Simply gazing at them would boil down to window shopping.
2. To make them yield to the temptation of buying as many of them as possible thanks to :
   - sales promotions : free gifts (give-aways), coupons that can be used for free gifts or rebates, free samples, cost-price sales, clearance sales, bargain basement sales, etc.
   - competitions : the prizes are cars, cruises, houses...
   - special credit facilities, etc.

TEST YOUR KNOWLEDGE

1 - Try and give a definition of marketing.

2 - What is the difference between marketing research, market research and merchandising ?

3 - What is a sample survey ?

4 - What are the three main purposes of advertising ?

5 - Which are the two greatest advantages of advertising for consumers ?

6 - Which criticisms would **you** level at advertising ?

7 - Why do producers think that packaging is important ? Do you agree ?

8 - How can producers exploit modernity snobbery ?

9 - What is built-in obsolescence ?

10 - Why is a reliable after-sales service so important ?

96 - TO MISTAKE-TOOK-TAKEN

■ - How can you mistake the balance of trade **for** the balance of payments , (how can you confuse the b.o.t. **with = and** the b.o.p.)

■ - There is no mistaking (confusing) the invoices : they are not dated the same day !

Il n'y a pas moyen de se tromper de factures : elles ne sont pas datées du même jour !

Contraire : - There is no telling (distinguishing) one invoice from another.

Il n'y a pas moyen de distinguer entre les factures (une facture d'une autre).

■ - I am afraid you are thoroughly (utterly) mistaken ; the success of the plan hinges on (rests on - turns on - depends on - is contingent upon) the unions' restraint.

Je crains que vous ne vous trompiez complètement ; le succès du projet dépend de la modération des syndicats.

Autres traductions de " se tromper " :

- Don't dial the wrong number, consult (refer to) the card-index !

Ne vous trompez pas de numéro, consultez le fichier !

- Don't take the wrong plane this time !

Ne vous trompez pas d'avion cette fois-ci !

" The chartered accountant is often out in his reckoning. Isn't it odd ? " - " Anybody can make a mistake ! "

L'expert comptable se trompe souvent dans ses calculs. N'est-ce pas étrange ? " Tout le monde peut se tromper ! "

- " He is FFr 1m out in his reckoning ! " - " Never mind if it is **to** our advantage ! "

" Il se trompe d'un million de francs français dans ses calculs ! " - " Ne vous inquiétez pas, si c'est à notre avantage ! "

Substantifs : - To **make** a (typing, spelling) mistake :

faire une faute (de frappe, d'orthographe).

- Sorry ! You've been summoned by mistake !

Navré ! On vous a convoqué par erreur !

- You have once more made an error of judgement : you have made one blunder too many !

Vous avez une fois de plus fait une erreur de jugement ! Vous avez fait une bourde (gaffe, impair, bévue, erreur) de trop !

97 - TO MOW-MOWED-MOWN

faucher (herbe, céréales), tondre (gazon = turf)

A lawn-mower : *une tondeuse à gazon* (textuel " *à pelouse* ") ;

a mower - a reaper : *une faucheuse.*

- Small farmers have set up (formed) a cooperative to buy agricultural machinery ; their latest acquisition (purchase) is a combine-harvester which reaps and threshes cereals : it is more cost-effective than a host of harvesters wielding scythes, sickles and flails !

Les petits fermiers ont formé une coopérative pour acheter des machines agricoles ; leur dernière acquisition est une moissonneuse-batteuse qui fauche (récolte) et bat les céréales : cela est plus rentable qu'une armée de moissonneurs maniant des faux, des faucilles et des fléaux ! (**mais** " scourge " : *fléau, calamité)*

98 - TO OUTRUN-RAN-RUN

■ *Dépasser* (comme dans une course)

Synonyme : to outstrip - to outpace - to get ahead of

- The Japanese automotive industry has outrun (outstripped-outpaced-got ahead of) its European and American competitors.

L'industrie automobile Japonaise a dépassé ses concurrents Européens et Américains.

Cf. to overtake - took - taken - to catch up with and pass - to come abreast with and pass : *rattraper et dépasser*

- Their steel industry started from scratch after World War II ; it has now overtaken ours as regards output, quality and price !

Leur industrie sidérurgique est partie de zéro après la Deuxième Guerre Mondiale ; elle a maintenant dépassé la nôtre sur le plan de la production, de la qualité et du prix !

- No overtaking ! (highway code).

Défense de doubler ! (code de la route).

Mot proche : *devancer, être le premier à :* to forestall
- When we tried to make a foray into that market, we discovered that the Americans had forestalled all their competitors there, and had secured all the orders !
Quand nous avons essayé de faire une incursion sur ce marché, nous avons découvert que les Américains y avaient devancé tous leurs concurrents, et qu'ils avaient enlevé toutes les commandes !
■ *Dépasser, surpasser*
a) en valeur, en magnitude ; *dépasser des limites :* to exceed, to go beyond, to outweigh
- Exports this year have outrun (exceeded, gone beyond) all our expectations.
Les exportations cette année ont dépassé tous nos espoirs.
- Building a nuclear plant outruns (exceeds) their potentialities.
La construction d'une centrale nucléaire dépasse leurs potentialités.
- The disadvantages outweigh the advantages :
Les inconvénients l'emportent sur les avantages.
b) en nombre. Préférer : to exceed, to top, to outnumber
- She hinted that our imports would top the £6m mark.
Elle a laissé entendre que nos importations dépasseraient le cap des 6 millions de livres.
- Our staff never exceeded 1,200 employees.
Notre personnel n'a jamais dépassé 1200 employés.
- The non-strikers (depreciatory : the blacklegs, the scabs) were outnumbered ten to one, so they had to beat a hasty retreat when they attempted to clock in, clamouring against the fact that " the right (freedom) to work was being flouted ! "
Les non-grévistes (péjoratif : les jaunes) étaient à un contre dix, si bien qu'ils durent précipitamment battre en retraite quand ils essayèrent de pointer, tout en protestant contre le fait que " la liberté du travail était bafouée ! "
c) en excellence. Préférer : to surpass, to outmatch, to outclass, to outshine ; **plus fort** : to dwarf, to eclipse
- We are really no match for them as regards the first place on the market (we really cannot vie **with** them **for** the first place), they outshine us (surpass, etc.) in all respects : know-how, expertise, craftmanship, business acumen, etc. !
Nous ne sommes vraiment pas de taille à lutter contre eux en ce qui concerne la première place sur le marché (nous ne pouvons vraiment pas rivaliser avec eux...), ils nous surpassent à tous égards : savoir-faire, compétence, talent, sens aigu des affaires, etc. !

Familier : to have the edge on : *avoir l'avantage sur, dépasser, être supérieur à* (to have **an** advantage over somebody).
- We still have the edge on them in the field of microchips.
Nous les dépassons encore dans le domaine des microprocesseurs.

99 - TO OVERCOME-OVERCAME-OVERCOME

surmonter, vaincre (to get the better of, to vanquish, to triumph over)
- The country is making strenuous efforts to overcome the difficulties encountered by its burgeoning (budding) industry in its attempt to export its lines, without bringing upon itself any economic retaliatory measures (economic reprisals) from industrialized countries.
Le pays fait des efforts acharnés pour surmonter (vaincre) les difficultés rencontrées par son industrie naissante dans sa tentative d'exporter sa production, sans encourir (attirer sur soi) des mesures de rétorsion économiques (des représailles économiques) de la part des pays industrialisés.
Autres traductions de " vaincre " : to vanquish, to triumph over, to get the upper hand
- If we want to defeat (vanquish) our opponents (adversaries), we must revamp the company and lower its operating costs.
Si nous voulons vaincre nos adversaires, nous devons réorganiser l'entreprise et diminuer ses frais d'exploitation.
- If we want to get the upper hand of our competitors...
Si nous voulons l'emporter sur nos concurrents...

15 - STRUCTURES

PRONOMS DIVERS

1 - POSSESSIFS :

Le mien, etc.

a) Pour traduire : c'est à moi, etc. après la question : à qui est, à qui sont... ? - Whose car is this ? It's mine, yours, his, hers, its own, ours, yours, theirs.

NB. On peut employer " to belong to " + Pronoms personnels compléments :

- This car belongs to me, you, him, her, it, us, you, them.

b) Pour traduire " un(e) " parmi d'autres...

- He is a friend of mine, etc.

Cf. Cas possessif incomplet :

- He is a friend of John's.
- He is a teacher of my daughter's.

c) Pour traduire " aucun(e) " parmi d'autres...

- No friend of theirs would dare attack us !

Variante : None of their friend**s** would dare attack us !

2 - DÉMONSTRATIFS :

This (pluriel : these) : proximité dans l'espace ou dans le temps au contraire de that (pluriel : those), comme pour les adjectifs.

- Here ! Drink this, and you'll feel much better !
- Did you hear what the President said last night ? : that will make many people think !
- " What do you think of the flowers ? " - " I prefer these to those ! "

NB. Mr X and Mr Y work here : **the former** is an accountant, **the latter** is an engineer : ... *le premier... ce dernier* (**invariable**).

3 - RÉFLÉCHIS ET RÉCIPROQUES :

a) Myself, yourself, himself, herself, itself, our**selves**, your**selves**, them**selves**.

- A man is selfish when he loves himself too much !
- She killed herself on learning the dreadful news.

NB. By oneself - alone :

- He has learnt English by himself, which accounts for his mistakes.

b) Each other (deux), one another (plus de deux).

- The parson says that we should love one another : *le pasteur dit que...*
- He doesn't speak the language but we understand each other all the same.

Exception : Après " among " employer les réfléchis :

- The thieves shared the booty among themselves.
  Les voleurs se partagèrent le butin.

Attention ! comparer :

- She has killed herself - she has committed suicide et
  She was (she got) killed **in an accident.**
- She was (she got) drowned when swimming in the lake et
  She has drowned herself out of despair. (to drown : *noyer*)

4 - MOI, TOI, ETC.

a) C'est à moi : Cf. it's mine, etc.

b) Pour moi : for me : après prépositions, pronoms personnels compléments.

- *Derrière lui* : behind him.

c) Forme d'insistance :

- ***She*** is the boss ! *C'est elle le patron !*
- ***He*** is a mere puppet ! *Lui n'est qu'une simple marionnette !*
- ***I*** did it. *C'est moi qui l'ai fait.*

Le pronom est en italiques dans un texte imprimé, souligné quand le texte est manuscrit, mis en relief à l'oral.

5 - CELUI DE, CELLE DE

a) That of (the one of) ou le cas possessif incomplet : êtres animés ou expressions de temps
- It's not **my** car, it's my father's - it's that of my father.
- ... " And so he cut off your cat's leg with his mowing machine ? " (*faucheuse*) " No, my dog's ! "
- " Is it today's mail ? " - " No, yesterday's ! "

b) That of, the one of (pluriel those of) : objets inanimés
- I asked the architect : " Is this the door of the kitchen ? " - " No ", he answered " it's that of (the one of) the bathroom ".
- I did not break the leg of the table, but that of the chair !

6 - CELUI QUI, CELLE QUE

a) **Personnes** : **l'éviter** : dire l'homme qui, etc.
The one who, whom, whose

■ Selon la fonction de celui, etc. et du relatif : he who, him whom, she whose, etc. (traduction très élégante).
- He who transgresses God's law will burn in Hell for ever and ever.
- Don't kill the one who is standing behind that tree : I want him alive !
- Do you like the actors ? I don't like the hero ; I prefer the one who plays the part of the villain !

Au pluriel : those who, whom, whose est courant
- Those who don't understand will raise their hands.

b) **Animaux et choses :** the one which (pluriel those which, the ones which)
- " Give me that tool " - " Which tool ? " - " The one which is on the sill " *(appui de fenêtre).*

7 - CE QUI, CE QUE

a) What : - Can you see what he's got in his right hand ? It's a gun !
b) Which (après une virgule en général) quand l'antécédent est un membre de phrase :
- It is freezing, which is extraordinary in June !
c) Tout ce qui, ce que : all that.

8 - QUEL, LEQUEL ?

a)**What** is your name ?
b) Avec idée de choix : **which**
- You are known to the police under the names of Smith, Martin, Thompson, Thomas... Which is your real name ?

THÈME D'APPLICATION NUMÉRO 15

1 - " A qui appartient ce numéro ? " - " C'est celui de notre expert-comptable (3 constructions) "

2 - Que pouvons-nous faire contre les Japonais et les Américains ? Nous ne sommes pas de taille à lutter contre les premiers, et ces derniers ont devancé tous leurs concurrents et enlevé toutes les commandes !

3 - Les petits fermiers s'entraident en formant des coopératives pour acheter du matériel agricole ; la nôtre possède une moissonneuse batteuse qui fauche et bat les céréables, ce qui est plus rentable qu'une armée de moissonneurs !

4 - Nos exportations ont dépassé tous nos espoirs cette année mais nous voulons nous surpasser (to surpass) : elles devront dépasser le cap des X millions de livres l'an prochain.

5 - Eux, ils ont l'avantage sur nous sur le marché national ; mais nous, nous les surpassons sur le marché étranger.

6 - Ils nous dépassent encore dans le domaine des microprocesseurs mais pas dans celui de l'industrie automobile !

7 - " Quel numéro as-tu composé (to dial) ? " - " Celui que j'ai trouvé en consultant le fichier ! "

8 - Les pays sous-développés ne sont pas satisfaits ; ceux qui (3 traductions) font des efforts acharnés pour exporter les productions de leur industrie naissante encourent des mesures de rétorsion économique.

9 - Nous allons réorganiser l'entreprise, ce qui nous permettra de diminuer nos frais d'exploitation et de vaincre nos adversaires.

10 - Un de nos industriels (2 constructions) a essayé de faire une incursion sur ce marché mais ses adversaires ont triomphé de lui en enlevant toutes les commandes.

11 - Aucun de leurs (2 constructions) fabricants ne surpasse les nôtres, à aucun égard : savoir-faire, compétence, talent, sens aigu des affaires, etc.

12 - Ces trois pays-là se répartissent les marchés ; si nous voulons les vaincre, nous devons réorganiser nos entreprises et diminuer leurs frais d'exploitation !

13 - C'est vous qui vous trompez complètement ! Moi, je ne me trompe jamais dans mes calculs !

14 - L'expert comptable fait trop d'erreurs ! Heureusement, celle qu'il a faite la dernière fois était à notre avantage !

15 - Personne ne peut rivaliser avec nous sur le plan de la production : nos potentialités dépassent celles de (3 constructions) nos concurrents.

16 - COMMUNICATIONS

(Première partie)

THE PARTIES CONCERNED

BUSINESS UNITS

Before you apply for a job, you are already interested to know in what kind of firm you are possibly going to work : your future is at stake ! If your application is successful, the owner of the firm or, in large ones, the Personnel Manager (the Human Resources Manager) will receive you for an interview during which he/she will acquaint you with the exact nature of the firm and that of your work. Both pieces of information are important as both can affect your prospects.
With yet stronger reason, if you want to venture into business, and set up your own firm, you will study closely which type of business organization would be best suited to your situation.
In the private sector, there is a large variety of business units.

- One-man businesses *(les entreprises individuelles)*. They belong to sole traders = *des propriétaires uniques* (sole owners, sole proprietors, owner-managers), for instance shop-keepers, plumbers, hairdressers, etc. The sole trader provides capital and labour (but he can be helped by one or two employees), he is accountable to no one as regards the management of the business, the profits are all his, but he runs a risk : if the business fails (becomes bankrupt) he must settle the debts off his own assets. His death entails that of the business if no one wants to take it over. His employees are then left without a job. On the other hand, it is often pleasant to work for a sole trader on condition of course that he and his employee(s) get along well !
- Partnerships = *les sociétés de personnes.*
  a) General partnerships (ordinary partnerships) = *les sociétés en nom collectif.*
  If for instance a sole trader's employees are at loggerheads with him, or if he goes bankrupt, or if he dies, they may decide to form a partnership (to go into partnership). It enables them to invest a larger capital in the business – their savings and perhaps bank loans – in order to expand it. It is probably the main advantage of partnerships, with also the fact that like sole traders, partners (fellow partners, co-partners) are accountable to no one as concerns the way in which they manage their business. They share the profits, but also the losses, and they face unlimited liability : they are personally liable (responsible) for all the debts of the firm. Partnerships are fairly common in the professions.
  b) Limited partnerships : *les sociétés en commandite*. In this type of partnership, there are two kinds of partners.
    1. The sleeping partners (the silent partners) = *les associés commanditaires, les commanditaires, les bailleurs de fonds*. They invest capital in the business and share in the profits, but they do not take part in its management. They face only limited liability : they are liable for the debts of the firm within the limits of their investments.
    2. The acting partners (active partners, general partners, working partners) = *les commandités.*
    They run the business, share in the profits, but they assume unlimited liability for the debts incurred.
    It can also be very pleasant to work in partnerships because they are small firms, and it makes good relations easier.
- Joint-stock companies : *les sociétés de capitaux.*
  They have three main features :
  a) They are legal entities, i.e, they have their own legal existence, unlike partnerships which are dissolved in the event of one partner's death, retirement or bankruptcy.
  b) The liability of investors is limited to the amount of their investments.
  c) Their capital consists in shares or debentures.
    1. Ordinary shares = *les actions ordinaires*. Their holders are entitled to a dividend, i.e, a part of the profits, if the company is fortunate enough to make profits !
    2. Preference shares = *les actions privilégiées ou prioritaires*. Their holders receive a fixed dividend which is paid before that of ordinary shares.
    By way of compensation for the financial risks

that they take, the holders of ordinary shares have a say in the running of the company : they elect the Board of Directors : *le Conseil d'Administration.*

3. Debentures : *les obligations.* They are not shares, but loans. Debenture holders *(les obligataires)* receive interest at a fixed rate on the money that they lend to the company ; they have no say in its management, but they have precedence on shareholders (US : stockholders) as regards the payment of interest.

There are two kinds of joint-stock companies :

a) The (Private) Limited Company, roughly equivalent to the French *" Société à Responsabilité Limitée " (SARL).*

1. Its name must end with Limited (= Ltd).
2. Its shares and debentures are not quoted on the Stock Exchange, and cannot be bought and sold (traded) publicly ; it makes expansion through an increase of capital more difficult since shares and debentures can be issued only to private investors (relatives, friends, etc.).

b) The Public Limited Company : it is broadly similar to the French *" Société Anonyme ".*

1. Its name must end with PLC or plc,
2. Its shares and debentures are quoted and traded on the Stock Exchange, which makes expansion easier since they can be issued to the general public,
3. Because it is usually larger than the (private) limited company, it secures economies of scale *(des économies d'échelle)*, i.e, lower costs per unit of production (e.g. in manufacturing) or per unit sold (e.g. in retailing).

■ The expansion of firms.
Firms will expand if the demand for their goods is soaring at home, or abroad if they have launched out into foreign trade, or if they want to diversify into new products. In both cases they need more money to have extensions built to their factories, to buy new machinery, engage new workers, etc. They can raise the necessary funds :

a) By ploughing back (reinvesting) part of their profits.

b) By issuing new shares or debentures.

They can also expand by combining with other firms.

a) Mergers : *les fusions.*
Two companies are said to have merged when they have joined together to form one new company. The merger is horizontal when both companies make the same product(s) at the same stage of production, e.g. two sugar refineries. It is vertical when the end-product of one company is the raw material of the other. A company that manufactures confectionery for instance can merge with a sugar refinery.

b) Absorption *(Intégration).*
Small business are very often absorbed (taken over) by larger ones because they are not competitive on the market. Not only are they no longer able to undercut their competitors, but they cannot even bring their prices into line with theirs. They have lost before they start when they put in (submit) tenders for contracts. No one in his senses would try to bail them out ! No matter how doggedly they strive to keep their business afloat, they must sooner or later file a petition in bankruptcy *(déposer leur bilan).* The business is eventually wound up. Absorption is probably the lesser of two evils because it can entail fewer redundancies.

c) Takeovers and takeover bids : *prises de contrôle et offres publiques d'achat (OPA).*
" Lame ducks " are doomed to absorption, if not liquidation, but takeovers concern healthy, profit-making firms, upon which a person or an organization are going to prey. The latter – appropriately called " corporate raiders " in the United States *(pirates ou pillards de sociétés)* make a takeover bid to the shareholders of the company that they covet : they make them the offer of buying at a named price, which is far higher than their market price, all the shares of the company, or enough shares to secure its control. The directors may accept or reject the bid. In the latter case, the raiders raise their bid to make it more alluring, and it may be the beginning of a staggering escalation.

d) Cartels are huge associations of producers in one particular branch of industry which aim, without merging, at avoiding competition among themselves, at regulating outputs and prices. Trust is the American word for cartel. In all countries there are anti-trust laws to prevent the creation of monopolies. A monopoly exists when a powerful company, a cartel or a trust, controls the market.

e) A holding company *(un " holding ", une société de portefeuille)* holds at least 51 % of the shareholders' equity *(le capital actions)* of several companies, but does not necessarily concern itself with their management. It is called the parent company *(la maison mère)* and it controls subsidiaries *(des filiales).*

f) Multinationals (multinational companies : GB ; multinational corporations : US).
They are companies whose ownership and headquarters (head offices) are located in a country, with

branches *(des succursales)* or subsidiaries *(des filiales)* abroad. A great many of them are American (General Motors, IBM, Kodak, etc.), but practically all large industrialized countries have theirs : e.g. BP, ICI in Great Britain ; Saint-Gobain, Carrefour in France ; Fiat, Olivetti in Italy ; Philips in Holland ; Nestlé in Switzerland ; Sony, Toyota in Japan, etc.
It may be profitable for companies to be multinational, or transnational, when ownership and head offices are located in two or more countries, because :

1. Their marketing departments abroad are in a privileged position to inquire into the needs, tastes or wishes of the local populations, and to distribute their lines.
2. Transport costs are reduced : raw materials are to be found on the spot, and finished goods are available there and then.
3. Host countries are usually tax havens.
4. They choose the countries where labour costs are lowest.
5. By setting up branches or subsidiaries in different countries, they protect themselves from economic or political difficulties in one of them : the others take over to weather the crisis.

Host countries stand to gain from the presence of multinationals because they create jobs, transfer their technological knowledge to them, invest or reinvest funds in their economies. However, multinationals are often reproached for spiriting away all the profits that they make, for neglecting the safety of their workers, and not caring at all about polluting the environment (cf. Union Carbide and the disaster in Bhopal). At home, people find fault with them for exactly the same reasons : why do they invest abroad when their own economy is in dire need of capital injections, and is suffering from high levels of unemployment ?

■ Co-operatives.

a) Consumer co-operatives. They are business organizations owned and run by a group of people whose aim is not to make a profit, but to break even, i.e. not to make either a profit or a loss. Wholesale and retail cooperatives want to enable their members to buy products that are good value for money (good quality products at fair prices). The profits are shared among the members in proportion to the amount of their purchases.

b) Producer co-operatives. They are business organizations owned and run by a group of producers (small manufacturers, farmers, wine growers, etc.) who join together, either to buy raw materials in bulk (and so at a discount), such as fertilizers, seeds, feedstuffs, etc., or equipment (agricultural machinery, etc.), or to sell their products or their produce.

■ The expansion of firms : advantages and drawbacks.
On the one hand, it seems desirable that business should expand. In this way they secure economies of scale which can translate into lower consumer prices. They buy new equipment to increase their outputs, and so create jobs, they fill their suppliers' order books and make them work at full capacity, they require a wider range of services from banks, insurance companies, haulage contractors, the Post Office, Telecommunications : they contribute to absorbing unemployment, they improve the country's adverse balance of trade when their products are successful abroad, in a word, they give a fillip to the economy. On the other hand, the collapse of one of those behemoths is always tragical as it affects so many people : even its suppliers and its subcontractors do not escape unscathed. If it does not fail, as its prosperity is contingent upon economic circumstances, the latter may require that it should undergo a thorough and painful restructuration : it entails slimming down the workforce, cutting back on orders, farming out less work to smaller firms, distributing leaner dividends – or none at all – for some time, etc.
Moreover, running a very large business is a feat : before a decision can be made, there are so many people to consult, whose views, aims, interests, are conflicting, and so many economic parameters to be taken into account ! As for employees, working for such a firm can be an asset, as it probably offers more opportunities for promotion than would a smaller one. Yet the majority of them must feel as if they were nothing more than tiny cogs in a gigantic machine.

APPLICANTS FOR A POSITION

By the end of 1992, the European Economic Community is at long last going to become a common market in which goods, people, services, capital, will be allowed to move freely. It implies that anybody living within this " Europe without frontiers " will be entitled to work in the member nation of its choice, and so to apply for a job there. Improved communications, thanks to high-speed trains and " the Chunnel " – the Tunnel under the Channel – will knit the Community all the more closely and will favour exchanges on the labour market.

■ Jobcentres and employment agencies.
If for one reason or other you are eager to work for a particular firm abroad, you can write to its Personnel Manager to enquire whether they have a vacancy for someone with your qualifications, stating of course why

you are so interested in working for them. Join a S.A.E. (stamped addressed envelope) of course ! The Chamber of Commerce, or the Consulate of the country concerned can help you to find the address of the firm. You may be lucky and receive an answer with further information, an application form, etc. Nothing venture, nothing gain !

During a stay in the country of your choice, you can go to an employment office – a Jobcentre in the United Kingdom – and consult display panels with cards on which there appear job vacancies : if one of them is suitable, give the reference number to one of the clerks, who will arrange an appointment with the employer.

You can also register your name, address, qualifications, etc., as well as the kind of job that you would like, and you will be contacted as soon as there is a vacancy.

Jobcentres are run by the State. You can also go to private employment agencies : they do not charge job-seekers for registering with them, the employer pays a fee if the job is taken. As from January 1993 Jobcentres and private agencies will probably run a regular international department for job vacancies abroad.

■ Advertisements for jobs : job ads (colloquial).

National, and sometimes local newspapers, already publish advertisements of that type – most often in a foreign language – in their " Situations Vacant " columns, and this practice will undoubtedly develop.

a) Some advertisements ask interested people, applicants or candidates, to telephone :
   - Please telephone John Smith on 01 842 4481 between 9.30 am and 6 pm.
   - Call Abigail on…
   - Kindly telephone…
   - Please ring Victoria…
   - Call in confidence Rebecca X on…
   - For an immediate, confidential discussion, call me Mildred…
   - If you would like further information (details), call in strictest confidence during normal office hours…
   - No telephone inquiries please… Apply in person on Tuesday…
   - Telephone : (Tel :)…
   - Please contact Lisa on…
   - Call N°… (24 hour ansaphone)
   - Phone me…

b) Most often applicants (candidates) are invited to write :
   - Interested applicants should send a full CV to…
   - Please send your CV in confidence to… Ref. …
   - Please send adequate particulars in confidence quoting Ref… to…
   - Applications to …
   - Send a full CV to …
   - If you would like to apply please write with full CV to …
   - Forward a comprehensive Curriculum Vitae to …
   - Further particulars and application forms are obtainable from…
   - Candidates of either sex…
   - Applicants, male or female …
   - Completed application forms should be returned by …
   - A job description and application form can be obtained from…
   - All replies will be aknowledged and dealt with in total confidence …
   - Please apply with CV and names of two referees to …
   - Closing day for applications is …
   - Closing day for receipt of applications is …

c) A few phrases to answer an advertisement :
   - I am interested in your advertisement in yesterday's issue of…
   - I have just seen your advertisement for the above vacancy …
   - In reply to your advertisement… could you please send me further details about this vacancy, together with an application form …
   - I wish to apply for the post of … as advertised in …
   - I would like to apply for the job of … advertised in …
   - Attached (= enclosed) please find a full CV
   - You have advertised a vacancy in… for an executive secretary, and I would be most grateful if you could forward me an application form …, etc.

d) Curriculum Vitae :

CURRICULUM VITAE (CV)

(US : Personal record = data sheet = *résumé*)

Family name (= surname)

First names (= forenames)

Address :

Telephone number :

Date of birth : Place of birth :

Nationality :

Marital status : single, married, children ? If any, number, dates of birth

Education : 1) Schools, University, dates of entering and leaving
2) Diplomas or degrees
3) Special qualifications : languages, shorthand, stays abroad, driving licence, etc.

Armed forces service : place and dates – Rank – Branch of service

Hobbies and other interests : music, data processing, stamp collection, etc.

Experience (Track record) :
1) Training periods, training courses. Dates, place, address, etc.
2) Successive jobs : company, address, dates, etc.

Referees : People who can testify to your qualifications, character, etc. Names, addresses, etc.

Testimonials (References) : enclosed photocopies of reports from referees

Photograph Date :

Signed :

(to be continued)

TEST YOUR KNOWLEDGE

1 - What is a sole trader ?

2 - What is the difference between a general partnership and a limited partnership ?

3 - What are the three main features of joint-stock companies ?

4 - What is the difference between a share and a debenture ?

5 - What is the difference between a (private) limited company and a public limited company ?

6 - How can firms raise funds in order to expand ?

7 - What is a takeover bid ?

8 - What are the pros and cons of multinationals ?

9 - Is the expansion of firms desirable ?

10 - Draw up your own curriculum vitae.

100 – TO OVERHEAR – HEARD – HEARD

surprendre (conversation, etc.)
– Our correspondent then overheard the President saying to the Ambassador that he was not averse to (opposed to) subsidizing (mais : loth : loath to subsidize) exports in order to absorb (mop up – soak up – sop up) agro-food surpluses : he had his scoop !
Notre correspondant surprit alors le Président en train de dire à l'Ambassadeur qu'il n'était pas hostile (opposé) au fait de subventionner les exportations afin de résorber les excédents agro-alimentaires : il tenait son article à sensation !

101 – TO OVERRIDE – RODE – RIDDEN

■ to trample underfoot : *fouler au pieds* ; to act counter to : *agir à l'encontre de* ; to refuse to comply with : *refuser de se plier à* ; to disregard – to ignore – not to pay attention to – not to heed : *méconnaître*
– A member state of the EEC cannot override with impunity the decisions of the European Court of Justice.
Un état membre de la CEE ne peut impunément passer outre aux (agir à l'encontre des) décisions de la Cour de Justice Européenne.
– Trade unions do not unreservedly approve of co-management (workers' participation : co-determination) ; they apprehend the Management's overriding the workers' wishes.
Les syndicats n'approuvent pas la co-gestion (la participation) sans réserve ; ils redoutent que la Direction ne tienne aucun compte des vœux des travailleurs.
■ to prevail over : *prévaloir sur* ; to get (gain) the better of – to get (gain) the upper hand of : *l'emporter sur.*
– It is sometimes normal that the interest of the State should override that of private citizens.
Il est parfois normal que l'intérêt de l'État l'emporte sur celui de simples citoyens.
– In the end, his viewpoint overrode that of his workmates : they would resume work the next morning.
Finalement son point de vue l'emporta sur celui de ses compagnons de travail : ils reprendraient le travail le lendeman matin.
■ **Adjectif :** overriding : *primordial, absolu, qui l'emporte sur toute autre chose.*
– Those are overriding considerations !
Ces considérations l'emportent sur toutes les autres !
– The new five-year plan comprises three overriding priorities.
Le nouveau plan quinquennal comprend trois priorités absolues.
– The overriding problem is to find the means of reviving an economy that a fifteen years' war has turned into a shambles !
Le problème primordial est de trouver le moyen de faire renaître une économie qu'une guerre de quinze ans a complètement dévastée (mise en ruines).
NB : " to overrule " a un sens proche de celui de " to override ", mais implique qu'une décision est prise en vertu d'un pouvoir, d'une autorité, d'un mandat supérieurs.
– The Court of Appeal can overrule a judgment passed by a court of law.
La Cour d'Appel peut casser (annuler) un jugement rendu par un tribunal.
– Of course, the Chairman will balk at (jib at – shy away from – shrink from) endorsing the majority's choice, but he is not empowered to overrule the Board's decisions ! He has not the right of veto.
Bien sûr, le Président répugnera à accepter le choix de la majorité, mais il n'est pas habilité à l'annuler. Il n'a pas le droit de veto.
– A veto is ruled out !
Un veto est exclu !

102 – TO OVERRUN – OVERRAN –OVERRUN

■ *Envahir*
– If we fail to stem the tide (the flow) of illegal immigration, this country will soon be overrun with (invaded by) hordes of desperate foreign job-hunters (job-seekers).
Si nous ne réussissons pas à endiguer le flot des immigrants clandestins, notre pays sera vite envahi par des hordes d'étrangers désespérés à la recherche d'un emploi.
■ *Dépasser :* to exceed, to go beyond (a limit)
– In those sweatshops, the boss used to deduct a " fine " from workers' meagre wages whenever they overran the time allotted to them to do their task.
Dans ces ateliers à main d'œuvre exploitée, le patron défalquait « une amende » du maigre salaire des ouvriers chaque fois qu'ils dépassaient le temps qui leur était imparti pour accomplir leur tâche.

Substantif : – The estimate states a maximum outlay of 15 millio**n** dollars, and no provision has been made for a possible overrun ! Who is going to foot the bill ?
Le devis fait état d'un débours de 15 millions de dollars et on n'a pas prévu de dépassement éventuel ! Qui va régler la note ? (payer l'addition ?)

Mots proches : – Without chemical weed-killers, fields would be overgrown with weeds.
Sans désherbants chimiques, les champs seraient envahis (= recouverts) par les mauvaises herbes.
– Sewers swarm with rats (= teem with ; are alive with).
Les égouts sont envahis par les rats (= grouillent de).
– In Frebruary, holiday-makers flock to (= throng to) winter-sports resorts.
En février, les stations de sports d'hiver sont envahies par les vacanciers (= ils affluent dans).
– We are swamped with orders : we have a three months' backlog of unfilled orders to catch up with !
Nous sommes envahis par (= submergés par) les commandes : nous devons rattraper un retard (un arriéré) de trois mois de commandes non honorées.

103 – TO OVERSEE – OVERSAW – OVERSEEN

to superintend, to control :
exercer son autorité sur, superviser
– The I.M.F. (International Monetary Fund) oversees world finance.
Le F.M.I. (Fonds Monétaire International) exerce son autorité sur la finance mondiale.

Substantifs : An overseer – a foreman : *un contremaître.*
– The Central Bank has intervened (to interven**e**) too late to support (to shore up, to prop up, to bolster, to buttress) our flagging currency.
La Banque Centrale est intervenue trop tard pour soutenir (consolider, renforcer) notre monnaie défaillante.
– In the wake of that unfortunate oversight, the tanker fell foul of a reef...
A la suite de cette malencontreuse inadvertance, le pétrolier heurta un récif...

104 – TO OVERSHOOT – OVERSHOT – OVERSHOT

aller au delà du but fixé
(≠ to undershoot)
– " Long-haul liner overshoots runway : hundreds of casualties " (Newspaper headline).
« Un avion de ligne long-courrier atterrit trop long (franchit la limite de la piste) : des centaines de victimes » (gros titre de journal).
– In the last **financial** year, public expenditure overshot the Government's targets by 3 %, but at the same time, the development plan undershot its targets by 6 %.
Lors du dernier exercice financier (budgétaire) les dépenses publiques ont dépassé de 3 % les objectifs du Gouvernement mais parallèlement le plan de développement est resté de 6 % en deçà de ses objectifs.
– The Japanese had agreed to restrain their exports to the EEC, but they keep overshooting the proposed quotas.
Les Japonais avaient accepté de limiter leurs exportations à destination de la Communauté Économique Européenne mais ils ne cessent de dépasser les quotas proposés.
– Public sector borrowing will overshoot in the current financial year !
Les emprunts du secteur public seront plus importants que prévus au cours du présent exercice bugétaire.
– There are signs of growth undershooting the target (= falling short of the target) set in the five year plan.
Il semble bien que la croissance n'atteindra pas l'objectif fixé dans le plan quinquennal.

PRONOMS DIVERS (suite)

9 – RELATIFS

a) Personnes : who, whom, whose.
b) Animaux et choses : which.
c) **That** relatif :

■ Quand l'antécédent est mixte.
– The furniture, the animals and the people **that** were in the building were all burnt to ashes (*cendres*).
■ Après un superlatif.
– She is the most glamorous actress **that** ever played in a film.
■ Souvent après " first, last, all, only ".
– He is the only chap **that** can do it : *c'est le seul gars qui sache le faire.*
– I have read all the books **that** dealt wih this question.
– He is probably the last man that saw her alive.
– He broke all that was in the room.

d) Dont :

■ **Exprimant un rapport de possession** : " whose " **jamais** suivi de l'article.
– The police are looking for the pilot whose plane crashed last night.
– She is a woman whose qualities everybody admires.
– The pig is an animal whose tail looks like a corkscrew (*un tire-bouchon*).
– I've thrown away the chair whose leg I broke yesterday.
■ **Sans rapport de possession** : dans une phrase comme " la viande dont il se nourrit " dont signifie de laquelle. Mais " de " se traduit différemment selon les verbes anglais : to live on, to talk about, to be afraid of, to be surprised at, to look after, to be in love with, to laugh at, to part with, to boast of, to feed on, to suffer from, etc.
Sans rapport de possession " dont " se traduira donc par la préposition que gouverne le verbe + le pronom relatif convenable.
– The exploits of which he is always boasting... *dont il se vante...*
– The food on which he lives.
– The ghost of which they are afraid.
– The girl about whom they were talking.
– The children after whom I look – of whom I take care : *dont je m'occupe.*
NB. La suppression du pronom relatif complément est toujours possible, **avec rejet de la préposition** :
– The food he lives on.
– The girl they were talking about.
■ **Attention !** avec certains verbes **transitifs** anglais :
To witness : *être témoin de* : the accident (that) I witnessed.
To remember : *se souvenir de* : the event (that) I remember.
To use : *se servir de* : the pen (that) I use.
To need : give me the money (that) I need.
To approach : the coast (that) we are approaching...
To enjoy : the reputation (that) he enjoys...
To evince : *faire preuve de* : the courage you evinced yesterday is extraordinary.

10 – " LE "

Se traduit par " so " après : to think, to believe, to suppose, to expect, to hope, to fear.
– " Is that girl of age ? " – " I think so " (≠ I don't think so).

THÈME D'APPLICATION NUMÉRO 16

Exprimer tous les pronoms

1 - C'est le premier journaliste qui ait surpris le Président en train de dire qu'il n'était pas hostile (3 traductions) au fait de subventionner les exportations !
2 - Nous ferons tout ce que nous pouvons pour résorber (4 traductions) les excédents agro-alimentaires !
3 - Nous avons besoin de désherbants chimiques pour éliminer les mauvaises herbes dont nos champs sont envahis.
4 - " Croyez-vous que les Japonais dépasseront les quotas proposés ? " " Je le crains ! "
5 - C'est le seul moyen que nous possédions pour soutenir (5 traductions) notre monnaie défaillante !
6 - Dans ces ateliers à main-d'œuvre exploitée, que restait-il du salaire dont le patron défalquait une amende ?
7 - Le problème primordial est de faire renaître un pays dont une guerre de 15 ans a complètement dévasté l'économie.
8 - Ils répugnent à (3 traductions) accepter le flot des immigrants clandestins à la recherche d'un emploi dont notre pays est envahi (différent de phrase 3).
9 - La co-gestion forcera-t-elle les patrons à satisfaire les vœux des ouvriers dont ils ne tiennent aucun compte jusqu'à présent ?
10 - " Quel était le tribunal dont la Cour d'Appel a annulé le jugement hier ? " " Celui, bien sûr, dont les journaux parlent depuis des semaines ! "
11- A quoi sert un devis dont le dépassement pourrait se chiffrer à deux millions de dollars ? Celui qui devra régler la note exige des chiffres précis !
12 - C'est le seul pays qui leur ait donné les produits chimiques dont ils avaient besoin pour tuer les rats dont grouillaient leurs égouts.
13 - " Les Japonais dépasseront-ils les quotas proposés cette année ? " " Je le suppose ! La duplicité dont ils font preuve est exaspérante ! "
14 - Comment le pétrolier a-t-il pu heurter les récifs dont il approchait malgré le système radar dont il était pourvu ? (to equip sb. with st.)
15 - Qui nous aidera à exécuter (to fulfil) les commandes dont nous sommes submergés à présent ?

17 - COMMUNICATIONS

Parties and equipment concerned (Deuxième partie)

THE COMPANY : AN ORGANIZATION CHART (ORGANIGRAMME)

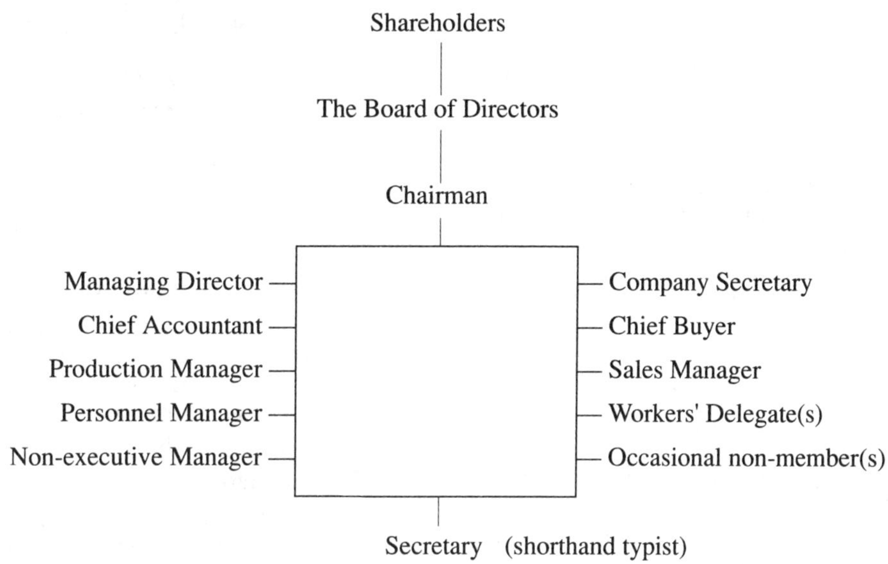

THE SHAREHOLDERS

The shareholders, or more precisely those who hold ordinary shares, elect the Board of Directors at the Annual General Meeting. Every year, at the AGM, they are apprised of the dividend that they will get, of the company's performance over the previous fiscal year (*l'exercice précédent*), and they are given the balance sheet (*le bilan*).

THE DIRECTORS

The Directors elect one of their number as Chairman (US : President), and another as Managing Director (*Directeur Général* ; US : CEO = Chief Executive Officer). Sometimes, one and the same person acts simultaneously as Chairman and Managing Director. He/she is then called Chairman and Managing Director (*Président Directeur Général : PDG*).

The Directors lay down the policy of the company. **Executive** Directors work full-time in the company, and are responsible for carrying out that policy : they are the Managers (the Heads) of the main departments. **Non-executive** Directors (*les Administrateurs*) simply attend Board meetings ; they are Advisors who give legal, financial or technical advice, but take no active part in management. Directors also elect the other officers (executives) of the company (*les autres cadres supérieurs de la société*).

THE MANAGING DIRECTOR

The Managing Director runs the firm : he/she sees to it that all the decisions taken at Board meetings are implemented.

THE COMPANY SECRETARY (*LE SECRÉTAIRE GÉNÉRAL*)

- He/she makes sure that all the operations of the company are conducted in accordance with the law.
- He/she is responsible for recording the proceedings (the minutes) of all Board meetings, which are kept in the Minute Book (*le Registre des délibérations, ou des procès-verbaux*).
- He/she is the link between the company and the shareholders.

- He/she also keeps a record of all the company's financial transactions.
- He/she may be in charge of insurance and security matters.
- In large firms, he/she may very well have overall responsibility for the inward and outward mail, the reception and telephone services, the computer department, the typing pool, the reprography and filing departments, etc.

The Chief Accountant (The Financial Director ; US : the Comptroller or Controller)

He/she is by definition in charge of the Company's accounts. Every year, the shareholders appoint an Auditor (*un Commissaire aux comptes*) who is not an officer of the company and who audits (*vérifie et certifie*) the accounts ; the balance sheet can then be drawn up and sent to the Shareholders together with the Auditor's report on the company's financial position.

The Chief Buyer (Head Buyer = Purchasing Officer)

- He/she buys all that the company needs to operate efficiently.
  1. Raw materials and component parts for the production department (the factory).
  2. Machinery.
  3. Office furniture and equipment.
  4. Stationery.
  5. Food for the staff canteen, etc.
- He/she is in charge of stock control (US : inventory management) i.e, he/she regularly determines the quantities of raw materials, components, work(s) in progress (the goods that are being processed), and finished goods that are to be found in the firm, and ascertains that they are held at the optimum level : if the firm runs short of supplies, its output is bound to plunge ; on the other hand, idle stock proves expensive.

The Production Manager = the Works Manager (*Le Directeur de la Production*)

He/she is by definition in charge of the Production Department, or in other words, of the factory which manufactures the goods that are subsequently sold through the agency of the Sales Department, whose head is obviously :

The Sales Director (Manager) : (*Le Directeur des Ventes*)

He/she heads up the Export, the Home Sales, the Marketing, and the After-Sales Departments, and is a key officer in the firm since the latter's life hinges upon the volume of goods that he/she and his/her collaborators manage to sell, at home and/or abroad : they combine their efforts so that the firm may always have a full order book, and work consequently at full capacity.

The Personnel Director (Manager, Officer) US : the Human Resources Manager

He/she is entrusted with tasks of paramount importance :

- He/she takes on (hires, recruits) the workers - of all categories - that the firm needs, after advertising vacancies for jobs, screening the applicants, and shortlisting those with suitable qualifications.
- He/she ensures the promotion of employees through training and further education (sandwich courses, work-study programmes), or makes it easier for those who have been laid off or transferred to adapt themselves to another job thanks to retraining courses.
- He/she is entrusted :
  1. With the unpleasant task of dismissing thoroughly incompetent employees, or those who are guilty of serious misconduct or negligence.
  2. With the no less unpleasant task of laying off such employees as have been made redundant in the wake of technological or economic upheavals (automation, mergers, takeovers, etc.).
- He/she is responsible for employees' safety, health and welfare.
- He/she endeavours to promote good industrial relations (labour relations) within the firm, based on collective bargaining, collective agreements, labour contract policies between Management and Trade Unions' representatives (shop-stewards).
- He/she writes testimonials for the employees who leave the firm and apply for a position elsewhere.
- He/she also takes charge of the employees who retire, of those who are dissatisfied and hand in (tender) their resignation.
- He/she tries to settle amicably all the disputes that cannot fail to arise about wages, working conditions, unfair treatment, etc., which requires from him/her a wealth of psychology and diplomacy.

Occasional non-members

They may be officers who have not board status, but must be consulted on one or several items of the agenda : they are the Heads of the Transport, the Research and Development, the Computer Departments, the Home Sales, the Export, the Warehouse Managers, etc.

Workers' delegates

Workers are no longer excluded from the decision-making ; their delegate(s) take(s) part on their behalf in the management of the firm within the framework of a policy intended to do away with the cleavage between Management and Labour, and which is called : workers' participation or employee participation, co-determination, co-management, or industrial democracy.

The secretary

She is a shorthand typist, or a stenotypist, in charge of taking down the minutes of the Board meeting, i.e, of making a record of all the decisions that have been reached at the meeting.

The topics which are to be discussed appear on the agenda (*l'ordre du jour, le programme*). It is nearly always set out as follows :

Agenda

1. Apologies for absence.
2. Minutes of previous (last) meeting.
3. Matters arising (*questions en suspens*) : issues that were raised during the previous meeting about which no agreement was reached.
4. Item
5. Item *questions à l'ordre du jour.*
6. Item
7. Any other business (*autre problème, autre question).*
8. Date, time, venue (*endroit*) of next meeting.

The minutes will follow the order of items on the agenda :

Minutes

1. Apologies for absence : a proxy (*un mandataire*) may represent the person who cannot attend the meeting.
2. Minutes of previous (last) meeting.

   They are supposed to be read, approved and signed there and then. To save time, as they have often been sent previously to all members of the Board, they are often " taken as read ". The Chairman will say for instance : " I move that the minutes of the last meeting be taken as read " (" *Je propose que nous passions directement à l'ordre du jour* "), and he signs them if everybody approves.
3. Matters arising : resolution adopted (carried = passed) this time.

4., 5., 6., Items : resolution carried for each one of them.

7. Any other business : resolution if any.
8. Date, time, venue of next meeting.

OFFICE EQUIPMENT TECHNOLOGY = OFFICE AUTOMATION : LA BUREAUTIQUE

A large part of a firm's activity consists in dealing with information and instructions, whether outward - or inward - bound, handled or exchanged within the firm.

For a long time, firms had to make do only with the post and the telephone to despatch and receive both information and instructions, and on the office-boy as an internal means of communication ! Much of the clerical work used to be done by hand, or with the help of manual calculators and typewriters.

The latter are doomed to become nothing more than museum pieces : thanks to the astounding breakthroughs achieved in electronics these last twenty years, firms now have at their disposal an impressive range of equipment which makes clerical work easier, less time-consuming, and consequently cheaper.

Computers and data processing (*l'informatique*)

The first big electronic computer was built in 1946. Its name was " ENIAC ", which stood for " Electronic Numerical Integrator and Calculator ". It was so bulky that it filled a huge room ! Then, American scientists at Bells Laboratories invented the transistor, a tiny piece of semi-conducting material (silicon or germanium) which was to spark off a genuine revolution, especially when other researchers at Intel Corp. managed to integrate thousands of transistors on a chip, thus creating the microprocessor chip, or microprocessor for short.

Though half the size of a fingernail, the microprocessor is much more powerful than ENIAC, and far cheaper too ! If the car industry had evolved as quickly, it would now produce luxurious limousines at roughly a hundred dollars each (= apiece) !

NB. Do not mistake one word for another :

- **silicon :** le silicium. Cf. " Silicon Valley " in California where high-technology firms sprouted up like mushrooms a few years ago.
- **silicone :** la silicone. Cf. the coating of non-stick frying pans.
- **silica :** la silice. It is a kind of sand which is used, for instance, for making glass.

There are different types of computers :

- Mainframes (*les ordinateurs centraux, les unités centrales*)
- Minicomputers (*les mini-ordinateurs*) which take up less space, and are to be found in a good many offices.
- Microcomputers (*les micro-ordinateurs*) or desk-top computers (*ordinateurs de table*) or home computers (*ordinateurs familiaux*) which are even smaller and are used in the office or at home.
- Portable computers that businessmen can take along with them on their business trips.

The conventional name for the machine itself is the hardware, (*le matériel*), whereas the programmes that are fed into it are the software (*les logiciels*).

Computers can be linked (connected) to others within or outside the firm through an adapter called " modem " - for " modulator-demodulator " - and the telephone network. A new umbrella term has been coined for the new technology resulting from the fusion of data processing and telecommunications : communication technology (*la télématique*). Information and messages can thus be transmitted by electronic mail (*courrier électronique*) from one computer terminal to another.

This possibility has given rise to " telecommuting (*le télé-travail*), i.e, doing one's work at home and not on the firm's premises. To keep in touch with the firm, or with its customers or suppliers, the only requisite for the " telecommuter " (*le télé-travailleur ; parfois : le télénavetteur*) is a workstation : a desk, a computer terminal, a printer (*une imprimante*), a modem and a telephone line. " Telecommuting " is the modern version of cottage industry, so much so that " telecommuters' " homes have been humorously referred to as " electronic cottages ! ". After " flexitime " a few years ago, working at " flexiplaces " is now much praised !

- The concept offers obvious advantages :
  1. Employees save money since they no longer commute to their offices, no longer have to buy car park tickets, or pay heavy fines for exceeding the time limit. They no longer need to be dressed up to the nines, and they economize as well on lunches, snacks and coffee from vending machines ! They do away with the stress and strain of rush hours, of traffic jams, of work under pressure, with the fear of being late, with the impression of being watched all the time by a demanding employer, like " Big Brother " in George Orwell's novel, " 1984 ". They now work at the time and at the pace of their choice. Mothers can look after their children, or see to it that the casserole is simmering on the cooker, or that the milk does not boil over.
  2. Employers economize on real estate expenses as they no longer need so much office space usually in or near town centres, and the price of computers and other items of hardware, such as printers, is becoming lower everyday. Moreover, and it is borne out by statistics, " telecommuting " tends to increase employees' productivity.
- These advantages are counterbalanced by a good many drawbacks :
  1. Employees are apt to suffer from loneliness : they miss human contacts. Besides, life at home is not always a bed of roses ! It also has its seamy side, and difficulties may arise with which it is sometimes difficult to cope. Tackling two tasks at a time can be detrimental to one or to the other, or to both ! There are also times when the atmosphere in the family is so heavy that the possibility of commuting again would be most welcome to recover some serenity. Employees are also afraid of being shunted to one side as regards promotion. Trade Unions agree with them on that point, and even suspect some employers of exploiting telecommuters, of trying to turn the electronic cottage into an " electronic sweatshop ! "
  2. Employers apprehend losing control over their employees, and legal problems crop up as regards industrial injuries : should an employee slip on the way from the kitchen to his/her workstation, and break his/her arm, or wrist, in which capacity will he/she claim for injury benefits and time off, as an employee or as a private individual ?

" Telecommuting " was heralded as a revolutionary work concept that was to bring about sweeping changes in the world of labour. It is undeniably making headway, but slowly as yet. It is probably due to the disadvantages that it presents, and to the reorganization that it entails.

What can be asked of a computer ? It can be programmed to perform at least the following functions :

- Calculate the salaries and wages of workers on the payroll (*le registre du personnel*), print out payslips (*bulletins, feuilles de paie*) and credit transfer slips (*avis de virement*).

- Keep the accounts of :
  – the Purchasing Department
  – the Sales Department
  – The Costing Department, in charge of calculating manufacturing costs and selling prices (*prix de revient et de vente*), etc.
- Control stocks. Cf. tome 2 : the Kanban inventory system = the Kanban method or the Just-in-time method (JIT) : *la gestion optimisée des stocks = la méthode du " juste-à-temps "*.
- Control Production through CAD/CAM = Computer aided design and Computer aided manufacturing : *la Conception assistée par ordinateur (CAO) et la Fabrication assistée par ordinateur (FAO)*. Cf. tome 2.

  " Kanban " and " CAD/CAM " are key elements of production technology (*la productique*).

Advantages and Drawbacks.

Computers save irksome labour, chiefly handwritten clerical work. They speed up the above-mentioned operations, and their calculations and projections are more accurate. They keep Management posted about all the particulars relating to the firm's life that are essential to ensure its smooth running.

More and more small-and-medium-sized concerns can afford to invest in such sophisticated equipment, as new breakthroughs in electronics, standardization, mass-production and competition concur to nibble at prices.

On the other hand, switching over to computerization leads up to an inevitable shake-up that may last for a great many months. Part of the staff must be trained or re-trained, not without grumblings as people loathe having to change their habits ; older employees who are soon to retire, or who would find it difficult to adapt themselves to those newfangled contraptions are apt to feel rejected, and are indeed the casualties of progress.

Furthermore, video-display terminals (VDTs) are reputedly not quite safe for full-time operators : they are said to impair vision, cause headaches and migraines, stiff necks and backs, and worse, miscarriages and birth defects. In any case, this has not yet been proved scientifically, and manufacturers do their utmost to make VDTs absolutely safe by shielding their devices against the leakage of radiation.

The Word Processor
(*la machine de traitement de texte*)

Manual typewriters are little by little yielding ground to the electric, the electronic, the memory typewriters, and to the most sophisticated, high-performance machine of them all, the Word Processor (WP). Text composition and editing (*la retouche, la correction*) are fast and simple on WPs : keyboards are standard, and just have a few extra " command " keys. The typist sees what she is typing on a visual display unit (*une console de visualisation, un visuel*), or screen for short. She edits the text when necessary, i.e, she deletes or adds a letter, puts in the required punctuation marks, changes the order of paragraphs or the layout of the text. When everything seems satisfactory, she pushes on the right keys for the text to be either printed or stored, or both.

Texts are stored (*mis en mémoire*) on floppy disks (*disquettes*), retrieved (*recherchés et extraits*), edited and printed at will.

The telephone (see chapter 18) ;
the intercom ; paging devices

All modern offices are fitted out with a telephone receiver for receiving or making external or internal calls. They may also be equipped with an intercom (*un interphone*), usually of the type with a built-in loudspeaker ; it is very common for communications between company officers and their secretaries.

As important people are not always in their offices, although somewhere in the firm, and as it is sometimes urgent to get in touch with them, they have on them a pocket pager, i.e, a small radio receiver. When it buzzes or bleeps, they go to the nearest telephone, or come back to their offices. That device is also called a bleeper (*un bip*).

Telex (see Chapter 18) and Fax
= the facsimile machine

This machine - no bigger than a typewriter - uses an optical scanner which " reads " all that appears on a document, and transforms it into electrical signals that can be transmitted over a telephone line. Another Fax machine at the other end of the line gives a faithful reproduction of the original, whether it is a text, a picture, a graph, a list of figures, etc. It is faster than a telex, and cheaper to run. Numerous firms now give their Fax number close to their Telephone and Telex numbers. " Fax " has become a noun and a verb. You can send " a fax " - for " facsimile copy " - to London, or " you fax " documents to New York ! Like a telex message, a fax is also proof positive (*est une preuve formelle*).

Videotex (Viewdata system)

In France, printed telephone directories have been replaced by low-cost terminals linked to central data banks : " Minitels ", or " Stand-alone Teletel videotex terminals ". Subscribers can not only obtain telephone numbers through their " Minitels ", they can also obtain information from any data bank on any subject.

The French system, " Teletel ", rivals the British " Prestel " system, but the latter's terminals are costly, and a good many subscribers prefer to use modified TV sets. The Netherlands and Australia have also adopted the " Prestel " system. As for the United States, Videotex is only just taking off.

Firms often use one or several Videotex terminals to obtain stock-market, or commodity market quotations, air-line time-tables, etc.

OTHER EQUIPMENT

- Duplicating machines : spirit duplicators, ink duplicators, and offset-litho duplicators are little by little being replaced by photocopiers.
- Mail-opening machines, time and date stamping machines, collating machines, folding machines, addressing machines, envelope sealing machines, franking machines.

  Most of these machines can be integrated into one single system (*ensemble ou système de façonnage*) which collates sheets, i.e, arranges them in order, inserts them into envelopes, seals the envelopes, stamps and counts them.

TEST YOUR KNOWLEDGE

1 - WHICH FUNCTION DOES THE COMPANY SECRETARY PERFORM WITHIN THE FIRM ?

2 - WHY ARE THE TASKS ENTRUSTED TO THE PERSONNEL DIRECTOR OF PARAMOUNT IMPORTANCE ?

3 - WHAT IS " CO-MANAGEMENT " ?

4 - WHAT IS " TELECOMMUTING " ?

5 - WHAT ARE THE ADVANTAGES OF " TELECOMMUTING " FOR EMPLOYEES ?

6 - WHAT CAN BE ASKED OF A COMPUTER IN A FIRM ?

7 - WHAT ARE THE DRAWBACKS OF COMPUTERIZATION ?

8 - WHAT IS A POCKET PAGER ? WHAT IS IT USED FOR ?

9 - WHAT IS A FACSIMILE MACHINE ?

10 - COMPARE THE RESPECTIVE ADVANTAGES OF A FAX AND A TELEX

105 – TO OVERTAKE – OVERTOOK – OVERTAKEN

Gagner de vitesse ; surprendre
– " No overtaking ! " (Roadsign)
" Défense de doubler ! " (Panneau de signalisation).
– It is said in the highway code that you are not to overtake on a level-crossing, on a bridge or at crossroads ; if they catch you in the act, the police will book you !
Il est dit dans le code de la route qu'on ne doit pas dépasser sur un passage à niveau, sur un pont ou aux carrefours ; si la police vous prend sur le fait, elle vous dressera une contravention (to book sb. **for** doing st.).
– The typhoon overtook the trawlers as they were heading for the harbour : the raging ocean was to take a heavy toll among the seamen !
Le typhon surprit les chalutiers alors qu'ils faisaient route vers le port : l'océan déchaîné devait faire beaucoup de victimes parmi les marins.
– The authorities are overtaken by events.
Les autorités sont dépassées par les événements.

106 – TO OVERTHROW – OVERTHREW – OVERTHROWN

renverser (figuré)
– The aim of those protracted strikes, those tumultuous demonstrations, and those violent riots is to overthrow the Government, and destabilize the country politically.
Le but de ces grèves prolongées, de ces manifestations houleuses et de ces violentes émeutes est de renverser le Gouvernement et de déstabiliser politiquement le pays.
– Physicists, chemists, biologists keep constructing new theories which overthrow such as were hitherto accepted.
Les physiciens, les chimistes, les biologistes ne cessent d'échafauder de nouvelles théories qui renversent celles qui étaient jusqu'ici admises.
NB. *" Renverser "* au sens propre cf. to spill – to upset

107 – TO PAY – PAID – PAID

■ *Payer, régler*
– You can pay in cash (in specie) or by cheque, so long as you settle (pay) your debts once and for all !
Vous pouvez payer en espèces ou par chèque, du moment que vous réglez vos dettes une fois pour toutes !
– You pay your due**s** to a trade union, your subscriptio**n** to a club and your contribution**s** to Social Security.
On paie sa cotisation à un syndicat, sa cotisation à un club et sa cotisation à la Sécurité Sociale.

Mots proches :
I want to settle up (to square up) with you before I leave the country.
Je veux régler mes comptes avec vous (payer mes dettes envers vous) avant que je ne quitte le pays.

Attention à la construction !
– How much did you pay **for** that hand-woven rug ?
Combien avez-vous payé cette carpette tissée à la main ?

Au figuré :
– France will have to pay one day or other for its lack of competitiveness in high tech(nology) industries (microelectronics, genetic engineering, robotics).
La France devra payer un jour ou l'autre son manque de compétitivité dans les industries de pointe (= la micro-électronique, le génie génétique et la robotique).
■ *Rapporter* (to be profitable)
– Drilling for oil on offshore rigs is tedious, strenuous, hazardous work, but it pays !
Le forage pétrolier sur les plateformes de forage est un travail fastidieux, ardu, dangereux, mais qui rapporte !
■ **Avec des particules**
+ **back** : *rembourser, rendre, restituer* (to restore st. to sb.)
– How can he pay back the money that he has swindled from you ? He has gambled it away !
Comment peut-il rembourser l'argent qu'il vous a escroqué ? Il l'a gaspillé au jeu !
– If you advance to me enough money to buy some seed and fertilizer, I will pay you back on the crop.
Si vous m'avancez assez d'argent pour acheter de la semence et de l'engrais, je vous rembourserai sur la récolte.
– I will pay him back in his own coin !
Je lui rendrai la monnaie de sa pièce !

Synonymes : – I will take my revenge on him – I will wreak vengeance on him :
Je me vengerai de lui.
– I will demand an eye for an eye !
J'appliquerai la loi du talion !

Autres traductions de " rembourser " : to repay, to reimburse, to refund
– Don't be so foolish as to lend him money, he would never repay you !
N'ayez pas la stupidité de lui prêter de l'argent, il ne vous rembourserait jamais ! (you would never get it back).

Au figuré : – Don't expect to be repaid for your generosity (don't expect your generosity to be requited) !
Ne vous attendez pas à ce que votre générosité soit payée de retour !
– The company reimburses me (for) all my travelling expenses.
L'entreprise me rembourse tous mes frais de voyage.
– In France, you pay for the medicines (the remedies) that you buy at the chemist's, but the National Health Service reimburses you for such medicines as appear on the doctor's prescription to a limit of (up to) 75 %. You get the remainder back if you subscribe to a Friendly Society.
En France, on paie les médicaments que l'on achète chez le pharmacien, mais la Caisse Maladie vous rembourse ceux des médicaments qui figurent sur l'ordonnance du docteur à concurrence de 75 %. Vous êtes remboursé du reste si vous appartenez à une mutuelle.
– This article is definitely defective (faulty ; there is a flaw in this article). Take it to the check-out with your receipt and you will be refunded (you will get a refund), unless you want to exchange it (**for** another one, **for** another model).
Cet article est vraiment défectueux (il y a un défaut dans cet article ; pour les pierres précieuses, a flaw *: un crapaud). Portez-le à la caisse avec votre reçu (votre ticket de caisse) et vous serez remboursé, à moins que vous ne vouliez l'échanger (**contre** un autre, **contre** un autre modèle).*
\+ **down** : *payer comptant, verser tout de suite* (to pay cash rightaway)
donner un acompte (to put down)
– They are so much interested in the patent that they offer to pay 10,000 dollars down for it.
Ce brevet les intéresse tant qu'ils offrent de verser 10.000 dollars de suite pour l'obtenir.
– You pay 10 % down now, and settle the balance over three months.
Vous versez maintenant 10 % d'acompte et vous réglez le solde en 3 mois.
\+ **for** :
– They reckon that a wind turbine on the island ought to be able to pay for itself in five years.
Ils estiment qu'un aérogénérateur sur l'île devrait pouvoir être amorti en 5 ans (que son seuil de rentabilité serait atteint en 5 ans – that it would reach break-even point in five years).

17 - STRUCTURES

SUBJONCTIF " FOSSILE "

PRÉSENT

1 – Verbe to be : be à toutes les personnes.

2 – Autres verbes : indicatif présent mais sans " s " à la troisième personne du singulier.

Emploi : le subjonctif présent ne s'emploie guère que dans des souhaits, des locutions toutes faites, la langue littéraire.

– God (Heaven) be praised ! *Dieu (le Ciel) soit loué !*
– Mathematics be hanged ! *Au diable les mathématiques !*
– Be that as it may. *Quoi qu'il en soit.*
– God bles**s** you. *Dieu vous bénisse.*
– God sav**e** the Queen. *Que Dieu protège la Reine.*
– Long live the Emperor ! *Vive l'Empereur ! etc.*

PASSÉ

1 – Verbe to be : were à toutes les personnes.

2 – Autres verbes : prétérit de l'indicatif. On l'appelle " prétérit modal " car on utilise un temps (prétérit) en guise de mode (subjonctif).

Emploi : le subjonctif passé est encore assez souvent employé et particulièrement dans les cas suivants :

1 – Après if : If I were a rich man. *Si j'étais un homme riche...*
– If there were no sun, nothing would live on earth !
S'il n'y avait pas de soleil, rien ne vivrait sur terre !

2 – Après as if (as though)
– He is staring at me as if I were mad !
Il me dévisage comme si j'étais fou !
– Don't treat him as though he were a child !
Ne le traite pas comme s'il était un enfant !

NB. Pour rendre l'expression : *on dirait que...* exprimant une improbabilité, traduction différente selon le sens concerné :
– It **looks** as if there were no one in the boss's office.
On dirait qu'il n'y a personne dans le bureau du patron.
– It **sounds** as if someone were playing the piano in those ruins !
On dirait que quelqu'un joue du piano dans ces ruines !
– It **smells** as if there were a rosebed right in the middle of this desert.
On dirait qu'il y a un massif de roses en plein milieu de ce désert.
– It **tastes** as if this soup were made with slops !
On dirait que cette soupe est faite avec de l'eau de vaisselle !
– It **feels** as if a snake were crawling up my leg !
On dirait qu'un serpent monte le long de ma jambe !
– It **looks** as though you did not understand !
On dirait que vous ne comprenez pas !

3 – Après it is time : *il est temps* ; it is **high** time : *il est grand temps.*
– It is time you told me the truth.
Il est temps que tu me dises la vérité.
– It is high time you stopped behaving like a child !
Il est grand temps que tu cesses de te conduire comme un enfant !

4 – Après suppose : *suppose, supposez que...*
– Suppose he were a murderer, would you marry him ?
Supposez que ce soit un criminel, l'épouseriez-vous ?

– Suppose the Third World War broke out tomorrow...
Supposez que la Troisième Guerre Mondiale éclate demain...

5 – Après I **would** rather : *j'aimerais mieux, je préfèrerais que...*
– I would rather you left me alone
J'aimerais mieux que tu me laisses seul.
– He would rather the doctor did not lie to him about his illness !
Il préfèrerait que le docteur ne lui mente pas au sujet de sa maladie !

NB. I **had** better : *je ferais mieux,* ne gouverne pas le subjonctif, mais l'infinitif sans to.
– You had better go right away !
Tu ferais mieux de partir tout de suite !

6 – Après to wish : *je voudrais,* exprimant un souhait irréalisable.
– She wishes she were the Sleeping Beauty.
Elle voudrait être la Belle au Bois Dormant.
– I wish my son listened to my advice !
Je voudrais que mon fils écoute mes conseils !

Remarque : *Je voudrais,* exprimant un souhait réalisable, se rend par le conditionnel de to like et la construction infinitive.
– She is a good pupil and she would like to be a secretary.
C'est une bonne élève et elle voudrait être secrétaire.
– He would like his wife to stay at home after they are married.
Il voudrait que sa femme reste à la maison après qu'ils seront mariés.

THÈME D'APPLICATION NUMÉRO 17

1 - Au diable le typhon ! Il a surpris les chalutiers alors qu'ils faisaient route vers le port et il devait faire beaucoup de victimes parmi les marins.
2 - Quoi qu'il en soit, je voudrais que (réalisable) vous versiez maintenant 10 % d'acompte et que vous régliez le solde en 3 mois.
3 - Le forage pétrolier sur les plateformes de forage est un travail ardu, fastidieux, dangereux, mais, Dieu soit loué, qui rapporte !
4 - " Il est grand temps qu'il rembourse l'argent qu'il m'a escroqué ! " " Comment (le) peut-il ? Il l'a gaspillé au jeu ! "
5 - Supposez que vous lui prêtiez de l'argent, il ne vous le rembourserait jamais !
6 - " On dirait que cet article est vraiment défectueux " " S'il y avait un défaut, Madame, il vous serait remboursé ou échangé ! "
7 - Les manifestations deviennent de plus en plus houleuses, les émeutes de plus en plus violentes, comme si le but de leurs organisateurs était de renverser le Gouvernement !
8 - J'aimerais mieux (pas de contraction) que vous régliez vos dettes une fois pour toutes, par chèque ou en espèces, si vous quittez le pays !
9 - Nous voudrions que la France (a : réalisable – b : irréalisable) accroisse (enhance) sa compétitivité dans les industries de pointe, sinon elle devra le payer un jour ou l'autre.
10 - " Supposez que la police me prenne sur le fait ! " – " Elle dresse une contravention à tous ceux qui doublent sur un passage à niveau ! "
11 - Comme la générosité n'est jamais payée de retour, je préfèrerais que tu te venges de lui ! Rends-lui la monnaie de sa pièce !
12 - Au diable le patron ! L'entreprise me rembourse tous mes frais de voyage mais pas ceux de (2 traductions) ma secrétaire, comme si elle était inutile !
13 - " Écoutez ! On dirait que l'aérogénérateur fonctionne ! " – " Il était grand temps que le vent se mette à souffler ! "
14 - Nous aimerions mieux que vous nous avanciez la somme maintenant ! Nous la partagerions entre nous pour acheter de la semence et de l'engrais !
15 - Je voudrais pouvoir vous aider, mais l'argent dont vous auriez eu besoin m'a été escroqué !

18 - COMMUNICATIONS

(Troisième partie)

THE TELEPHONE

GENERALITIES

– All industrialized countries are now on STD (Subscriber trunk dialling).

Tous les pays industrialisés ont maintenant l'automatique interurbain.

– Most British large towns have a (number) code which must be dialled before the susbscriber's number. For example :

Birmingham : 021	Bristol : 272
Edinburgh : 031	London : 01
Southampton : 703	Sheffield : 742

NB. Do not dial the initial 0.

La plupart des grandes villes britanniques ont un indicatif, (chiffré) que l'on doit composer avant le numéro de l'abonné : Par exemple ...

NB. *1. Ne pas composer le 0 initial*
2. L'indicatif départemental : the area code.

– Push-button telephones are now becoming more common than telephones with dials.

Les téléphones à touches deviennent maintenant plus courants que les téléphones à cadrans.

– There are several telephone sockets in modern offices : as you can plug in your telephone where you like, you can easily alter the office lay-out.

Il y a plusieurs prises téléphoniques dans les bureaux modernes : comme on peut brancher son poste où on veut, on peut facilement modifier l'agencement du bureau.

– When you do not know someone's telephone number, you can look it up in the directory (the phone book) or in your own card-index. Businesses are listed in the yellow pages of the directory (the Classified Trade Directory), according to the goods or the services that they supply.

Quand on ne connaît pas le numéro de téléphone de quelqu'un, on le cherche dans l'annuaire ou dans son fichier. On trouve la liste des entreprises dans les pages jaunes de l'annuaire (l'annuaire par professions), suivant les biens ou les services qu'elles fournissent.

– In France, an electronic telephone directory has replaced the printed version ; it is consulted through a Minitel terminal.

En France, un annuaire téléphonique électronique a remplacé la version imprimée ; on le consulte par le truchement d'un Minitel.

– All large firms have a switchboard operator. He/she receives all outside (external) or inside (internal) calls.

Toutes les grandes entreprises ont un(e) standardiste. Il/elle reçoit tous les appels de l'extérieur et de l'intérieur.

– Always have a notebook and a pen by the side of the telephone, possibly a pad of telephone message forms : you may have to take down (write down) notes or a message.

Ayez toujours un bloc-notes et un stylo près du téléphone, éventuellement un bloc de formules de message téléphonique : il se peut que vous deviez prendre des notes ou un message.

– A loudspeaking telephone will make that task easier : you will not have to hold the receiver !

Un poste à amplificateur vous facilitera la tâche : vous n'aurez pas à tenir le combiné !

– You can always switch off the loudspeaker to discourage inquisitive eavesdroppers !

On peut toujours couper le haut-parleur pour décourager les oreilles indiscrètes.

– A telephone answering machine (= an ansafone) will enable customers for instance to leave messages even after office hours.

Un répondeur permettra aux clients par exemple de laisser des messages même après les heures de bureau.

– Freefone (US toll-free) numbers enable people to obtain information free of charge : the firm foots the bill !

Les Numéros Verts permettent d'obtenir des renseignements gratuitement : c'est l'entreprise qui paie la note !

– Telephone boxes (booths – kiosks) are to be found everywhere, as well as payphones installed in stores, pubs, museums, stations, etc.

On trouve partout des cabines téléphoniques, ainsi que des téléphones publics dans les grands magasins, les cafés, les musées, les gares, etc.

– They are most useful for the public at large, for commercial travellers in particular, who thus can keep in touch with their company, when the latter cannot afford to equip their cars with a carphone.

Ils sont des plus utiles pour le public en général, pour les voyageurs de commerce (les représentants) en particulier, qui peuvent ainsi rester en contact avec leur entreprise quand cette dernière ne peut se permettre d'installer le téléphone dans leurs voitures.

– Payphones work with coins. The more modern ones – cardphones – work with prepaid, disposable cards that you can buy at post offices, tobacconists and newsagents. You slot in your car which " empties " of its units according to the length, the distance of the call, the time of day and the day of the week.

Les téléphones publics fonctionnent avec des pièces de monnaie. Les plus modernes – les téléphones à cartes – fonctionnent avec des cartes jetables payées d'avance que l'on peut acheter dans les bureaux de poste, chez les marchands de tabac et les marchands de journaux. On introduit sa carte qui " se vide " de ses unités selon la longueur et la distance de l'appel, l'heure du jour et le jour de la semaine.

– You can use an analogical alphabet to spell difficult words. Telephone operators use the following one in the Anglo-saxon world.

On peut utiliser un alphabet analogique pour épeler les mots difficiles. Les téléphonistes (standardistes) utilisent le suivant dans le monde Anglo-saxon.

A : Alfred	N : Nellie
B : Benjamin	O : Oliver
C : Charlie	P : Peter
D : David	Q : Queen
E : Edward	R : Robert
F : Frederick	S : Samuel
G : George	T : Tommy
H : Harry	U : Uncle
I : Isaac	V : Victor
J : Jack	W: William
K : King	X : X-ray
L : London	Y : Yellow
M: Mary	Z : Zebra

Example : A **for** Alfred, etc.

Exemple : A ***comme*** *Alfred, etc.*

– You can also resort to the alphabet which is used in international maritime communications, in air-traffic control, police or army communications, and which has been popularized by the cinema, the radio and television.

On peut aussi recourir à l'alphabet qui est utilisé dans les communications maritimes internationales, dans le contrôle du trafic aérien, les communications de la police ou de l'armée, et qui a été popularisé par le cinéma, la radio et la télévision :

A : Alpha	N : November
B : Bravo	O : Oscar
C : Charlie	P : Papa
D : Delta	Q : Quebec
E : Echo	R : Romeo
F : Foxtrot	S : Sierra
G : Golf	T : Tango
H : Hotel	U : Uniform
I : India	V : Victor
J : Juliet	W: Whiskey
K : Kilo	X : X-ray
L : Lima	Y : Yankee
M: Mike	Z : Zulu

MISCELLANEOUS PHRASES

■ Calling a subscriber : *Appel d'un abonné.*

– " Cork and Screw, Ltd. " Good morning (Can I help you ?)

" Cork and Screw. Ltd. " Bonjour (Vous désirez ? – J'écoute !)

– Good morning. Could you give me (put me through to) Extension 605, please ?... Could I speak to Mr Burton, please ? (Could you put me through to Mr Burton, please ?) This is Marcel Piduche (Marcel Piduche speaking).

Bonjour. Pourriez-vous me donner le Poste 605, s'il vou plaît ?... Pourrais-je parler à Mr Burton, svp ? (Pourriez-vous me passer Mr Burton, svp ?) De la part de Marcel Piduche (Marcel Piduche à l'appareil).

– Who is calling – who is speaking – who is that speaking, please ?

De la part de qui ? (qui est à l'appareil ?)

– Sorry, can you spell your name, please ?

Excusez-moi, pouvez-vous épeler votre nom, svp ?

– Hold on a moment, please (= hold the line a moment, please), I'll see if he is in.

Un instant, ne quittez pas, je vais voir s'il est là.

– Mr Burton is on (the) line, Sir.

Vous avez Mr Burton, Monsieur.

– ... Thank you, Mr Burton. Can you put me back through to the switchboard operator, please ?

Merci, Mr Burton. Pouvez-vous me repasser le standard, s'il vous plaît ?

■ Setbacks (hitches). *Incidents (contretemps)*

– Sorry, I can't hear you... Can you speak louder, please ? Can you speak more slowly, please ?... The line is very (terribly, awfully, dreadfully) bad !

Excusez-moi, je ne vous entends pas... Pouvez-vous

parler plus fort, s'il vous plaît ?... Pouvez-vous parler plus lentement, svp ?... La ligne est très (terriblement) mauvaise !

– Sorry, the private (direct) line with our factory is out of order.

Je regrette, la ligne directe avec notre usine est en dérangement.

– Whom are you calling, please ?... What number are you calling, please ?... You must have dialled the wrong number !... Don't mention it !

Qui appelez-vous, s'il vous plaît ?... Quel numéro voulez-vous, svp ?... Vous avez dû faire une erreur ! - ...Je vous en prie !

– Sorry, Madam, nobody answers... Would you like me to put you through (Shall I put you through) to someone else ? Would you care to speak to someone else ?

Je regrette, Madame, personne ne répond... Voulez-vous que je vous passe quelqu'un d'autre ? Voulez-vous parler à quelqu'un d'autre ?

– Sorry, Sir, the Sales Manager is in conference. Would you like to speak to his secretary ?

Je regrette, Monsieur, le Directeur des Ventes est en conférence. Voulez-vous parler à sa secrétaire ?

– Jill ? It's Frances. There's a French customer on the line, would you take the call for Mr Peacock ? Thank you.

Jill ? C'est Frances. Il y a un client français au bout du fil, pourrais-tu prendre la communication pour Mr Peacock ? Merci.

– Aren't you " The Doggie's Delight " Company, in York ?... I'm sorry to have disturbed you – excuse me for disturbing you... Do forgive me, I'm so sorry !

Vous n'êtes pas " The Doggie's Delight " Company, à York ? Pardonnez-moi de vous avoir dérangé(e)... Pardonnez-moi, je regrette vraiment ! (Toutes mes excuses !)

– Don't ring off (Don't hang up) – Hold the line – Hold on, I'm still trying to connect you.

Ne raccrochez pas, j'essaie encore d'obtenir votre communication.

– " Why can't you get on to Extension 819 ? " – " The line (the number) is engaged (US busy) ".

" Pourquoi n'arrivez-vous pas à joindre le Poste 819 ? " – " La ligne (le numéro) est occupé(e) ".

– Mrs Bossy is not in her office. Shall I try to locate her ? It might take some time... Would you like her to call you back ? Can you give me your address and telephone number ? (How can we get in touch with you ?)

Mrs Bossy n'est pas dans son bureau. Voulez-vous que j'essaie de la trouver ? Il se peut que cela prenne du temps... Voulez-vous qu'elle vous rappelle ? Pouvez-vous me donner vos coordonnées ?

– Would you rather call her back later ? ...Would you like to leave a message for her ?... Can I take a message for her ?

Préférez-vous la rappeler plus tard ?... Voulez-vous lui laisser un message ? Puis-je prendre un message pour elle ? (Puis-je lui faire une commission ?)

– " Have you finished ? (Is your call over ?) " – " Don't cut off, please, Miss Proud is going through her files for me ! "

" C'est terminé ? (Avez-vous terminé ?) " – " Ne coupez pas s'il vous plaît, Mademoiselle Proud consulte ses dossiers pour moi ! "

– Sorry, Sir, we are working under pressure this morning ! "

" Excusez-moi, Monsieur, mais nous sommes débordés ce matin ! "

– The line has gone dead ! I can't hear the dialling tone... !

La ligne est morte ! Je n'entends pas la tonalité... !

TELEPRINTERS AND TELEX

GENERALITIES

– The devices at both ends of a telegraph line which send and receive Telex messages are teleprinters (US : teletypewriters).

Les appareils aux deux extrémités d'une ligne télégraphique qui envoient et reçoivent les télex sont des télescripteurs.

– The Telex service operates 24 hours a day, whether or not the teleprinter is manned : messages can come in after office hours and overnight.

Le service du Télex fonctionne 24 heures sur 24, qu'il y ait une permanence ou non au télescripteur : les messages peuvent arriver après les heures de bureau et pendant la nuit.

– The advantage of a Telex (message) over a telephone conversation is that it is proof positive. Both the sender of the message, and the person who receives it, have a record – in black and white – of that message.

L'avantage d'un Télex sur une conversation télépho-

nique est que c'est une preuve formelle. L'expéditeur du message et la personne qui le reçoit ont tous deux une copie – noir sur blanc – de ce message.

– How can one supply proof on one's sincerity or of another person's dishonesty by referring to a telephone conversation ?

Comment peut-on faire la preuve de sa bonne foi ou de la mauvaise foi d'une autre personne en se référant à une conversation téléphonique ?

– As charges for Telexes are based not only on distance between subscribers but also on the length of messages, these should be as concise as possible, written in " telegraphese ", that is to say, omitting all unessential words.

Comme le coût des Télex dépend non seulement de la distance qui sépare les abonnés mais aussi de la longueur des messages, ceux-ci doivent être aussi concis que possible, écrits en style télégraphique, c'est-à-dire en omettant tous les mots qui ne sont pas essentiels.

A FEW POSSIBLE ABBREVIATIONS

acc, acct	: account Y/acc overdue. Please settle. *Votre compte impayé. Veuillez régler.*
A/C	: Account Please transfer the amount to Brighton Bank A/C 88496.
addnl (Xtra)	: additional – extra Goods prepacked without addnl (Xtra) cost.
ad val.	: ad valorem : Prices exclusive of ad val tariffs *Les prix ne comprennent pas les droits de douane calculés suivant la valeur des marchandises.*
agcy, agt	: agency, agent
a.m	: matin, du matin (ante meridiem) ≠ p.m (post meridiem)
amt	: amount Amt invoice inexact. Please vfy (verify) *Montant facture inexact...*
appro.	: approval Pls (please) forward order X on appro. *Veuillez expédier commande X à l'essai.*
approx.	: approximately
arr.	: arrival ≠ dep. departure Arr. (≠ dep.) ship scheduled Oct. 27.
Attn.	: attention Attn. Mr Cox : *à l'attention de...*
bal.	: balance : solde Pls settle bal. before March 31.
bbl.	: barrel A barrel of oil : *un baril de pétrole (159 litres)*
BO	: Branch Office (HO : Head Office) Please contact our BO in York or our HO in London. *Veuillez contacter notre succursale de York ou notre siège social à Londres.*
Bro, Bros	: Brothers
C/A	: current account Pls credit our C/A N°... *Veuillez créditer notre compte courant N°...*
C.	: circa Delivery c. Jan. 17. *Livraison aux alentours du 17 janvier.*

cgo.	: cargo Owing to strike cgo left on quay. *A cause d'une grève, cargaison laissée sur le quai.*
CH.	: Customs House Documents withheld CH. Casablanca : *Documents retenus Bureaux de Douane de Casablanca.*
chk, chq	: cheque, check (US) Pls remit chq. promptly
C/N	: crédit note : *avoir*
Co.	: Company
com, comm.	: commission Our agent's 10 % (10pc) com. included.
C/O	: care of : *aux bons soins de*
cont.	: contents Contents damaged in transit (in trans. – in trnsp. – in trsp.). *Contenu endommagé pendant le transport.*
ctf.	: certificate CH demand ctf. of origin.
dely.	: delivery
d., ds.	: day, days Pmt (payment) at 30 ds. *Paiement à 30 jours.*
d/d, dtd	: dated Y/Letter d/d Feb. 2
deld., delvd.	: delivered
Dept., Dpt.	: Department The Exp. (≠ Imp.) Dpt. The Import ≠ Export Department
desp.	: despatch(ed) : *expédier (expédié)*
dis., disc.	: discount 2.5 % dis. acc. (accepted). *Remise de 2,5 % acceptée.*
dmg.	: damage Pls send adjuster to assess dmg. *Veuillez envoyer expert pour évaluer les dommages.*
do.	: ditto : idem
doz.	: dozen Pls desp. 10 doz. shirts Ref. X. *Veuillez expédier 10 douzaines de chemises Référence X.*
E & OE	: Errors & Ommissions Excepted : *Sauf erreur ou ommission (dans le bas des factures).*
Fwd.	: forward. Pls fwd. (desp.). *Veuillez expédier.*
FAO	: for the attention of
gds.	: goods
gr.	: grade : *qualité*
gtd.	: guaranteed. High gr. gtd. *: Haute qualité garantie.*

gr. wt	: gross weight (≠ n. wt) *poids brut* (≠ net weight : *poids net*)
guar.	: guarantee A three year guar.
H. O. : HQ	: Head Office – Headquarters *Siège social – Quartier général*
Hgt.	: height : *hauteur* cf. lgth. and wdt. : length and width – *longueur et largeur.*
HP.	: hire-purchase To pay for something, to buy something on hire-purchase : *… à tempérament, par versements échelonnés.*
hr (s)	: hour(s)
Inc.	: Incorporated Equivalent US de Ltd (Limited) pour les sociétés
incr.	: increased Prices higher due to incr. tariffs.
info.	: information Please send further info. about… *Veuillez envoyer des renseignements complémentaires sur…*
ins., insce.	: insurance
int.	: interest 3 mths credit w/o int. *3 mois de crédit sans intérêt.*
inv.	: invoice : *facture*
Jnr., Jr.	: Junior ≠ Snr., Sr. : Senior
max., mxm	: *maximum* ≠ min. : *minimum*
memo.	: memorandum : *note de service*
mdse.	: merchandise
msg.	: message
mgr.	: manager
mgt.	: management
n.a.	: not available : *indisponible* ≠ X stre : ex store – X whse : ex warehouse. *En magasin, disponible.*
N/C	: no charge : *gratuit*
No, Nos, n.	: number(s) : *numéro(s)*
O/C	: overcharge : *trop-perçu* We send C/N 188 dol. O/C your inv. N°…
ord.	: order Y/ord. Ref. XYZ *Votre commande Réf…*
p.a	: per annum cf. per mth., per w., p.d (per diem). *par an, par mois, par semaine, par jour* Int. rt 8 % p.a : *Taux d'intérêt 8 % par an.*
payt, pmt, pt	: payment
pend.	: pending : *en attendant* Pend. Y/instructions…
pkge.	: package

pkg.	: packing
POB, PO box	: Post Office Box : *Boîte Postale.*
prod.	: product. production
PTO	: Please turn over : *TSVP*
qy.	: query : *demande de renseignements, question.* Regarding your qy. on our inv. …
qlty.	: quality
quot.	: quotation. Pls. send quot. items X, Y, Z on your cat. *Veuillez nous envoyer les prix des articles X, Y, Z sur votre catalogue.*
rcv (d)	: receive(d)
rcpt.	: receipt We acknowledge rcpt of your ship. (shipt.) – of your csgt. (consignment) *Nous accusons réception de votre envoi.*
redg.	: registered. By regd. post : *en recommandé*
rem., remit.	: remittance : *versement*
repl.	: replacement Pls send Model W in repl.
rng.	: range : *gamme, éventail* A wide rng. of prices.
rpt.	: repeat : *répéter ou renouveler* Unexpected demand. Pls rept. our order n. 876.
rt.	: rate
rtd.	: returned Containers rtd. as reqd. (as required) *Containers retournés comme demandé.*
s.a.e	: stamped addressed envelope Pls send s.a.e with C.V (curriculum vitae)
satis. ≠ unsatis.	: (un) satisfactory
sat. ≠ unsat.	: Quality gds in csgt. (shipt) unsatis.
sched.	: schedule. On sched. – *dans les temps* behind ≠ ahead of sch. – *en retard ≠ en avance*
sgd.	: signed. Contract sgd. last Mon. (Monday)
ship., shipt.	: shipment – consignment : *envoi, expédition*
ster., stg.	: sterling Pt in ster. *Paiement en livres sterling* (in dol. : *en dollars*)
std.	: standard Up to std : *conforme aux normes, satisfaisant.*
stge.	: storage . To be kept in cold stge. : *en entrepôt frigorifique.*
STN.	: Station : *gare* Delivery (dely.) in Dover Central Stn.
stk.	: stock. Gds in stk. ≠ out of stk. *Marchandises en magasin* (stock), *disponibles ≠ épuisées, indisponibles.*
sz.	: size : *taille, dimension*
tfr.	: transfer : *virement, transfert*

tlx. tx.	: telex
trnsp., trsp.	: transport
unpd.	: unpaid
urg.	: urgent Bill unpd. Remit. urg. Pls. *Facture impayée. Réglement de toute urgence svp.*
u.s.c	: under separate cover : *sous pli séparé*
UW, u/w	: underwriter : *assureur*
wc.	: without charge :*gratuitement, sans frais*
wk.	: week
w/o	: without
wt.	: weight : *poids*
X	: ex : X stk, *sur stock ;* Xstre (store) – Xwhse (warehouse) : *disponible ;* X factory, X mill, X wks (works) : *départ usine.*
Xtra.	: extra (addnl) : *en sus, supplémentaire*
yr (s)	: year(s)
yr. Y/	: your. – Yr. ref. – Y/ref.
Yrs.	: *salutations*
Jours de la semaine	: Sun., Tues., Wed., Thurs., Fri., Sat.
Mois	: Jan., Feb., Mar., Apr., May, Jun., Jul., Aug., Sept., Oct., Nov., Dec.
Quelques mesures	: in(s) : inch, inches : *pouce(s)* ft : foot, feet yd(s) : yard(s) ml(s) : mile(s) gal. : gallon. GB : 4,546 litres. US : 3,785 litres lb. : livre (*poids* ; du latin : libra) cu. : cubic. One cu. metre : *un mètre cube* sq : square. Three sq. miles : *trois miles (milles) carrés*

(to be continued)

TEST YOUR KNOWLEDGE

NB. Le texte sera lu à haute voix par le professeur ou l'assistant(e).

A) VOUS TRAVAILLEZ EN FRANCE DANS UNE SOCIÉTÉ MULTINATIONALE OU CERTAINS CADRES NE PRATIQUENT QUE L'ANGLAIS.

1 – PRENDRE L'ESSENTIEL DU MESSAGE ET LE TRANSCRIRE SUR LA FORMULE DE MESSAGE TÉLÉPHONIQUE

2 – AVEC L'AIDE DU TEXTE, TRANSPOSER CET APPEL EN MESSAGE TELEX TEL QUE L'AURAIT ENVOYE LINDA BAKER

Hello ! " Gamp and Brolly " in Toulouse ? Good morning ! Could I speak to Mr John Drizzle, Extension 349, please ? From Linda Baker, Secretary to John Start, Managing Director of " The International Umbrella Manufacturing Company, Ltd ", in Birmingham.

Ho ! he is off for the day, is he ? Then, could you put me through to his secretary, please ? Thank you.

Hello, Mr Drizzle's Secretary ? Good morning. I hear Mr Drizzle is off for the day, but could I leave a message for him, it's fairly urgent. Thank you. Well, I'm Linda Baker, Secretary to John Start, Managing Director of " The International Umbrella Manufacturing Company, Ltd ", in Birmingham.

You see, our Managing Director is a good friend of Alex Mac Pherson, a regular customer of yours, I think. Well, Mr Mac Pherson is so satisfied with the quality and the price of your lines that he recommended you warmly and advised us to get in touch with you.

Now, we are interested in your latest creation, " The Automatic Panoramic Umbrella ", which is a great success in your country, so we are told, and Mr start would like to meet Mr Drizzle as soon as possible to discuss the possibility of manufacturing that article in our own factory, under licence of course.

Mr Start asked me to get in touch with Mr Drizzle as quickly as possible as competition from Hong Kong or Taiwan manufacturers is very keen these days, and we don't want to miss this opportunity.

Postal delays being awful at the present time, it was safer to call you up !

Well, can you ask Mr Drizzle to contact Mr Start as soon as he can, or can you tell me when we can be sure to talk to him ? Tomorrow morning, half-past-nine ? Right. I will call tomorrow then.

I think I haven't given you our address and our telephone number. Can you take it down ? So, it's " The International Umbrella Manufacturing Company, Ltd ", 38, Lancashire Road, Birmingham B32 8LG (England) Telephone 021 135793 Extension 264.

Well, thank you for your help. Good bye.

APPEL TÉLÉPHONIQUE / **TELEPHONE MESSAGE**	
DATE :	*HEURE* / TIME :
DE / FROM :	
Société / Company :	
Adresse / Address :	
Tel.	Poste / Extn :
☐ *Rappellera* / Will call back	
☐ *A rappeler* / To be called back	
☐ URGENT	
Objet / Subject :	

B) TRADUIRE LES TELEX SUIVANTS EN UTILISANT AUTANT D'ABRÉVIATIONS QUE POSSIBLE SANS TOUTEFOIS QUE LE CORRESPONDANT EN TROUVE LE DÉCRYPTAGE DIFFICILE !

1 – Nous vous expédions 10 caisses de boulons et écrous dimensions 12x8 demain Mercredi 8 Janvier. Vous pouvez en prendre livraison à la gare centrale de Deal. Veuillez virer le montant de la facture à notre Compte bancaire 123456 Banque Européenne. Salutations.

2 - Merci pour votre demande du 18 Juin concernant votre facture. Les prix sont nets, les droits de douane sont inclus et l'emballage est gratuit. Salutations.

3 – Notre service exportation peut expédier votre commande du 30 avril Référence X à la fin du mois si nos fournisseurs nous livrent dans les temps. Seul le modèle GKL peut être livré sur stock. Salutations.

4 – Merci pour votre envoi du 1er Juin. Les containers vides seront retournés comme vous nous l'avez demandé. La qualité des articles N° 18 et 24 n'est pas satisfaisante. Pouvez-vous nous accorder une ristourne complémentaire sur ces articles ? Salutations.

5 – Nous accusons réception des marchandises expédiées le 7 de ce mois. Pourquoi les prix sur la facture ne correspondent-ils pas aux prix que vous nous avez envoyés ? Veuillez, je vous prie, vérifier. Êtes-vous toujours d'accord pour nous accorder un crédit de 3 mois sans intérêt ? Salutations.

107– TO PAY (suite)

+ in (sans complément) **+ into** (avec complément circonstanciel)
– Tradesmen queue up at the bank on Monday mornings : they pay in the previous week's takings – they pay the previous week's takings into their accounts.
Les commerçants font la queue à la banque le lundi matin : ils versent la recette de la semaine précédente – ils versent (font porter) la recette de la semaine précédente à leur compte.
– As proof of their payment they are issued (handed over) a deposit receipt.
Comme preuve de leur versement on leur délivre (remet) un reçu de versement.

Mots proches :

To credit an account **with** X pounds – to credit X pounds to an account ≠ to debit an account **with** X pounds – to debit X pounds **against** an account.
Créditer un compte de X livres ≠ débiter un compte de X livres.
+ off :
Régler en totalité, s'acquitter de, amortir une dette (to amortize)
– He is bent on paying off all his creditors (on paying off all his debts) before he leaves the country.
Il tient absolument à régler tous ses créanciers (à régler toutes ses dettes) avant de quitter le pays.
– Thanks to the recovery, we were able to pay off all our debts within a comparatively short span of time.
Grâce à la reprise, nous avons pu amortir nos dettes (nous acquitter de nos dettes) en un laps de temps relativement court.
***NB.* Attention !** *Amortir un emprunt* : to redeem a loan, a mortgage
Licencier, congédier – to lay (laid-laid) off – to make redundant
– When employees are paid off – laid off – made redundant, they apply for unemployment benefits (they sign on the dole : GB).
Quand les salariés sont licenciés, ils s'inscrivent au chômage.
Réussir, avoir des effets heureux, fructueux (fruitful)
– His determination paid off in the long run (he was repaid for his determination).
Son acharnement a été fructueux à la longue (il a été récompensé pour son acharnement).
– The Government's inflation-fighting policy is exacting, but it seems to be paying off.
La politique gouvernementale de lutte contre l'inflation est exigeante, mais elle semble réussir.
+ out : to lay out – *débourser*
– I wish I knew a way of going to the United States without paying out a penny.
Si seulement je connaissais un moyen d'aller aux États Unis sans débourser un sou !

Expressions :

To pay attention to : to pay heed to (to heed ≠ to ignore) : *faire (prêter) attention à*
– You should have paid attention to my advice.
Vous auriez dû écouter mes conseils.
– Nobody paid heed to economists' warnings (nobody heeded – economists' warnings went unheeded).
Personne ne prêta attention aux avertissements des économistes.
– They do not take any heed of the nation's plight.
Ils méconnaissent l'état critique dans lequel se trouve la nation.
To pay homage to : to pay tribute to : *rendre hommage à*
– In the notice of dismissal, they pay tribute to his unremitting dedication to the firm !
Dans la lettre de licenciement, on rend hommage à son infatigable dévouement envers l'entreprise !
To pay a call (short visit) on sb. : to pay a visit to sb. : *rendre visite à quelqu'un.*
– She has been on sick leave (on maternity leave) for a fortnight : I pay a call on her every so often to keep in touch.
Elle est en congé de maladie (en congé de maternité) depuis quinze jours : je lui rends une petite visite de temps en temps pour garder le contact.
To pay sb. a compliment : to pay a compliment to sb. on st. : *faire un compliment à quelqu'un pour quelque chose.*
– She exerts herself (she takes pains) to keep the business going, but he never pays her any compliments on it.
Elle s'efforce tant qu'elle peut de faire tourner l'affaire, mais il ne lui en fait jamais compliment.

To pay lip service to : *ne soutenir qu'en paroles, n'approuver que du bout des lèvres, accorder un hommage verbal à*
– They pay lip service to the Chairman's initiative, but in their heart of hearts, they all know that it is doomed to failure !
Ils louent pour la galerie l'initiative du Président mais en leur for intérieur, ils savent tous qu'elle est vouée à l'échec !
To pay through the nose : *payer les yeux de la tête*
– We paid through the nose for that cruise, and it disappointed us !
Nous avons payé cette croisière les yeux de la tête, et elle nous a déçus !

Substantifs : Pay : *la solde (d'un militaire)* cf. wage**s** : *le salaire (d'un ouvrier)* ; salary : *le traitement (d'un employé)* ; fee : *honoraires (professions libérales), cachet (artistes).*

Figuré : – Technicians in the pay of unscrupulous foreign firms engage in industrial espionage in high tech(nology) sectors ; it saves the latter long and expensive R & D programmes.

Des techniciens à la solde de sociétés étrangères sans scrupules se livrent à l'espionnage industriel dans les secteurs de pointe ; cela évite à ces dernières de longs et coûteux programmes de recherche théorique et appliquée (**R**esearch and **D**evelopment).
– Severance pay – redundancy pay – lay-off pay – *indemnité de licenciement.*
Aussi : " the golden handshake " (text. " *la poignée de mains dorée* " ; s'emploie aussi pour la prime de départ en retraite anticipée). To give sb. the golden handshake. (concerne les cadres)
– Pay claims – wage claims : *les revendications salariales*
– Pay settlements – wage settlements : *les accords salariaux*
– The shop stewards made a petition to the Management in which they put forward their workmates' pay claims : then they organized a day of action (of protest) in support of those claims during which workers also gave vent to other grievances (conditions of work, etc.)
Les délégués syndicaux adressèrent une pétition à la Direction dans laquelle ils présentaient les revendications salariales de leurs compagnons ; puis ils organisèrent une journée revendicative en faveur de ces revendications au cours de laquelle les travailleurs exprimèrent aussi d'autres griefs (conditions de travail, etc.).
– The Management agreed to setting up a joint commission to enter into collective bargining. They eventually reached a wage (pay) settlement (they eventually struck a wage bargain) according to the terms of which workers are granted a (pay) rise (a rise in wages ; U.S. : a raise) ; workers will also get backpay as the pay settlements are backdated.
La Direction a accepté de mettre sur pied une commission paritaire pour engager des négociations collectives. Ils ont fini par parvenir à un accord sur les salaires (ils ont finalement conclu un accord salarial) aux termes duquel une augmentation de salaire est accordée aux travailleurs ; les travailleurs toucheront également un rappel puisque ces accords ont un effet rétroactif.
– They will take a nice pay-packet back home !
Ils rapporteront une belle enveloppe chez eux !
– A pay-in slip : *un bordereau de versement (qui accompagne un versement).*
– Payload : Aircraft : passengers + cargo, for which payment is received.
Avions : les passagers + la cargaison pour lesquels on perçoit un paiement – l'emport.
(Spacecraft) : crew + instruments : *l'équipage + les instruments – la charge utile.*
– Payroll : *la paie de tout le personnel*
– The firm has 10,000 people on the payroll – has a payroll of 10,000 people.
L'entreprise emploie 10 000 personnes.
– You cannot be a civil servant, and on a private firm's payroll at the same time !
On ne peut être fonctionnaire et en même temps émarger au budget d'une entreprise privée !
– P.A.Y.E. – pay-as-you-earn – method of collecting income tax ; employers deduct it from earnings.
Méthode de perception de l'impôt sur le revenu ; les employeurs le déduisent des gains.
– The payee ≠ the drawer : *le bénéficaire ≠ le tireur (d'un chèque)*
– A taxpayer – a ratepayer : *un contribuable*
– Payment. To **make** a payment by cheque : *effectuer un réglement par chèque.*

– They enclosed a cheque to the amount of X pounds in payment of their purchases.
Ils ont joint un chèque d'un montant de X livres en réglement de leurs achats.
– In our store, newly weds can equip their homes from cellar to attic on easy terms – by easy payments.
Dans notre magasin, les jeunes mariés peuvent monter leur foyer de la cave au grenier avec facilités de paiement.
– They pay (put) 10 % down and settle the balance in 24, 48 or even 72 monthly payments (of X pounds) (payments = instalments).
Ils versent un acompte de 10 % et réglent le solde en 24, 48 ou même 72 versements de X livres par mois.

Adjectif : – This cheque is payable to bearer, payable at sight.
Ce chèque est payable au porteur, payable à vue.
– Make out a cheque payable to (the order of) X.
Faites un chèque à l'ordre de X.

18 - STRUCTURES

ÉQUIVALENTS DU SUBJONCTIF FRANÇAIS

MAY OU MIGHT, SELON LA CONCORDANCE DES TEMPS

May : verbe principal au présent ou au futur
Might : verbe principal au passé ou au conditionnel

1 – Après " that ", contraction de " in order that " : afin que, pour que, ou de " so that " : de telle façon que, de telle manière que, **dans les phrases affirmatives.**

– I give you the report that you may judge by yourself.
Je vous donne le rapport pour que vous jugiez par vous-même.
– He opened the door of the cage that the bird might fly away.
Il a ouvert la porte de la cage pour que l'oiseau s'envole.
NB. Dans les phrases négatives, employer " for fear " avec **should** à toutes les personnes.
– I have not told him anything for fear he should reveal the secret.
Je ne lui ai rien dit pour qu'il ne révèle pas le secret.
– Start earlier for fear you **should** arrive late !
Pars plus tôt de telle façon que tu n'arrives pas en retard !

Construction plus simple : la construction infinitive avec " for " que la forme soit affirmative ou négative.
– I give you the report for you to judge by yourself.
– He opened the door of the cage for the bird to fly away.
– I have not told him anything for him not to reveal the secret.
– Start earlier for you not to arrive late.

2 – Après certains composés de " ever " mais jamais " whenever " chaque fois que (everytime) qui gouverne l'indicatif.

– Whenever I think of it, I feel depressed !
Chaque fois que j'y pense, j'ai le cafard !
– Whatever we may do, we shall die one day !
Quoi que nous fassions, nous mourrons un jour !
– Whichever girl you may marry, make her happy !
Quelle que soit la jeune fille que tu épouses, rends la heureuse.
– Wherever you may go in Europe, you will find filling-stations.
Où que vous alliez en Europe, vous trouverez des stations-service.
– However intelligent you may be, you will not solve that problem.
Quelque intelligent que vous soyez, vous ne résoudrez pas ce problème.

Attention au temps du verbe principal ;
– He **said** that wherever we **might** go in Europe, we should find filling stations.
Il a dit que où que nous allions en Europe, nous trouverions des stations-service.
– However intelligent he **might** be, he was not able to solve that problem.
Quelque intelligent qu'il fût, il n'a pas été capable de résoudre ce problème.

Constructions plus simples :

- No matter what, which, where, how + indicatif
  – No matter **what** we do, we shall die one day.
  – No matter **which** girl you marry, make her happy.
  – No matter **where** you go in Europe, you will find filling-stations.
  – No matter **how** intelligent you are, you will not solve that problem.

Attention cependant à la concordance des temps :

■ – No matter how intelligent **he was**, he **was** not able to solve that problem.

Au lieu de however + adjectif + may ou might : adjectif + as + indicatif

– Intelligent as you are, you will not solve that problem.

– Strong as he is, he will not beat the record.

Quelque fort qu'il soit, il ne battra pas le record.

THÈME D'APPLICATION NUMÉRO 18

1 - Hier, j'ai versé à mon compte la recette de la semaine : on m'a délivré un reçu afin que j'aie (2 constructions) une preuve de mon versement.

2 - Il est grand temps que tu écoutes mes conseils afin que tu ne sois pas licencié (2 constructions).

3 - Quelque décidé qu'il soit (3 constructions), il ne pourra pas payer toutes ses dettes en ce laps de temps relativement court !

4 - Quels que soient les avertissements que les économistes donnent (2 constructions) aux Gouvernements, ils n'y prêtent pas attention !

5 - Où que vous travailliez (2 constructions) dans les secteurs de pointe vous trouverez des techniciens sans scrupules qui se livrent à l'espionnage industriel.

6 - Quoi que dise le Président (2 constructions), nous savions tous en notre for intérieur que son initiative était vouée à l'échec.

7 - Quelles que soient les revendications que vous présentiez (2 constructions), la Direction n'engagera pas de négociations collectives.

8 - Elle s'est efforcée tant qu'elle a pu de faire tourner l'affaire pour que le patron amortisse son emprunt (2 constructions).

9 - Nous lui rendrons une petite visite pour que vous la complimentiez (2 constructions) pour son infatigable dévouement envers notre entreprise.

10 - " Supposez que nous versions un acompte de 10 % et que nous réglions le solde en 24 mois " – " J'aimerais mieux que vous fassiez un chèque à mon ordre immédiatement ! "

11 - Quel que soit votre emploi (2 constructions), vous pouvez vous inscrire au chômage dès que vous êtes licencié, où que vous ayez travaillé (2 constructions).

12 - Leur politique exigeante est un échec mais ils la poursuivent, comme si l'économie de la nation n'était pas dans un état critique !

13 - Ne l'écoutez pas, afin que vous ne soyez pas déçus (2 constructions) : comme si il existait un moyen d'aller aux États Unis sans débourser un sou !

14 - Si belles que soient leurs " enveloppes " (3 constructions), des jeunes mariés ne peuvent monter leurs foyers de la cave au grenier qu'avec des facilités de paiement !

15 - Quelque initiative que vous preniez (2 constructions), ils ne vous soutiendront qu'en paroles !

19 - COMMUNICATIONS

Business Letters : Commercial Correspondence (Quatrième partie)

LAY-OUT : PRÉSENTATION (GB AND US)

HEADING – LETTER-HEAD : *EN TETE*

No heading : name and address of sender at the top, on the right-hand side (in the top right-hand corner).

DATE

On the right-hand side, underneath (below-under) the heading or the sender's address.

NB. – Do not mention the name of the place
– Always a comma before the year
– Several possibilities : 21st February, 198...
21 February, 198...
February 21st, 198...
Date as postmark

Originally American, February 21, 198... is becoming frequent even in GB.

The names of months and days always begin with a capital letter.

Never write the date in figures :

12.2.198... : 12th February, 198... : **GB**
December 2nd, 198... : **US**

REFERENCE – REF. : *RÉFÉRENCE*

On the left-hand side (on the same line as the date for instance)

Possibilities :

- Our reference : Our ref.
  Your reference : Your ref.
- When answering (in your reply) please quote (please refer to) our ref... *(référence à rappeler dans toute correspondance).*

MAILING INSTRUCTIONS : *DIRECTIVES D'EXPÉDITION*

Air Mail, Registered Post, Recorded Delivery, Express, etc. : *par avion, en recommandé, avec accusé de réception, urgent, etc.* (On the left-hand side, below the Reference).

INSIDE (INTERNAL) ADDRESS : *ADRESSE INTÉRIEURE,* SUSCRIPTION (NAME AND ADRESS OF THE ADDRESSEE : *DESTINATAIRE)*

On the left-hand side, against the margin, below mailing instructions (The transparent panel of window envelopes : aperture envelopes is on the left-hand side).

Different types of addressees :

1. One person :
   - Mr John Gordon.
   - Mrs Sarah Gordon.
   - Miss Sarah Gordon.
   - Ms, originally American, is frequently used for women. Always write first name or initial before the surname : in American, use 2 initials or the first name + one initial :
   - Mr L.M. Thomson, or
   - Mr Lewis M. Thomson.

   Other possibilities :
   - Doctor S. Roger, (Dr S. Roger).
   - Major Marmaduke Baxter, (Major M. Baxter).
   - Professor R.A. Gordon, etc.
   - The Manager, (The President, The Secretary, The Sales Manager, etc.) Hong kong Bank, etc.

   NB. In GB only, for men only, becoming old-fashioned :
   - R. Gordon, Esq. (Roger Gordon, Esq.)
     (Esq. – esquire : *écuyer)*

2. Several people, a company :

   Use " Messrs " when the name does not include Limited (Ltd)
   - Messrs Gordon and Sons,
   - Messrs Martin and Partners, etc.

   Do not use " Messrs " :
   - when the name includes " Limited " (Ltd)
     - Thomas Morris and Co, Ltd, etc.
   - when the name starts with " The " or a title
     - Dr John Willicott and Co., etc.
     - The Provincial Bank, etc.
     - The Comfortable Home Company, etc.

3. The letter is addressed to **one person within the firm :**
   – Mrs Gladys Peacock.
   c/o Sussex Gardening Tools, Ltd, etc.

   or – Sussex Gardening Tools, Ltd,
   For the attention of Mrs Gladys Peacock, etc.

   or – Sussex Gardening Tools, Ltd,
   Attention of Mrs Gladys Peacock, etc.

   or – Sussex Gardening Tools, Ltd,
   Confidential : for the attention of Mrs Gladys Peacock, etc.

NB. – GB : a comma at the end of each line, except the last one.
– US : a comma between the name of the town and that of the state, on the same line.

– Never underline the names of towns or cities (GB or US),
– The attention lines, underlined (underscored), can be placed under the internal address :

The Comfy Nappy Co, Ltd,
Elms Drive,
St Andrew Road,
EDINBURGH EN2 2YB

The Cleaning Equipment Corporation,
2247 Avenue of the Americas,
Portland, Oregon 18124

– **Do not forget the Postcode (GB), the Zip Code (US)**

ThePostcode consists of two groups of letters and figures : Bristol BT17 6BM ; Manchester M32 7LF.

The Zip Code consists of a five digit number.

– Sometimes the address includes the number of a Post Office Box :

The Maple Sugar Company,
PO Box 649,
Town of Mount Royal,
Quebec, Canada, H4P 2C9

SALUTATION (GREETING) : *L'INTITULÉ*

Against the left-hand margin, **not** in the middle.

1. One person :

■ **G.B.**

Usual – Dear Sir,
– Dear Madam (even if the lady is single),
– Dear Sir/Madam,
– Dear Sir or Madam,
Do not forget the comma.

Formal – Sir,
– Madam,

Cordial – Dear Mr Gordon,
– Dear Mrs Gordon,
– Dear Miss Gordon,

■ **US + colon**

(My) Dear Mr Carter :
(My) Dear Mrs Carter :
(My) Dear Miss Carter :

■ **GB and US**

Ms Carter, or : (woman, single or not).

2. Several people, a limited company (société par actions).

■ **GB + comma**

Usual – Dear Sirs,
– Mesdames.

Formal – Gentlemen,
– Sirs,
– Mesdames,

■ **US + colon**

– Gentlemen :
– Mesdames :

SUBJECT-MATTER – SUBJECT : *OBJET*

GB : below the salutation) underlined (underscored)
US : above the salutation)

Subject : your letter Ref. XY/WZ dated 8 Dec. 198…
Subject : Frankfurt International Fair.

BODY OF THE LETTER

– Divided into paragraphs
– Indented form : *presentation décalée*
– Block form : *présentation compacte*

COMPLIMENTARY CLOSE : *FORMULE DE POLITESSE*

– On the right-hand side (indented form) ;
– On the left-hand side (block form).

It depends on the salutation :

Salutation	**GB**	**US**
Dear Sir, Dear Madam, Dear Sir/Madam, Dear Sir or Madam,	Yours faithfully	Yours truly Truly yours Yours very truly Very truly yours
Dear Mr Gordon, Dear Mrs Gordon, Dear Miss Gordon,	Yours sincerely (Yours truly)	Sincerely yours Very sincerely yours
Sir, Madam, Gentlemen, Sirs, Mesdames,	Yours respectfully	Respectfully yours

SIGNATURE : *PARAFE*

Below the complimentary close, above the name of the person signing the letter with his/her position.

Yours faithfully
Signature
H. Gordon (Mr) or (Mrs) or (Ms)
Personnel Manager

1. The letter is signed by an employee who has power of attorney (*qui a une procuration*)

   Yours truly
   p.p. The Happy Baby, Ltd,
   Signature
   or per pro The Happy Baby, Ltd, etc.

NB. per pro – per procurationem – by proxy = *par procuration*

2. The employee has not power of attorney

   Yours sincerely
   for The Happy Baby, Ltd
   Signature
   Secretary

   Yours truly
   Gladys Simpson
   Secretary to Alfred Blump
   General Manager

ENCLOSURE(S) – ENCL(S) – ENC(S) : *PIECE(S) JOINTE(S)*

Against the left-hand margin, below the signature.

Enclosures : Receipt of your remittance (paiement)
Latest price list
Leaflet with list of our agents abroad

NB. To be known, not to be used :

- Re : Objet. Employé dans les documents juridiques,
- We thank you for your favour of the 14th inst. (instant), ult. (ultimo). *Nous vous remercions pour votre honorée du 14 courant, du 14 du mois dernier.*
- The goods will leave London on the 14th prox. (proximo) : *... le 14 du mois prochain.*

NB. Despatching the mail : types of letters

You can send a letter :

- by Registered Post : *en recommandé*
- by Recorded Delivery : *avec accusé de réception*
- by Air Mail
- Poste Restante

BUSINESS LETTERS : MISCELLANEOUS PHRASES

INTRODUCTORY PHRASES : *FORMULES D'INTRODUCTION*

– We acknowledge receipt of your letter dated (of) 3rd January, of your order, of your remittance, of your consignment, of your catalogue, of your (current) price list, of your quotations, etc.

Nous accusons réception de votre lettre du 3 Janvier, de votre commande, de votre réglement, de votre envoi, de votre catalogue, de vos prix courants, de vos tarifs, etc.

– We have just received your letter of June 1st... we thank you for your letter of... with great interest... we are pleased to answer in the affirmative to your enquiry of... we duly received the literature that we had requested from you in our letter of...

Nous venons de recevoir votre lettre du 1er Juin... Nous vous remercions pour votre lettre du... Nous avons lu avec grand intérêt votre lettre du... Nous avons le plaisir de répondre par l'affirmative à votre demande de renseignements du... Nous avons bien reçu la documentation que nous vous avions demandée dans notre lettre du...

– We acknowledge with thanks your order for... N° X...

Nous accusons réception de votre commande de... N° X et nous vous en remercions (" receipt " est sous entendu).

– We are very pleased to book your order for... N° X...

Nous avons le plaisir d'enregistrer votre commande de ... N° ...

– As requested in your letter of 29th February, we are sending you under separate cover (≠ herewith) a few samples of our knitting wools together with our terms of sale and delivery.

Comme vous nous le demandez dans votre lettre du 29 Février, nous vous envoyons sous pli séparé (≠ sous ce pli – ci-joint) quelques échantillons de nos laines à tricoter ainsi que nos conditions de vente et de livraison.

– We have much pleasure in informing you that... We have pleasure in enclosing our latest quotations... We are pleased to inform you that... We are writing to inform you that...

Nous avons l'honneur de vous informer que... Nous nous permettons de joindre nos derniers tarifs... Nous avons l'honneur de vous apprendre que... Nous vous écrivons pour vous informer que...

W e beg to inform you that... (Formal)

Nous avons l'honneur de (nous tenons à) vous informer... (Formel)

– We request you to be so kind as to supply us with the following (the undermentioned) items... : Would you be so kind as to...

Nous vous prions d'avoir l'amabilité de nous fournir les articles suivants (ci-dessous).

– We are happy to let you know that... It is with pleasure that we write to inform you that...

Nous avons le plaisir de vous apprendre que... C'est avec plaisir que nous vous écrivons pour vous apprendre que...

– Referring to your letter (in answer to – in reply to – in response to your letter – further to your letter), to your enquiry of July 25th...

Comme suite à (par suite à) votre lettre, à votre demande de renseignements du 25 juillet...

– Following your phone call, we beg to confirm (Formal) – we would like to confirm (Informal) our order of March 8th...

A la suite de votre coup de téléphone, nous avons l'honneur de (Formel) – nous tenons à (Informel) vous confirmer notre commande du 8 mars...

– We wish to advise you that..., to remind you that..., to inform you that..., to let you know that...

Nous tenons à vous faire part..., à vous rappeler... à vous informer..., à vous apprendre que...

– We are exceedingly (extremely) grateful to you for attending so carefully to our intererests in this delicate transaction...

Nous vous sommes extrêmement reconnaissants d'avoir veillé aussi soigneusement à nos intérêts dans cette délicate transaction...

– We thank you very much for honouring our firm with your confidence...

Nous vous remercions beaucoup de bien vouloir honorer notre société de votre confiance... Moins formel : for having confidence in our firm : for showing.

– We hasten to confirm by the present letter (by this letter) that... (Formal).

Nous nous empressons de confirmer par la présente... (Formel).

– I am writing to place with you a trial order for... If the goods come up to our expectations (meet our requirements), we propose (intend) to place regular orders with you in future.

J'ai l'honneur de passer auprès de vous une commande à l'essai de... Si les marchandises répondent à notre attente (satisfont nos besoins) nous nous proposons d'effectuer des commandes régulières auprès de vous à l'avenir.

– We are very much indebted to you for entrusting us with this substantial order...

Nous vous sommes très obligés de nous avoir confié cette commande importante

FINAL PHRASES : *FORMULES DE CONCLUSION*

– We look forward to (we are looking forward to) receiving your order... further orders from you... to hearing from you soon... to doing further business with you in future...

Nous espérons recevoir une commande de votre part... d'autres commandes de votre part... recevoir bientôt votre réponse... continuer à travailler avec vous à l'avenir...

– We hope to hear from you soon and remain... Hoping to hear from you soon... Hoping for an early reply, for an early delivery... we remain (Formal).

Dans l'espoir d'une prompte réponse, d'une livraison rapide, nous vous prions d'agréer... (Formel).

– Pending your reply...

Dans l'attente de votre réponse...

– Hoping that you will favour us with an order, we remain... (Formal).

En espérant que vous voudrez bien nous honorer d'une commande, nous vous prions... (Formel).

– We should appreciate an early reply – an early reply-would be much appreciated.

Nous vous serions obligés de bien vouloir répondre dans les plus brefs délais.

– Awaiting your instructions as regards the shipment... Awaiting your order, we remain... (Formal).

Dans l'attente de vos instructions en ce qui concerne l'expédition... Dans l'attente de votre commande, veuillez agréer (Formel).

– You can be confident that we shall not fail to execute (carry out-fulfil-fill-complete) your order in due course.

Vous pouvez être assuré que nous ne manquerons pas d'exécuter votre commande en temps voulu.

– Please do not hesitate to get in touch with us again (contact us)...

Veuillez ne pas hésiter à nous recontacter...

– Should a difficulty arise, we shall be glad to reciprocate your assistance : our lorries will be at your disposal !

En cas de difficulté, nous serons heureux de vous aider en retour : nos camions seront à votre disposition !

– We thank you in advance for your understanding...

Nous vous remercions à l'avance (d'avance) pour votre compréhension...

– We are only too glad to comply with your wishes...

Nous ne sommes que trop heureux de satisfaire vos désirs...

– We trust that the goods will meet your requirements...

Nous espérons vivement que les marchandises vous satisferont...

– We trust that you will dispatch the goods at your earliest convenience ; we will acknowledge receipt on arrival.

Nous espérons vivement que vous expédierez les marchandises dans les meilleurs délais ; nous en accuserons réception dès leur arrivée.

– We are counting on you to forward the documents by return of post.

Nous comptons sur vous pour expédier les documents par retour.

– Barring events entirely beyond our control, we undertake (we promise) to ensure delivery within the time limit.

Sauf événements entièrement indépendants de notre volonté, nous nous engageons à assurer la livraison dans les délais.

(to be continued)

TEST YOUR KNOWLEDGE

A VERY BUSY EMPLOYER, WHO IS ALL AT SEA IN HIS SECRETARY'S ABSENCE, LEAVES THIS MESSAGE TO HER ON THE DICTATING MACHINE.

PUT YOURSELF IN HER PLACE, WRITE THE LETTER AND TYPE IT, RESPECTING THE LAY-OUT OF BUSINESS LETTERS IN THE U.K. AND THE U.S.A.

A FEW NECESSARY WORDS OR PHRASES ARE TO BE FOUND IN CHAPTER 20.

Mathilde,

Vous savez que je suis parti à la foire commerciale de Lyon, mais il est urgent de répondre à une lettre d'une firme anglaise que j'ai reçue avant que vous ne rentriez de congé et que j'ai égarée ! Heureusement j'avais pris quelques notes ! Au fait, notre papier à en-tête n'est pas encore revenu de chez l'imprimeur, alors débrouillez-vous pour " faire bien " : " MM Henri et Wallon, Mobilier Scolaire ", adresse, téléphone, Telex, Fax, etc... faites pour le mieux !

D'après mes notes, ils habitent Bromswood, dans le Lancashire, Knightsley Road, T45 7BC. Comme vous n'étiez pas là, j'ai essayé de traduire moi-même et je pense en gros que j'ai compris. Et puis j'ai bien rangé la lettre mais impossible de la retrouver ! Leur raison sociale est : ' Modern Furniture, Ltd ", et jusqu'à présent il paraît qu'ils ne travaillaient qu'avec des firmes britanniques mais avec la perspective du marché unique de 1992 ils veulent diversifier leurs fournisseurs et ce que nous faisons les intéresse. C'est la Chambre de Commerce du Hainaut-Cambraisis qui nous a transmis leur lettre.

Alors vous leur dites que nous serions heureux de les avoir comme clients. Excusez le retard par des histoires d'inventaire ou ce que vous voudrez de plausible, la vérité peut-être ! Au fait j'espère que votre bébé va bien !

Vous vous rendez compte, ils ont écrit à la Chambre de Commerce il y a 15 jours ! Il faudrait vous adresser à Madame ou Mademoiselle Genevieve Whistletune, responsable du Service Achats.

Envoyer-leur notre catalogue (le nouveau), nos tarifs, nos conditions de vente, etc.

Vous leur dites que nous sommes à leur entière disposition s'ils veulent venir visiter l'usine par exemple ou nos salles d'exposition. Il faudrait qu'ils prennent rendez-vous avec nous (après la fermeture de la foire dans huit jours). Tenez, envoyez-leur donc la série de photos de notre stand que nous avons prises avant l'ouverture.

Enfin, faites pour le mieux ! Tâchez de faire chic parce qu'on a besoin de clients. Au fait, la référence de la lettre m'avait frappé : SN/CF !

Vous leur dites que nous pouvons livrer n'importe quel article sur stock, c'est notre fierté, et que nous livrons par camion à domicile. Donc délais de livraison relativement courts. Remise évidemment pour les grosses commandes !

Vous signerez pour moi avec toutes mes excuses bien sûr, tournez cela bien !

Je pense ne rien avoir oublié.

Si, vous leur dites que la série de tables et chaises ainsi que les armoires Type BTS 2 sont épuisées (Ref. catalogue S.414) mais c'est vraiment le seul article qui nous manque, nos ateliers en refont une série qui sera disponible dans six semaines.

Écrivez dès aujourd'hui.

Dites-leur ce que sont les photos que vous leur enverrez de notre stand à Lyon !

Je compte sur vous.

A bientôt !

PS. *Si vous avez une minute de libre, pouvez-vous mettre un peu d'ordre dans mes papiers. Peut-être retrouverez-vous l'original de la lettre ! Merci.*
Envoyez la lettre par avion.

108- TO PUT - PUT - PUT

■ *Placer, mettre, poser*
■ *Dire, exprimer*
– How shall I put it ? *Comment dire ? Comment l'exprimer ?*
– As the Chairman put it in his address yesterday...
Comme l'a dit le Président dans son allocution hier...
– To put it bluntly... *pour parler sans ménagement (sans mettre de gants)...*
– To put it in a nutshell, European industrialists are in disarray because the Japanese corner the market.
(Pour le dire) en un mot (textuellement : coquille de noix), les industriels européens sont en plein désarroi parce que les Japonais accaparent le marché.

Expressions :

– We cannot endorse (approve of) the Union's latest move : we will put the matter into the hands of our solicitors.
Nous ne pouvons approuver la dernière manœuvre du syndicat : nous allons mettre l'affaire entre les mains de nos avocats.
– High interest rates put **the** brake(s) on (put **a** curb on) investments, and therefore put a great strain on competitiveness.
Les taux d'intérêts élevés freinent les investissements (slow investments down – *ralentissent les i.) et par conséquent mettent la compétitivité à rude épreuve.*
– Microelectronics **has** (ou **have**) put an end to (put the lid on) an industrial era, and spearhea**ds** (spearhea**d**) yet another economic revolution.
La microélectronique a mis fin à (text. " a mis le couvercle sur ") une ère industrielle et est le fer de lance d'une nouvelle révolution économique.
– The new technique will soon be put to the test (on trial), and we pin all our hopes on its efficiency.
Cette nouvelle technique sera bientôt mise à l'épreuve (à l'essai) et nous fondons tous nos espoirs sur son efficacité.
– We must adjust to a changing world : the survival of industry hinges on (hangs on – rests on – is contingent upon) computerization, but it will put it to great expense.
Nous devons nous adapter à un monde en transformation : la survie de l'industrie dépend de l'informatisation, mais cela lui occasionnera de grosses dépenses.
– Economic life was hobbled (shackled – fettered) by too many finicky (pernickety) regulations ; deregulation is going to put that state of affairs to right**s** (to set... to right**s**).
La vie économique était entravée par trop de réglements tatillons : la libéralisation va mettre bon ordre dans cet état de choses.
– " Europe must cash in on (capitalize on – avail itself of – take advantage of) the United States' economic recovery to put its own economy right (to set... right – to redress) " – " I am sure that it will profit by (from) – benefit by (from) that long-awaited revival, and that it will climb (jump) on (aboard) the bandwagon ! "
" L'Europe doit profiter de la reprise économique aux États Unis pour redresser sa propre économie " – " Je suis sûr qu'elle tirera profit de cette reprise longtemps attendue, et qu'elle prendra le train en marche ! "
– If Italy and Spain try to carve out a larger share of the European wine market, it will put (place) the income of French wine growers in jeopardy.
Si l'Italie et l'Espagne essaient de se tailler une part plus grande du marché du vin européen, cela compromettra le revenu des viticulteurs français.
– Garbage (refuse) is now being put to good use in order to eke out dwindling natural resources : they retrieve from **it** all that can be reprocessed – recycled.
On tire parti désormais (on met désormais à profit – on fait désormais bon usage) des ordures afin de faire durer (afin d'économiser) les ressources naturelles qui s'épuisent : on en retire (on en extrait) tout ce qui peut être recyclé (retraité).
– The concept of Quality Circles is gradually being put to practical use (implemented – applied – put into practice) in French industry.
Le principe des Cercles de Qualité est mis peu à peu en application dans l'industrie française.
– As soon as he was put in charge of (entrusted with) the revamping of our production methods, he undertook (set off – set out) to incite all the stick-in-the mud members of the Board to launch out into computerized production technology (to incite sb. to do – to stimulate sb. to do – to urge sb. **on** to do – to egg sb. **on** to do – to spur sb. **on** to do – to prod sb. into doing – to goad sb. into doing).

Dès qu'il fut chargé de la réorganisation de nos méthodes de production, il entreprit d'inciter tous les membres encroûtés du Conseil D'Administration à se lancer dans la productique.
To put right : *corriger* (to correct), *remédier à* (to remedy), *réparer* (to mend).
– You can put right an error, a defect (a fault), a theory, a judgment, an abuse.
– The word processor is out of order, and no one here can put it right.
La machine à traitement de textes est en panne, et personne ici ne peut la réparer.
– A few days off will put you right !
Quelques jours de congé vous remettront d'aplomb !
To put straight : to tidy up : *mettre de l'ordre dans*
– Gladys, can you put the office straight before you leave, please ?
Gladys, pouvez-vous mettre le bureau en ordre (mettre de l'ordre dans le bureau) avant de partir, s'il vous plaît ?

To put + particules

+ aside :

■ *mettre de côté* (propre et figuré), *économiser* (to save, to put away, to put by).
– By cutting down on luxuries (by contenting themselves with the bare essentials) they managed to put aside enough money to buy a second home in the country.
En rognant le superflu (en se satisfaisant du strict minimum) ils ont réussi à mettre assez d'argent de côté pour acheter une résidence secondaire à la campagne.

■ putting aside the fact that... *mis à part le fait que, outre que, hormis le fait que.*

+ away :

■ *économiser* (to put aside, to put by)
– You cannot know what the future has in store for you : put away (put aside, put by) a little money for a rainy day !
Tu ne peux savoir ce que l'avenir te réserve : mets un peu d'argent de côté en cas d'imprévu !

■ *ranger*
– I demand from my apprentices to be orderly (tidy) ; as soon as a task is completed, they are to put their tools away.
J'exige de mes apprentis qu'ils aient de l'ordre ; dès qu'une tâche est achevée, ils doivent impérativement ranger leurs outils.

+ by : to put aside, to put away : *économiser*

+ down :

■ *déposer*
– The hitch-hiker asked me to put him down in the town center.
L'auto-stoppeur m'a demandé de le déposer au centre ville.

■ *verser*
– He never pays cash ; he has everything put down (chalked up, charged) to his account, and he settles the bill (he foots the bill) at the end of each month.
Il ne paie jamais comptant ; il fait tout porter à son compte (mettre sur l'ardoise) et il règle la facture à la fin de chaque mois.
– We bought it on the hire-purchase : we had to put 20 % down, and we paid the remainder (the balance) over 24 months.
Nous l'avons acheté à tempérament ; nous avons fait un premier versement de 20 % et nous avons payé le reste (le solde) en 24 mois.
– May I ask you to put FF 1,000 down as a deposit ?
Puis-je vous demander de verser 1000 Francs d'arrhes ?

■ *réprimer, réduire* – to quell, to repress
– In the wake of (following, following upon, as a sequel to) the Government's austerity measures the police **have** had to put down a good many riots.
A la suite des mesures d'austérité prises par le Gouvernement, la police a dû réprimer bon nombre d'émeutes.

Expressions :
– We are sick and tired of all that wheeling and dealing : we need a President who will put his foot down and clamp down on (crack down on) all those profiteers.
Nous en avons assez de toutes ces manigances (toutes ces combines) : il nous faut un Président qui fasse preuve d'autorité et qui serre la vis à tous ces profiteurs.

– The Unions refuse to knuckle under (to buckle under) to the Management's demands ; they have asked workers to put down their tools (to down tools) right away.
Les Syndicats refusent de céder aux exigences de la Direction ; ils ont demandé aux ouvriers de débrayer immédiatement. Cf. *céder* : to yield, to give in, to cave in, to give way ; to submit, to surrender.

■ *attribuer, imputer* – to attribute, to ascribe, to impute
– Can we put down the decline in the birth-rate to people's fear of the future ?
Peut-on attribuer le déclin de la natalité à la peur qu'ont les gens pour l'avenir ?

19 - STRUCTURES

ÉQUIVALENTS DU SUBJONCTIF FRANÇAIS (suite)

SHOULD À TOUTES LES PERSONNES

1 – Après " for fear " (lest : littéraire) : de peur que ; afin que... ne... pas, pour que... ne... pas, et après "in case " : au cas où ; " in case " se sous-entend très souvent grâce à **l'inversion hypothétique.**
– Confirm your phone call in writing for fear the receptionist should forget to reserve the room.
Confirme ton coup de téléphone par écrit de peur que le préposé à la réception n'oublie de réserver la chambre (pour qu'il n'oublie pas).
– In case your subscription should already be renewed, please ignore this letter.
Au cas où votre abonnement serait déjà renouvelé, veuillez ne pas tenir compte de cette lettre.
– **Inversion hypothétique :** Should your subscription already be renewed, please ignore this letter.
– In case he should not comply with the deadline, we would bring an action against him.
Au cas où il ne respecterait pas le délai, nous lui intenterions un procès.
OU : Should he not comply with the deadline, etc.
NB. Autres inversions hypothétiques comportant des subjonctifs :
– Should the occasion arise : *le cas échéant* (if the case arises).
– **Were it not for** my wife and children, I would give in my resignation.
N'était ma femme et mes enfants, je donnerais ma démission.
– **Had I known** that he was lying, I would have dismissed him.
Si j'avais su qu'il mentait, je l'aurais mis à la porte.

2 – Après les locutions impersonnelles : it is just, it is normal, etc. (forme impersonnelle de to be + adject. ou partic. présent).
– It is just that murderers should be punished severely.
Il est juste que les criminels soient punis sévèrement.
– It is unthinkable that you should not avail yourself of that opportunity !
Il est impensable que vous ne profitiez pas de cette occasion !
Construction plus simple : proposition infinitive avec " for "
– It is just for murderers to be punished severely.
– It is unthinkable for you not to avail yourself of that opportunity.

3 – **Rappel :** pour rendre le subjonctif après " afin que, pour que " **dans une phrase négative :**
– Take your ignition key with you for fear someone should steal your car.
Prenez votre clé de contact afin que l'on ne vous vole pas votre voiture.

4 – De préférence à " may " ou " might " chaque fois que le sujet de la principale **intime un ordre, exprime une injonction** ou **une requête.**
– The policeman at the cross-roads raises his arm in order that cars should stop : ... *pour que les voitures s'arrêtent.*
– The judge has written to him in order that he should pay to his wife the alimony to which she is entitled.
Le juge lui a écrit pour qu'il paie à sa femme la pension alimentaire à laquelle elle a droit.

5 – Après " to be anxious " : tenir beaucoup à ce que et diverses expressions.
– The doctor is anxious that you should take a few days' rest.
... à ce que vous preniez quelques jours de repos.
– It is not to be expected that... *Il ne faut pas s'attendre à ce que...*
– I don't see why... : *Je ne vois pas pourquoi...*
– There is no reason why... : *Il n'y a pas de raison que...*

6 – Après les verbes exprimant **un ordre :** to order, to command
une revendication, une exigence : to demand, to claim ; to require
une insistance : to insist ;
une suggestion, une proposition : to suggest, to propose ;
une recommandation : to recommend, to urge ;
une préférence : to prefer ;
une requête : to request ;
une décision : to decide ;
une motion : to move ;
un avis : to be of the opinion that : *être d'avis que*
une acceptation ou **un refus :** to accept, to refuse, etc. ou leurs **substantifs :** an order, a claim, a proposal, a suggestion, a request, a decision, a motion, an agreement, a refusal, etc.
surtout lorsque le verbe est au passé ou le substantif dans une **phrase au passé.**

On peut aussi dans ce cas utiliser le **subjonctif fossile avec concordance des temps.** Usage très courant en Américain sans concordance des temps. Il en ira de même en Américain pour tous les verbes de volonté (cf. D).

– He suggested that we should adopt the project – that we adopted – that we adopt (surtout US).
– What do you think of his suggestion that we should adopt. – that we adopted – that we adopt (US).

THÈME D'APPLICATION NUMÉRO 19

1 - Nous ne pouvons pas approuver la dernière manœuvre des Japonais, nous nous battrons afin qu'ils n'accaparent pas le marché ! (2 constructions)
2 - Nous tenons beaucoup à ce que cette nouvelle technique soit bientôt mise à l'épreuve : nous fondons tous nos espoirs sur son efficacité !
3 - Il est normal que nous mettions (2 constructions) un peu d'argent de côté en cas d'imprévu : nous ne pouvons savoir ce que l'avenir nous réserve.
4 - Je lui ai écrit pour qu'il règle la facture avant la fin du mois, au cas où il ne pourrait (2 constructions) payer comptant.
5 - Quand j'étais le patron, j'exigeais que mes apprentis rangent leurs outils (3 constructions) dès qu'une tâche était achevée.
6 - La Commission a suggéré que l'Europe profite (3 constructions) de la reprise économique aux États-Unis pour redresser sa propre économie.
7 - Nous insistons pour que le Gouvernement fasse preuve d'autorité (2 constructions) de peur que l'Italie et l'Espagne n'essaient de se tailler une part plus grande du marché du vin européen.
8 - Dès qu'il a été chargé de la réorganisation de nos méthodes de production, il a proposé que nous nous lancions (3 constructions) dans la productique !
9 - Tous les syndicats recommandent que les ouvriers débrayent (2 constructions) immédiatement au cas où les patrons refuseraient (2 constructions) de céder à leurs exigences.
10 - Il est normal que les experts attribuent (2 constructions) le déclin de la natalité à la peur qu'ont les gens pour l'avenir, mais ce n'est pas la seule raison !
11 - La proposition, que la police serre la vis (3 constructions) à tous ces délinquants, a été adoptée à l'unanimité (unanimously).
12 - Le Président Directeur Général a envoyé une note de service (a memorandum) à toutes les entreprises du groupe pour que le principe des Cercles de Qualité soit mis peu à peu en application dans chacune d'entre elles.
13 - Il n'y a pas de raison que nous ne tirions pas parti des ordures afin que les ressources naturelles s'épuisent moins rapidement : faisons-les durer de cette façon !
14 - Quelque coûteuse que soit l'informatisation (3 constructions) la survie de notre industrie en dépend : il est essentiel qu'elle s'adapte (2 constructions) à un monde en transformation.
15 - Avant la libéralisation, il était logique que les industriels soient (2 constructions) en désarroi : il était anormal que la vie économique soit entravée par tant de réglements tatillons.

20 - COMMUNICATIONS

Business Letters : Miscellaneous Sentences (Cinquième partie)

REGRETS AND APOLOGIES : REGRETS ET EXCUSES

– Will you please accept our apologies for the delay in replying to your letter... We must apologize for the delay... (for the late reply to your letter...).

Veuillez, je vous prie, accepter nos excuses pour le retard apporté à répondre à votre lettre... Nous vous devons toutes nos excuses pour le retard...

– Would you very kindly excuse us for the delay in delivering your order... for the late delivery of your order... It was beyond our control...

Veuillez avoir l'amabilité de nous excuser pour le retard apporté à la livraison de votre commande... Il était indépendant de notre volonté...

– We apoligize for the inconvenience this delay may have caused you, but we cannot be held responsible for it...

Nous vous présentons nos excuses pour les inconvénients que ce retard a pu vous causer mais nous ne pouvons pas en être rendus responsables.

– We are sorry to inform you that we shall not be able to meet our commitments if railwaymen do not soon resume work.

Nous avons le regret de vous informer que nous ne serons pas en mesure de respecter nos engagements si les cheminots ne reprennent pas vite le travail.

– We regret to hear that the items in our consignment were in poor (defective) condition (were faulty) ; they must have been damaged in transit.

Nous avons le regret d'apprendre que les articles de notre envoi étaient en mauvais état ; ils ont dû être endommagés pendant le transport.

– Much to our regret, we shall consider your order N°... as cancelled, unless you confirm it by the end of this week at the latest.

A notre grand regret, nous considèrerons votre commande N°... comme annulée, à moins que nous n'en ayons confirmation pour la fin de cette semaine au plus tard.

– We must regretfully inform you that we cannot supply you with the goods from stock (ex stock).

Nous vous informons à regret qu'il nous est impossible de vous fournir les marchandises sur stock.

– We very much regret to hear that you are at present out of stock for most of the goods listed in our order N°...

Nous regrettons beaucoup d'apprendre que la plupart des marchandises inscrites sur notre commande N°... sont pour le moment épuisées.

– For reasons beyond (outside) our control (Owing to unforeseen circumstances), we must unfortunately cancel our order...

Pour des raisons indépendantes de notre volonté, (A la suite de circonstances imprévues), nous devons malheureusement annuler notre commande...

– We can only say once again how sorry we are for having to cancel that order...

Nous ne pouvons qu'une fois de plus exprimer nos regrets de devoir annuler cette commande...

– Will you please accept our regrets at having to decline your offer...

Nous vous prions de bien vouloir accepter tous nos regrets de devoir décliner votre offre...

ENCLOSURES : PIÈCES JOINTES

– We are happy to forward our enclosed current price list, together with our terms of sale, delivery and payment.

Nous avons le plaisir de vous faire parvenir ci-joint nos prix courants ainsi que nos conditions de vente, de livraison et de paiement.

– Enclosed is a pro forma invoice...

Ci-joint une facture pro forma.

– Enclosed please find literature about our latest lines...

Veuillez trouver ci-joint de la documentation sur nos productions les plus récentes...

– We are sending under separate cover...

Nous vous envoyons sous pli séparé...

– The appended brochure (pamphlet)..., leaflet will give you a general idea of our services... The attached (enclosed) brochure...

La brochure..., le dépliant (le prospectus) ci-joint vous donnera un aperçu de nos services...

– The literature apprended to this letter...

La documentation qui accompagne cette lettre...

– We send herewith – please find herewith – herewith please find – we herewith enclose... – herewith, as requested, ...

Veuillez trouver ci-joint... Ci-joint, selon votre demande, ...

– Attached please find...

Ci-joint veuillez trouver...

– May we draw your attention to the attached document.

Permettez-nous d'attirer votre attention sur le document ci-joint...

INQUIRIES, REQUESTS : DEMANDE DE RENSEIGNEMENTS, DEMANDES

– We should like to receive...

Nous aimerions recevoir...

– We should appreciate your supplying...

Nous vous serions obligés de bien vouloir nous fournir (procurer)

– We shall be much obliged if you will send us... We shall be grateful if you will send us...

Nous vous serons reconnaissants – nous vous saurons gré de bien vouloir nous envoyer...

– Would you please be so kind as to let us know at your earliest convenience whether... We would appreciate it if you could let us know...

Auriez-vous s'il vous plaît l'obligeance (l'amabilité) de bien vouloir nous dire dans les meilleurs délais si...

– Will you please... Can you please... quote us for the supply of (give us a quotation for the supply of...)

Veuillez, s'il vous plaît, ... Pouvez-vous, s'il vous plaît, ... nous indiquer vos prix pour la fourniture de...

– Please be kind enough to send us a certified copy of the adjuster's report...

Veuillez avoir l'amabilité de nous envoyer une copie certifiée conforme du rapport de l'expert en assurances...

– We would very much like further particulars (details) about...

Il nous serait très agréable d'avoir d'autres détails (des renseignements complémentaires) sur...

FINANCIAL STATUS – CREDIT RATING – CREDIT WORTHINESS SITUATION FINANCIÈRE – DEGRÉ (OU RÉPUTATION) DE SOLVABILITÉ

– Before dealing with people with whom they have never had any business relations, firms want to know whether those people are financially sound. They may also want to prove to other firms that they enjoy a solid financial reputation.

Avant de traiter avec des personnes avec qui elles n'ont jamais eu de relations commerciales, les sociétés veulent savoir si ces personnes sont financièrement saines (solides). Il se peut qu'elles veuillent également prouver à d'autres sociétés qu'elles jouissent d'une solide réputation financière.

INQUIRIES : *DEMANDES DE RENSEIGNEMENTS*

- Direct ones (they must be done tactfully !)

  Directes (elles doivent être faites avec tact !)

  – We should be very much obliged if you could supply (provide, furnish) (if you could cite) the name of your bankers (the names of one or two firms) as (a) reference(s).

  Nous vous serions très obligés de bien vouloir fournir (de bien vouloir citer) le nom de votre banque (les noms d'une ou de deux sociétés) en référence.

  – We have taken good note of your request for credit, and in this respect, we should appreciate your supplying the name of your bankers as a reference.

  Nous avons pris bonne note de votre demande de crédit, et à cet égard, nous vous serions reconnaissants de bien vouloir nous fournir en référence le nom de votre banque.

- Indirect ones : *indirectes*

  – Harrington and Sons have placed a very large order with us, and as it is the first time we are doing business with them, we should be grateful if you could give us some information about their reliability (= their financial standing = their financial position = their financial status).

  H § S. nous ont passé une commande très importante, et comme c'est la première fois que nous traitons avec eux, nous vous saurions gré de bien vouloir nous donner des renseignements sur leur sérieux.

– Hanley Publications, Ltd, have given your name as a reference (have cited your name as reference – have referred us to your firm) with respect to their financial standing. Could you please give us all relevant information about it, in strict confidence of course, and without any responsibility on your part ?

HP, Ltd, nous ont donné votre nom en référence en ce qui concerne leur situation financière. Pourriez-vous, je vous prie, nous donner toutes informations utiles à ce sujet, de façon tout à fait confidentielle, bien sûr, et sans que votre responsabilité ne soit engagée.

– Before signing a substantial contract with Parkinson and Joyce, Ltd, could you please let us know whether we can safely extend to them the credit that they request ?

Avant la signature d'un contrat important avec P and J, Ltd, pourriez-vous, je vous prie, nous dire si nous pouvons sans risque leur accorder le crédit qu'ils sollicitent ?

– We would very much appreciate an appraisal (assessment) of the creditworthiness of Slatham and Marker, Ltd, with whom we are dealing for the first time.

Il nous serait fort utile d'avoir une évaluation de la solvabilité de S and M, Ltd, avec qui nous sommes en affaires pour la première fois.

ANSWERS : *RÉPONSES*

– In answer to your letter dated of June 27th, we beg to refer you to the Peninsular Bank, with whom we have had an account (with whom we have been in account) for some 12 years.

En réponse à votre lettre du 27 Juin, nous vous prions de bien vouloir vous adresser à The P.B., où nous avons un compte depuis quelque 12 ans.

– In reply to your status enquiry of January 30th, we are pleased to be able to tell you that Stove and Sons, Ltd, have always settled their bills promptly... are enjoying a solid financial reputation... are financially trustworthy.

En réponse à votre demande de renseignements financiers du 30 Janvier, nous avons le plaisir de pouvoir vous dire que St § S, Ltd, ont toujours réglé leurs comptes dans les meilleurs délais... jouissent d'une solide réputation financière... sont financièrement dignes de confiance.

– We unreservedly recommend " Computer Services " as trading partners. We have been doing business with them for more than 5 years, and we are glad to be able to testify to (to vouch for) their reliability... their sound finances.

Nous recommandons sans réserves C.S comme partenaires commerciaux. Nous traitons avec eux depuis plus de cinq ans, et nous sommes heureux de pouvoir nous porter garants de leur sérieux... de la solidité de leurs finances.

– Following your request, we checked up with Martin and Partners' bankers. We are pleased to say that they rate them as sound.

A la suite de votre requête, nous avons vérifié auprès de la banque de M § P. Il nous est agréable de vous dire qu'elle les juge (estime) solides.

– We are satisfied (convinced) that you can safely deal with Mr Brown as he has always met his liabilities in due course.

Nous sommes persuadés que vous pouvez en toute sécurité faire affaire avec M. B. car il a toujours fait face à ses engagements (financiers) dans les meilleurs délais.

– We unfortunately have reservations about that firm's financial position. They were on the verge of bankruptcy last year, and we advise you to be very cautious in your dealings with them.

Nous devons malheureusement émettre des réserves en ce qui concerne la situation financière de cette société. Elle était à deux pas de la faillite l'année dernière, et nous vous conseillons d'être prudents dans vos transactions.

– I am very much surprised at Mr Pennywise's citing me as financial referee : he has never honoured us with his custom ! ...he has not been established here for long, and we cannot yet assess (appraise) his financial standing...

Je suis très surpris que M. P. m'ait cité comme (à titre de) répondant : il ne nous a jamais honoré de sa clientèle ! ... Il n'est pas établi ici depuis longtemps, et nous ne pouvons encore estimer sa situation financière...

COMPLAINTS : RÉCLAMATIONS

■ From consignees about quality, number of items, damage, packaging, etc.

De la part des destinataires au sujet de la qualité, du nombre d'articles, des dommages, du conditionnement, etc.

– We are sorry to inform you that the quality of the appliances in your latest consignement has disappointed us... does not come up to our expectations (falls short of our expectations).

Nous avons le regret de vous informer de ce que la qualité des appareils de votre dernier envoi nous a déçus... ne répond pas à notre attente.

– We regret to have to inform you that the components that you sent to us as a replacement for (in place of) Model XYZ do not meet our requirements... are thoroughly unsuitable... do not fit (cannot be fitted on) that type of engine.

Nous avons le regret de vous apprendre que les pièces que vous nous avez envoyées en remplacement du Modèle XYZ ne répondent pas à nos besoins... ne conviennent absolument pas... ne conviennent pas à (ne peuvent être montées sur) ce type de moteur.

– Your shipment was duly delivered on June 1st, but the contents of the containers do not correspond with (tally with) the list of items that appears on the invoice... on the delivery note.

Votre envoi a bien été livré le 1er Juin, mais le contenu des containers ne correspond pas à la liste des articles qui figure sur la facture... sur le bon de livraison.

– We have no option but to send the goods back to you at your expense : they are not in conformity with our order, with the samples (they are not up to sample).

Nous n'avons pas d'autre choix que celui de vous retourner les marchandises (nous ne pouvons faire autrement que de vous renvoyer) : elles ne sont pas conformes à la commande... aux échantillons.

– We acknowledge receipt of your shipment ; unfortunately, three out of the eight cases that are invoiced... three out of the eight crates, drums, casks, barrels, cardboard boxes (cartons) that appear on the invoice... are missing.

Nous accusons réception de votre envoi ; malheureusement, trois des huit caisses qui sont facturées... trois des huit cageots, tonneaux, fûts, barils, cartons qui figurent sur la facture... sont manquants.

– The carrier disclaims responsibility (liability) for the missing crates, and we would appreciate it if you could sort out what has happened with your delivery department... your storekeeper (your warehouse-keeper).

Le transporteur rejette toute responsabilité pour les caisses manquantes, et nous vous serions obligés de bien vouloir éclaircir ce qui s'est passé avec votre service d'expédition... votre magasinier.

– We are at last in receipt of your latest consignment, but we must regretfully inform you that the goods were in very poor condition when they reached us : the enamelled sides on most of the appliances are either scratched or dented... the paintwork on the kitchen units is cracked... the paint is flaking off (peeling off)... the coating is coming unstuck... the drums are leaking... the handles are twisted... the doors are warped... can you please ask your insurers to send an adjuster to assess (appraise) the damage ?

Nous avons enfin reçu votre dernier envoi, mais nous regrettons de devoir vous informer de ce que les marchandises étaient en piteux état lorsqu'elles nous sont parvenues : les parois émaillées de la plupart des appareils sont soit griffées soit cabossées (bosselées)... la peinture des éléments de cuisine est craquelée... la peinture s'écaille... le revêtement se décolle... les fûts fuient... les poignées sont tordues... les portes sont déformées (gauchies)... Pouvez-vous, je vous prie, demander à votre assureur d'envoyer un expert pour évaluer les dommages ?

– I regret to have to point out that the packing left much to be desired... was defective. There was not enough foam plastic... there were not enough wood-shavings... polystyrene chips... The china sets have been smashed to smithereens (broken to bits).

J'ai le regret de vous signaler que l'emballage laissait beaucoup à désirer... était défectueux. Il n'y avait pas assez de mousse de plastique... de copeaux de bois... de billes de polystyrène. Les services de porcelaine ont été réduits en miettes.

– The cartons, I am sorry to say, suffered a lot in transport and were badly damaged on arrival ; in spite of the warnings : " Caution : handle with care " ... " Fragile... This side up... ", stevedores must have handled them roughly.

Les cartons, je le regrette, ont beaucoup souffert pendant le transport et étaient en très mauvais état à l'arrivée ; malgré les avertissements : " Attention : manier avec précaution "... " Fragile "... " Haut ", les dockers ont dû les malmener.

– We have, I think, every right to complain of your delay (of your being so late) in carrying out our order N° X... although we had agreed upon the 15th of April as being the absolute deadline. If we have not received your consignment by the end of next week, we will regretfully be obliged to cancel the order.

Nous sommes, je pense, en droit de nous plaindre du retard apporté à l'exécution de notre commande N° X alors que nous avions convenu du 15 Avril comme étant le tout dernier délai. Si nous n'avons pas reçu votre envoi avant la fin de la semaine prochaine, nous serons à regret dans l'obligation d'annuler la commande.

– We are sorry, but we cannot extend the deadline (time limit)... we cannot allow you a further deadline for delivery.

Nous regrettons mais nous ne pouvons prolonger le délai... Nous ne pouvons vous accorder un délai supplémentaire pour la livraison.

– Production constraints compel us to accept another supplier's offer.

Des impératifs de production nous contraignent à accepter l'offre d'un autre fournisseur.

– We thank you for the prompt delivery of our order Ref. X. On reading the invoice however, we were surprised at your making no mention whatever of the special discount that you had agreed upon for that trial order !

Nous vous remercions de la livraison rapide de notre commande Ref. X. En lisant la facture cependant, nous avons été surpris que vous ne fassiez absolument aucune mention de la remise exceptionnelle que vous nous aviez accordée pour cette première commande !

– ... We do not understand why you sent us the screws... the nails... in bulk, whereas they were to have been sent in plastic sachets – as per order. As this is going to put us to extra expense, could you please rectify the invoice accordingly ?

... Nous ne comprenons pas pourquoi vous nous avez envoyé les vis... les clous... en vrac, alors qu'ils devaient être envoyés sous sachets de plastique – conformément à la commande. Comme ceci va nous occasionner des frais supplémentaires, pourriez-vous, je vous prie, modifier la facture en conséquence ?

■ From consignors about outstanding payments.

De la part d'expéditeurs au sujet d'impayés.

– We are sorry to have to remind you that you have not yet settled our invoice dated...

Nous regrettons de devoir vous rappeler que vous n'avez pas encore réglé notre facture en date du...

– In spite of your telex of May 2nd, Ref..., which read : " we hasten to remit a cheque to you to settle our account... " we do not seem to be in receipt of any remittance from you yet.

Malgré votre télex du 2 Mai, Ref..., qui disait : " nous nous empressons de vous envoyer un chèque pour régler notre compte... ", il ne semble pas jusqu'à présent que nous ayons reçu un règlement de votre part.

– Our Accounts Department would appreciate a prompt settlement, in any case before the end of the 198... fiscal year (= financial year).

Notre Service Comptabilité vous serait obligé de bien vouloir régler rapidement, de toute façon avant la clôture de l'exercice 198...

– ... Consequently, could you please pay the sum owing – X pounds, as per invoice – on receipt of this reminder ?

... En conséquence, pourriez-vous, je vous prie, régler la somme dûe – X livres sterling, conformément à la facture – dès réception de ce rappel ?

We rely on your sending (= we trust that you will send) your remittance in good time to save us both the unpleasantness of litigation.

Nous espérons que vous voudrez bien envoyer votre règlement dans les meilleurs délais pour nous éviter, à vous comme à nous, le caractère désagréable d'un contentieux.

– You have not answered our third reminder ! Should you not remit (In case you should not remit...) the sum owing within a week, we would regretfully have to take legal action (start legal proceedings) against you.

Vous n'avez pas répondu à notre troisième rappel ! Au cas où vous ne régleriez pas la somme dûe dans un délai d'une semaine, nous devrions à regret engager des poursuites contre vous (nous aurions le regret de devoir engager...).

– We note that you have fallen into arrears with your monthly instalments... that you are in arrears with (that you are behind with) your instalments...

Nous constatons que vous avez pris du retard dans le versement de vos mensualités... que vous avez du retard dans vos versements...

– As extending your credit period is out of the question, could you please pay off the arrears (make up the arrears) – settle the overdue amount (pay off the outstanding amount) by the end of the month ?

Comme la prolongation de votre crédit est hors de question, auriez-vous, je vous prie, l'obligeance de bien vouloir régler l'arrièré – régler le montant en souffrance (impayé) avant la fin du mois ?

– Your account has been outstanding (overdue) for too long... There is no trace of your remittance in our ledgers... You have ignored our reminders (reminder letters)... Your cheque has been dishonoured (has been rejected)... We regret to inform you that we will put the case in the hands of our Legal Department (we will devolve the case upon our Legal Department).

Votre compte est en souffrance depuis trop longtemps... Il n'y a aucune trace de votre réglement dans nos registres... Vous avez ignoré nos rappels... Votre chèque a été refusé... Nous sommes au regret de devoir vous informer que nous allons remettre l'affaire entre les mains de notre Service du Contentieux (nous allons transmettre l'affaire...).

TEST YOUR KNOWLEDGE

– Imaginer les noms des sociétés françaises, leurs adresses, etc., ainsi que les dates, les références, etc.
– Les conversations téléphoniques se feront face à face, apres un temps de préparation.
– Comme il s'agit d'un exercice, employer toutes les variantes possibles, des plus simples aux plus formelles par exemple.

SUJET 1

Vous etes responsable du Service Achats d'un grand magasin. Le rayon " Peche à la ligne " a un probleme : la firme britannique " Trout and Sons ", Ltd, 48 Fishery Road, Plymouth PL5 3AB, Tel : 752 38672, Telex : 83147 TROPLY, a livré votre commande du... N°... dont vous accusez réception, mais :

1 – Il manque la caisse de moulinets (reels) que vous aviez pourtant commandés (Modele WHIZZ 2000). La saison vient d'ouvrir, vous en avez un besoin urgent.
2 – Le carton contenant les hameçons (hooks) est arrivé endommagé ; 15 sachets de plastique contenant les Modeles 8, 10 et 12 sont manquants.
3 – Le rabais de 3 % pour commande importante ne figure pas sur la facture.

Vous intervenez a) par lettre b) par télex c) par téléphone aupres de Mr Pike, Chef du Service Exportation (Poste 124).

SUJET 2

Le port de la cravate revient à la mode. Créateur d'entreprise nouvellement lancé dans la fabrication de cet article, vous contactez de nombreux grossistes et grands magasins en Grande-Bretagne.

1 – Adresser un exemplaire de cette lettre à " Clad and Partners " Weaver's Crescent Manchester M23 8LG, Tel : 928 8485, Telex : 87122 CLAMAN.
Vous tenez à disposition des échantillons de tissus ou de cuir, un catalogue avec modeles de tous genres, une large gamme de prix, etc.
2 – " Clad and Partners " est intéressé. Jennifer Frills, secrétaire particulière de Michael Dapper, responsable du Service Exportation (Poste 187) en voyage d'affaires, vous répond a) par lettre b) par telex c) par téléphone en souhaitant recevoir de plus amples renseignements : échantillons, prix, remise éventuelle, crédit.

SUJET 3

" Clad and Partners " font une commande importante – FF 20,000 – à livrer rapidement ; ils sollicitent un crédit et citent en référence " The Indo-European Bank " 18, Liverpool Street, Manchester M28 7LH, Tel : (061) 434 2272, Telex : 57781 INDOBA.
Vous contactez " The Indo-European Bank " a) par lettre b) par telex c) par téléphone (au vu de l'urgence de la commande).

SUJET 4

" The Indo-European Bank " vous répond a) par lettre b) par telex c) par téléphone.
Imaginer dans chaque cas, que la réponse est a) favorable b) évasive c) défavorable.

SUJET 5

Vous écrivez chez " Clad and Partners " pour les remercier de leur commande, que vous vous proposez d'honorer rapidement. Accord d'une remise exceptionnelle de 3 % – c'est une premiere commande – si le réglement vous parvient dans un délai de 30 jours. Crédit possible de 60 jours mais sans remise. Vous espérez qu'ils seront satisfaits, etc.

TO PUT + PARTICULES (SUITE)

+ forward : *proposer* (to propose, to propound), *avancer* (to advance), *suggérer* (to suggest)

–The theory recently put forward by a team of research-workers (= researchers, US) is attractive, but it does not meet with universal approval.
La théorie récemment proposée par une équipe de chercheurs est séduisante, mais elle ne remporte pas tous les suffrages.

– All the delegates that the shopfloor had put forward for the post were eventually rejected (= turned down).
Tous les délégués qu'avaient proposés les ouvriers pour ce poste ont fini par être rejetés.

+ in :

– If we do not accept the compromise, they threaten us to put in a claim for damages.
Si nous n'acceptons pas ce compromis, ils nous menacent de présenter une demande de dommages et intérêts.

– After staging that token strike, the Unions have put in a claim for a 15 % rise, but they eventually settled for 10 %.
Après avoir organisé cette grève d'avertissement, les Syndicats ont revendiqué une augmentation de 15 %, mais ils ont fini par transiger à 10 %.

+ into :

– All those lay-offs (redundancies) in smokestack industries consequent upon (following upon) computerization, and after years of over-manning (featherbedding), have put the Government into an awkward position.
Tous ces licenciements dans les industries traditionnelles, consécutifs à l'informatisation, et après des années de sur-effectifs, ont placé le Gouvernement dans une position inconfortable.
Cf. a mass lay-off, a labour shake-out ; labour shedding ; *un licenciement collectif ; le licenciement collectif.*

+ off : to postpone ≠ to bring forward

– The meeting of the Board has been brought forward to Monday. ≠ put off until
La réunion du Conseil a été avancée à Lundi. ≠ remise à

– " Procrastination is the thief of time " : the Central Bank ought not to put off shoring up our currency, or it might repent it !
" Il ne faut pas remettre à demain ce qu'on peut faire le jour même " : la Banque Centrale ne devrait pas différer de soutenir notre monnaie, ou elle pourrait s'en repentir ! (to procrastinate, littéraire : *remettre à plus tard, temporiser, atermoyer).*

Rappel : to shore up – to prop up – to buoy up – to bolster – to support – to sustain – to underpin – to buttress – to stay up.

Expressions :

+ on :

– The recovery is putting on (is picking up – is gathering) speed (the recovery is speeding up).
La reprise s'accélère.

– They put **an** embargo on all the imported goods that could well pose a serious threat (a serious challenge) to those that are manufactured in the country.
Ils mettent l'embargo sur tous les biens importés qui risquent de concurrencer ceux qui sont fabriqués dans le pays.

– In the car industry, thousands of workers are on the verge of being put on short time.
Dans l'industrie automobile, des milliers d'ouvriers sont sur le point d'être mis au chômage partiel (le chômage partiel : short-time working).

– The development of high tech(nology) industries bids fair to put the nation's economy on its feet again.
L'essor des industries de pointe promet de remettre sur pied l'économie nationale.

+ out :

– The night watchman is supposed to make sure (to see to it that) all the lights have been put out.
Le veilleur de nuit est censé veiller à ce que toutes les lumières soient éteintes.

– With that fire-extinguisher, you can put out any type of fire.
Avec cet extincteur, on peut éteindre n'importe quel type de feu (d'incendie).
– Don't put yourself out ! (Don't go to any inconvenience on my account !).
Ne vous dérangez pas pour moi !
– Imports of cheap textiles have put a good many firms (have driven a good many firms) out of business.
Des importations de textiles bon marché ont mené beaucoup de firmes à la faillite.
– The floods have put (thrown) thousands of people out of work.
Les inondations ont réduit des milliers de gens au chômage.

+ **through** :

■ to connect

– " Operator, can you put me through to Extension X ?
" Mademoiselle, pouvez-vous me passer le Poste X ?

■ to subject to, to cause to undergo : *soumettre, faire endurer*

– The world-wide recession has put the economies of the Western World through hard times.
La récession (à l'échelle) mondiale a fait connaître des temps difficiles au Monde Occidental (has subjected them to, has caused them to undergo hard times).

■ Our clerical staff are put through intensive training before we entrust them with such costly devices as computers or word processors.
On impose à notre personnel administratif une formation intensive avant de leur confier des appareils aussi coûteux que les ordinateurs ou les machines à traitement de texte.

Expressions diverses :

+ **to** :

– Before an operation, they put you to sleep.
Avant une opération, on vous endort.
– The riot police have put the demonstrators to flight.
La police anti-émeute a mis en fuite les manifestants.
– I would not like to put you to any trouble (inconvenience) on a Sunday.
Je ne voudrais pas vous causer d'ennui (vous déranger) un Dimanche.
– May I put a question to you ? (ask you a question ?)
Puis-je vous poser une question ?
– If the Union puts the matter (the issue) to a secret ballot, a great many workers will vote in favour of resuming work.
Si le Syndicat s'en remet pour cette affaire à un scrutin secret, beaucoup de travailleurs voteront en faveur de la reprise du travail.
– By putting the machines, your time and your money to good use, we can pull the firm out of the receiver's clutches !
En faisant bon usage des (en tirant parti des) machines, de votre temps et de votre argent, nous pouvons arracher notre firme aux griffes du syndic de faillite ! (wrench – wrest the firm from)
– Several schemes have been put to the test (have been experimented with) in order to put an end (to put a stop) to the rise in absenteeism.
Plusieurs procédés ont été mis à l'épreuve afin de mettre fin (un terme) à la montée de l'absentéisme.
– It would put us to great expense to replace the machinery now, but we would soon get a good return on that investment !
Cela nous engagerait dans de grandes dépenses de remplacer maintenant les machines, mais nous retirerions vite un bon bénéfice de cet investissement.
– Most developing countries are hard put to it to secure loans that would enable them to service their debts.
La plupart des pays en voie de développement ont beaucoup de mal à obtenir des prêts qui leur permettraient de servir les intérêts de leurs dettes.

+ **together** : *joindre, réunir, assembler*

– Put your hands together ! *Joignez les mains !*
– Let us put our desks together, thus we can spread the blueprint on them.
Réunissons nos bureaux, ainsi nous pourrons y étaler le bleu (le plan).
– Buying in kits proves cheaper, but with do-it-yourself kits you are sometimes at a loss to put the different parts together (to assemble).
L'achat en kit s'avère meilleur marché, mais avec des kits à monter soi-même on est parfois embarrassé pour monter les différentes pièces.

+ under :

– You have not paid the sum owing after the third reminder : it puts us **under an** obligation to take legal proceedings against you.
Vous n'avez pas payé la somme due après le troisième rappel ; cela nous met ***dans l'****obligation de vous poursuivre en justice.*

+ up :

– Increasing taxes will put prices up.
Les impôts en hausse font monter les prix (to raise, to increase, to force up, to send up, to push up).
– As the heirs could not reach an agreement, the estate was put up for sale (put up for auction), and they shared the procee**ds** of the sale among themselves.
Comme les héritiers n'arrivaient pas à s'entendre, la propriété a été mise en vente (mise aux enchères), et ils ont partagé entre eux le produit de la vente.
– We will put up at the Hilton for the night.
Nous descendrons au Hilton pour la nuit.

+ up with : to bear, to endure, to tolerate

– Workers can no longer put up with so many layoffs. (put up with so many of them **being** laid off)
Les ouvriers ne peuvent plus tolérer tant de licenciements.

20 - STRUCTURES

ÉQUIVALENTS DU SUBJONCTIF FRANÇAIS

La proposition infinitive

1 – Après les verbes de volonté : to want, to like (≠ to dislike, to hate) to wish (*souhaiter, désirer*), to order (*ordonner*), to prefer, to accept, to refuse, etc.
– She would like her daughter to become a secretary.
Elle voudrait que sa fille devienne secrétaire.
– Any parents would hate their children to become drug-addicts.
N'importe quels parents détesteraient que leurs enfants deviennent des drogués.
– The Captain ordered the spy to be shot at dawn.
Le Capitaine a ordonné que l'espion soit fusillé à l'aube.
– I would not accept an employer to regard me as a slave !
Je n'accepterais pas qu'un employeur me considère comme un(e) esclave !
NB. Autres constructions possibles. Cf 6 – chapitre 19

2 – Après les verbes exprimant une attente :
to wait for : *attendre* ; to expect : *s'attendre à ce que.*
– I often have to wait for my wife to be ready !
Je dois souvent attendre que ma femme soit prête !
– He did not expect me to arrive so early !
Il ne s'attendait pas à ce que j'arrive si tôt !
NB. Après to wait on peut employer l'indicatif avec " till "
– I often have to wait till my wife is ready !

3 – Après " too " et " enough " : proposition infinitive et " for "
– This box is too heavy for you to carry it alone !
Cette caisse est trop lourde pour que vous la portiez seul !
– He is not good enough at English for the firm to engage him as an interpreter !
Il n'est pas assez bon en anglais pour que la maison l'engage comme interprète !

L'indicatif

1 – Après un superlatif ; après **first** et **only**
– She is the prettiest girl that I know.
C'est la jeune fille la plus jolie que je connaisse.
– The priest was the only person that knew the secret.
Le prêtre était la seule personne qui connût le secret.
– You are the first person that congratulates me **on** my accent.
Vous êtes la première personne qui me félicite **de** mon accent.

2 – Après les verbes exprimant un doute : not to think, not to believe. Le temps est différent selon la nuance.
– I don't think that he has understood / that he understands / that he will ever understand !
Je ne pense pas qu'il ait compris / qu'il comprenne / qu'il comprenne jamais.
– Don't believe that I am intoxicated !
Ne croyez pas que je sois ivre !
NB. Après to doubt : *douter*, employer " whether " lorsque le verbe est à la forme affirmative.
– I doubt whether he will pass his examination.
Je doute qu'il réussisse son examen.
Mais : I do not doubt that he will fail his examination.
Je ne doute pas qu'il échoue à son examen.

– I doubt whether she has followed my advice !
Je doute qu'elle ait suivi mes conseils !
Mais : I do not doubt that she has followed my advice !
Je ne doute pas qu'elle ait suivi mes conseils !

3 – Après certains conjonctions : **unless** : *à moins que* ; (**al**) **though** : *quoique, bien que* ; **till**, **until** : *jusqu'à ce que* ; **provided – on condition that – so long as – as long as** : *pourvu que, à condition que* ; **before** : *avant que.* ***Attention !*** avant que = " **until** " après une forme négative.
– Repair the damage before the boss notices it !
Répare les dégâts avant que le patron ne s'en aperçoive !
Mais : I will **not** leave **until** you have apologized !
Je ne partirai pas avant que vous ne vous soyez excusé !
– She is quite willing to lend us that sum provided we sign an I. O. U. (I owe you).
Elle veut bien nous prêter cette somme pourvu que nous signions une reconnaissance de dette (phonétiquement : un " *je vous dois* ").

4 – To see (to it) – to make sure : *veiller à ce que, faire en sorte que, s'assurer que*
– Make sure that all the passengers have fastened their seatbelts.
Veillez à ce que tous les passagers aient attaché leurs ceintures.
– See to it that my instructions are carried out right away !
Faites en sorte que mes instructions soient exécutées sur le champ !

THÈME D'APPLICATION NUMÉRO 20

1 - Le Président du Conseil d'Administration veut que la réunion du Conseil soit avancée à Lundi.
2 - Mettons l'embargo sur les importations de textiles ; nous n'attendrons pas qu'elles mènent (2 constructions) nos entreprises à la faillite.
3 - La théorie proposée par notre équipe de chercheurs est séduisante : nous nous attendons à ce qu'elle remporte tous les suffrages.
4 - L'essor des industries de pointe est assez important pour qu'il remette sur pied l'économie nationale.
5 - La dépense est trop grande pour que nous remplacions dès à présent les machines : je ne crois pas que ce soit un bon investissement.
6 - Nous fabriquons le seul extincteur qui puisse éteindre n'importe quel type de feu !
7 - Ce n'est pas le premier procédé qui ait été mis à l'épreuve pour mettre fin à l'absentéisme et je ne pense pas qu'il soit plus efficace que les autres !
8 - Je doute qu'ils confient des appareils aussi coûteux à leur personnel administratif sans formation intensive !
9 - Personne ici ne doute que nous puissions encore arracher notre société aux griffes du syndic, à condition que nous fassions bon usage de notre temps et de notre argent !
10 - Ils nous menacent de présenter une demande de dommages et intérêts à moins que nous n'acceptions ce compromis.
11 - Tant que le Syndicat ne s'en remettra pas pour cette affaire à un scrutin secret, les ouvriers n'oseront pas voter en faveur de la reprise du travail !
12 - Nous ne pouvons pas accepter que des milliers d'ouvriers soient mis au chômage partiel, nous pourrions nous en repentir !
13 - Quoi que la récession ait fait connaître des temps difficiles au monde occidental, nous restons optimistes car nous nous attendons à ce que la reprise s'accélère.
14 - Nous veillerons à ce que les impôts n'augmentent pas car cela ferait monter les prix !
15 - Les pays en voie de développement ont été incapables de servir les intérêts de leurs dettes avant que la Banque Mondiale ne leur accorde des prêts complémentaires (= supplementary).

SOMMAIRE

Imprimé par Impressions DUMAS – Saint-Étienne
Dépôt légal 4e trimestre 1988 – Collection n° 52 – Édition n° 01 - 58/5523/4
Imprimeur n° 28 834